Shonu

Sengupta

Ultimate Psychometric Tests

Mike Bryon

Ultimate
Psychometric Tests

Over 1000 practical
questions for verbal,
numerical, diagrammatic
and personality tests

FOURTH EDITION

KoganPage

Publisher's note

Every possible effort has been made to ensure that the information contained in this book is accurate at the time of going to press, and the publishers and author cannot accept responsibility for any errors or omissions, however caused. No responsibility for loss or damage occasioned to any person acting, or refraining from action, as a result of the material in this publication can be accepted by the editor, the publisher or the author.

First published in Great Britain and the United States in 2005 by Kogan Page Limited
Second edition 2012
Third edition 2015
Fourth edition 2018

Apart from any fair dealing for the purposes of research or private study, or criticism or review, as permitted under the Copyright, Designs and Patents Act 1988, this publication may only be reproduced, stored or transmitted, in any form or by any means, with the prior permission in writing of the publishers, or in the case of reprographic reproduction in accordance with the terms and licences issued by the CLA. Enquiries concerning reproduction outside these terms should be sent to the publishers at the undermentioned addresses:

2nd Floor, 45 Gee Street	c/o Martin P Hill Consulting	4737/23 Ansari Road
London EC1V 3RS	122 W 27th St, 10th Floor	Daryaganj
United Kingdom	New York, NY 10001	New Delhi 110002
www.koganpage.com	USA	India

© Mike Bryon, 2005, 2012, 2015, 2018

The right of Mike Bryon to be identified as the author of this work has been asserted by her in accordance with the Copyright, Designs and Patents Act 1988.

ISBN   978 0 7494 8163 6
E-ISBN   978 0 7494 8162 9

British Library Cataloguing-in-Publication Data

A CIP record for this book is available from the British Library.

Typeset by Integra Software Services, Pondicherry
Print production managed by Jellyfish
Printed and bound by CPI Group (UK) Ltd, Croydon, CR0 4YY

CONTENTS

PREFACE

From now on, treat a psychometric test as the route to the career of your dreams. Use this book to ensure that you stand head and shoulders above the crowd of other applicants.

At some stage in the selection process for a great many jobs and courses you have to take a psychometric test. Many are completed online early in the application process. For the unprepared candidate they represent a significant challenge; fail and you risk not gaining the job or training of your choice. Take them seriously, as many more people are failed than pass.

Let me help you become one of the candidates that really stand out from the crowd. The secret is practice and mindset. The right sort, the right amount, at the right time and you will succeed.

This is the 'ultimate' psychometric test book because it contains 1,000 realistic practice questions. It is expressly designed for self-study, covers the major types of test and provides essential advice on the winning mindset. It also signposts the reader to the best sources of further practice in the Kogan Page Testing Series.

It is the ideal starting point for the reader who wants to do really well in a psychometric test at the intermediate level and it is the perfect introduction for candidates of graduate-level tests.

You will not find another book with so many practice questions. This means that you can really get down to some serious score-improving preparation. I will describe how to best organize your study and provide many hundreds of explanations and explanatory notes to help make sure you realize where you might be going wrong.

Success in a psychometric test is hard work and I will ask you to make a significant commitment in terms of time and effort. The choice is entirely yours – rise to the challenge and your dream career could become a reality. The alternative is to risk failure.

If you face a test that contains questions of a type not covered by this title or the suggested further reading, then contact me via the publisher and if I know of one I will be glad to let you know of a source of suitable practice material.

May I apologize in advance if you find an error in this book; please do not let it undermine your belief in the value of practice and do please take the trouble to notify Kogan Page, so that it can be removed at the next reprint.

PSYCHOMETRIC TESTS AND QUESTIONNAIRES: WHAT ARE THEY?

A psychometric test is not like a blood sample test where you simply roll up your sleeve and feel the discomfort of the needle. You have no control over the outcome of a blood test but in a psychometric test you should be totally in control. You achieve this through hard work, systematic preparation and a good test technique.

They may be taken online, with paper and pen or when performing a task in a workplace.

Whatever the task, it will be designed so that a score can be awarded, usually decided by how many questions were completed correctly. The test will allow the test administrator to draw comparisons between candidates, and the whole point when used for recruitment is that it will allow the administrator to conclude that candidate A got a better score than candidate B and that candidates F, G, H, I, J and K failed!

If you face a psychometric test or questionnaire as a part of a recruitment process for a job or course of study, then it is reasonable to assume that lots of people have applied and there are fewer vacancies or places than applicants. Some organizations attract as many as 40 applicants for every vacancy. The employer or college relies on the test to identify the more suitable candidates in as fair and objective a way as is economically possible. Every applicant will be invited to take the test and the results will be compared to decide who should be invited to the next stage of the recruitment process. The remaining candidates will be rejected.

There are many types in use. Some are specific to a particular role or profession, others are general. The most common sort involve a questionnaire completed online. Later in the recruitment process you might face a series of sub-tests taken one after the other over a number of hours with only a short pause between the papers. They may be designed to test your stamina and endurance as well as your interests, personality and abilities. Examples include:

personality questionnaires;

situational awareness questionnaires;

interest and motivational inventories;

Tests of verbal reasoning;

numerical analysis;

mechanical and technical reasoning;

diagrammatic and abstract analysis;

work sample tests;

in-tray exercises;

trainability tests;

fault diagnosis;

data interpretation.

These are very broad headings and each would include many different styles and types of question. A questionnaire will not normally have a time limit, while a test will be strictly timed.

As soon as you realize that you need to pass a test or complete a questionnaire, go about finding out as much as you can about it. The internet is a great source of this kind of information but the organization that has invited you may provide you with, or direct you to, a description of the test and some sample questions. You will not be able to get hold of past papers or real copies of the test.

If you suffer a disability that will adversely affect your ability to complete the test or any aspect of the recruitment process, then inform the organization at the first opportunity. It should be prepared to organize things differently to better accommodate your needs, and for certain conditions they may allow extra time to complete the test.

Why employers use them

Employers use tests and questionnaires to obtain information unavailable from CVs, application forms or interviews. They do this to ensure a fairer and more informed employment decision.

For example, f the Procter and Gamble website explains that they use employment assessments to ensure they hire the right people. It's a strartergy that has worked very well for them and they manage a series of world leading brands including Gillette, Oral-B and Pampers to name just a

few. You can read all their reasons for using psychometrics and work through free practice material for their reasoning test at: https://pg.sitebase.net/pg_images/taleo/practicetest.htm.

Big players in the testing industry

You get a good feel for the way psychometrics is used by organizations if you consider who publishes them and how major corporations use them. Consider the following examples:

> SHL is a leading publisher of tests, including ability screening online. The company has an extensive client list, and giants like L'Oréal, Colgate-Palmolive, Ford, Sony, Philips, Kraft Foods, Ericsson, Vodafone and many others use its psychometric products, which include a wide range of behavioural, ability and situational judgement assessments.

> Sainsburys PLC is typical of how major employers use psychometrics. Early in the application process you are invited to complete an online questionnaire that investigates your approach to customer service. You have to choose from suggested answers and indicate which you consider the best and worst response to a series of hypothetical situations. Take this style of question very seriously because a great many applicants are rejected on the basis of their answers.

> Recruitment to BT's professional services division involves a battery of tests and if you pass you are invited to an assessment day; it comprises an analysis exercise, interview, one-to-one exercise and group exercise.

> Psychometric Services Ltd (PSL) produces online and pen-and-paper questionnaires and ability tests with titles such as Occupational Personality Inventory, Dynamic Personality Questionnaire, Motivational Questionnaire,

Customer Service Questionnaire, Advanced Sales Questionnaire. Its client list includes, for example, Cadbury Schweppes, HMV, Lloyds TSB and Toyota.

Ernst & Young requires you to sit two numerical tests. The first is online, and if you pass that, there follows a second, invigilated, pen-and-paper test. Companies such as Land Rover do the same. Deutsche Bank is currently using a numerical test in which a calculator is not allowed. You have to work pretty quickly in the Citigroup online numerical test, and the time limit is also tough in the numerical test used by Deloitte.

Cathay Pacific uses an online numeracy test that consists of 33 questions and is time limited to 30 minutes. A favourite assignment involves the conversion of currencies. No one seems to make it through the whole exam.

Test publisher cut-e assesses millions of people a year in over 70 countries and 20 languages. Its online tests and questionnaires are used by, for example, IKEA, Nestlé, Vodafone and Siemens. The company offers numerical, verbal logical and spatial reasoning sub-tests and an English language proficiency test which examines fluency and vocabulary.

The Watson-Glaser Critical Thinking Appraisal is very widely used and examines five skills: accurate inferences, recognition of assumptions, proper deduction, interpretation of information, and evaluation of arguments. You usually sit it alongside the RUST advanced numerical reasoning appraisal which examines comparison of quantities and sufficiency of information.

What to expect

You may well have completed a psychometric questionnaire online or attend a training or recruitment centre to take a battery of psychometric tests.

Before you complete a questionnaire do some research about the organisation and the sort of personal qualities they expect from their employees. Take time over each question and answer them in a way that stresses the parts of your personality that matches your understanding of the organization's culture and preferred way of working. The best candidates approach the questionnaire with confidence in themselves and their abilities. Allow yourself sufficient time.

Do not underestimate how long it can take to give proper consideration to the hypothetical situations and suggested answers. Only answer the questions in the context of how you would respond at work. You might give a very different response if you were out with friends or relaxing at home. But such responses might be inappropriate at work so for every situation in the questionnaire remind yourself that the context is strictly how you would respond at work.

When you attend a test don't be late! And dress smartly. You are likely to be one of many candidates attending that day. If you are to undertake a physical test as well as written papers, then you may need to bring along sports clothes and shoes; you may be expected to attend for most of the day. All this detail will be included in your letter of invitation, so read it carefully.

Turn up prepared to work very hard indeed. Doing well in any test is not simply a matter of intelligence or ability. Hard work and determination play a big part too. If at the end of the day you do not feel completely exhausted, then you may have not done yourself justice. So go for it.

Expect to attend on the day able to adopt the right mental approach. The candidates that do best are not usually the ones who are fearful or who feel resentment about having to take a test. The winning approach is one in which you attend looking forward to the challenge and the opportunity it represents. You are there to demonstrate your abilities and prove to the organization that you are a suitable candidate. This should not discourage you. Everyone can develop this approach. The secret is preparation. Attend the test fully prepared for the challenge and use it to demonstrate how good you have become.

Turn up fully prepared, having spent many hours practising for the test, ready to take full advantage of your strengths and having addressed any areas of weakness. Do not underestimate how long it can take to prepare for a test. Start as soon as you receive notice that you must attend.

It is really important that you listen carefully to the instructions provided before a test begins. You may well be feeling nervous and this may affect your concentration, so make yourself focus on what is being said. Much of the information will be a repeat of the test description sent to you with the letter inviting you to the test. So read and reread this document before the day of the test.

Pay particular attention to instructions on how many questions there are in each sub-test and be sure you are familiar with the demands of each style of question. Look to see if at the bottom of the page it says 'Turn over'. You will be surprised how many people reach the bottom of a page and wrongly conclude that they have reached the end of the questions. They stop working and wait when they should be working away at the remaining questions.

Keep track of the time during the test and manage how long you spend on any one question. You must keep going right up to the end. Aim to get the balance right between speed and accuracy. It is better that you risk getting some questions wrong but attempt every question rather than double-check each answer and be told to stop because you have run out of time before you have finished. Practice can really help develop this skill.

If you hit a difficult section of questions don't lose heart. Keep going – everyone gets some questions wrong. You may find that you come next to a section of questions in which you can excel.

If you do not know the answer to a question, then educated guessing is well worth a try. If you are unsure of an answer to a multiple-choice question, then look at the suggested answers and try ruling some out as wrong. This way you can reduce the number of suggested answers from which to guess and hopefully increase your chances of guessing correctly.

2

HOW TO PASS PSYCHOMETRIC TESTS AND QUESTIONNAIRES

Doing well in a psychometric test or questionnaire is not just down to intelligence but also requires determination and hard work. If passing is important, then be prepared both to set aside hours in which to research and practise and to work hard.

The value of preparation and practice

You must achieve the best possible score to be sure that you pass. Other candidates will be trying to do this, so you must too, otherwise you risk coming a poor second.

The secret is preparation and practice. Everyone can improve their score and for many candidates practice will mean the difference between pass and fail.

Practice works best on material that is as much like the real questions as possible. Select from this book questions that are similar to those in the real test or questionnaire and restrict your practice to these questions. I have included material that will benefit most readers but this may mean that not all the material is appropriate to you in terms of the level of difficulty. So select the most appropriate material and if necessary obtain more from other titles in the Kogan Page Testing Series. Look online as well. Lots of sites offer free practice.

Before you complete a questionnaire complete your research on the organisation and the qualities they are looking for in their employees. Before taking a test practice for a number of days and up until the day of the test. In the case of a test, practice must be challenging, painful even. If it stops being a pain, then there really will be very little gain! But before you start practising, first you must get wise.

Get wise

Most psychometric questionnaires occur during the early stages of the application process so do your research first. Before you answer a personality questionnaire, find out about the organization and decide whether you like its culture and if it's the kind of place you will thrive in. If it is, then apply confident in that knowledge, take time over each question and answer it in a way that shows you as the ideal candidate for the role and company. Treat every question as an opportunity to show just how suitable you are. Many candidates do not take sufficient care or time over the questionnaire and fail to allow themselves enough time to reflect on every question, ensuring that they answer it in a way that best supports their application.

If you face a test, then be sure to get test wise. Most psychometric tests comprise a series of smaller tests or sub-tests taken one after the other, with a short pause between the papers. They might include, for example, first a sub-test on verbal reasoning, then a numerical reasoning sub-test and finally a non-verbal reasoning sub-test. But this is only one of many possible combinations. The series of sub-tests is called a battery.

It is really important that you understand what the test you face involves. You will be astonished at how many people attend not knowing what to expect. The first time they learn of the type of questions involved is when the test administrator describes them just before the test begins for real. Don't make this mistake. You need to know the nature of the challenge as soon as possible.

The organization to which you have applied may provide a description of the type of questions and the format of the test If they do then be sure to get details on:

how many sub-tests the test battery comprises;

what the title of each sub-test is;

what sort of question makes up a sub-test (ask them to describe an example of each type of question);

how many questions each sub-test includes;

how long you are allowed to complete each sub-test;

whether it is multiple choice or short answer;

whether you complete it with pen and paper or at a computer terminal;

whether or not a calculator is allowed.

Armed with this information you can now find hundreds of practice questions on which to set about a systematic programme of preparation.

How much and what kind of practice

Once you have a very clear idea of the test you face, you need to set about finding hundreds of relevant practice questions. You need hundreds because to get the most from practice you should undertake a minimum of 20 hours. If you are weak in maths or English, then you may well have to practise a lot more than this. This book contains 1,000 practice questions and will be an ideal source of practice material for many candidates. But you are unlikely to find all the practice material you need in one publication. This book will best suit the candidate at the intermediate level and introduces material at the graduate level, so if you face a psychometric test for a graduate, managerial or professional position you should move on from this title to other more advanced material also available in the Kogan Page Testing Series. In each chapter I have suggested sources of further material.

Undertake two sorts of practice

Type 1

Practise on realistic questions in a relaxed situation without time constraint. The aim is to become really familiar with the types of question and to realize what skills are being examined. Take one question at a time, looking at the answer and any explanation. If you get any wrong, try to understand why. Use this time to recognize which part of the test represents the greatest challenge for you and use this information to plan the amount of practice you need to undertake for each part of the test. Spend most time on your personal areas of weakness.

Type 2

Once you feel confident in each of the types of question that you face, start practising on realistic questions under strict time constraints and under realistic exam-type conditions. You can make up these 'mock tests' by taking, for example, 40 questions and allowing yourself 25 minutes to attempt them. Use a watch to time yourself and be sure to stop when you have run out of time. Even get someone to administer the test for you, telling you when to turn over the page and begin and to stop when you have run out of time. If you don't find your first mock test much of a challenge, then either increase the number of questions or reduce the time you allow yourself. The aim of this second sort of practice is to get used to answering questions under the pressure of time and to build up your speed and accuracy. Take this practice seriously, try to make every point count and work very quickly against what should feel like a tight time limit.

Set yourself a personal challenge

To get the most out of your practice and to help make it feel more realistic, set yourself the challenge of trying to beat your own score. To do this you will have to try hard and take the challenge seriously, and then you will have to try harder still. Try the following 10-step approach:

Become wise about the organization and qualities they seek in their employees.

Undertake the type 1 familiarization practice described above and make up three 'mock tests' for each of the sub-tests that you face

Take the first practice test under exam-type conditions and against a tight time constraint.

Mark your test and go over the questions you got wrong, working out why; if you did not finish the test, then resolve to work faster next time. Record the number of answers you got right in the first box below.

Set yourself the challenge of beating your first score, get yourself in the right frame of mind and be ready to really go for it in your second mock test.

Take your second mock test, making sure it contains the same number of questions and allowing yourself the same amount of time. Mark your answers, record your score and see if you did in fact beat your first score.

Go over the answers and explanations to your second test and, if you got any wrong, work out why.

Take a third test, trying once again to beat your best score.

Record your third score and go over any questions you may have got wrong.

Repeat this challenge for each of the sub-tests that make up the real test you face.

Record of mock test scores

Title of mock test _____

Test 1 [_____]   *Test 2* [_____]   *Test 3* [_____]

Copy this form to ensure that you can record your score in each sub-test.

The winning mindset

Doing well in a psychometric assessment takes practice but also the right mental approach. The winning candidate looks forward it. . They have long ago left behind any sense of resentment or irritation. So put aside any negative thoughts. They will not help. Focus on the opportunity that passing will afford you. Decide how much you want that opportunity and resolve to set about getting it.

It will take courage to make the necessary commitment, especially if you have previously experienced failure. But you must decide to take the risk! The winning candidate has committed everything to passing. They are fully prepared to risk not passing because they have concluded they have nothing to lose and everything to gain.

Typically the strongest candidate can't wait for the assessment to start. They work incredibly hard during the it and make every second and question count. They are test wise and very well prepared. They never forget why they are there. They attempt every question, which means they don't slow down or reflect for too long. When the questions are easy they maximize their speed while gaining every mark. When they are more difficult their preparation really begins to pay off. They have addressed their personal challenges and worked out beforehand how to deal with many of the more difficult questions, and when they reach some they cannot answer they sparingly apply educated guessing. They never give up. When they have finished they feel truly exhausted from the mental effort.

What to do if you fail

If you are reading this book having failed a psychometric test and this has prevented you from realizing a career goal, then take heart. It is entirely normal for candidates to fail on the first few attempts at many of the more popular tests. It certainly does not mean that you do not have the ability to do the job or course in question. However, it does mean that you need to improve on your performance in the test used to recruit to that position.

Failure will not mean that the company will not welcome a future application from you. Should you be successful at a later stage, once you are employed you will be judged by your performance in the job, not your past test scores, so it will not impinge on your future career prospects within the organization.

It is likely that over half the candidates who sit a psychometric test will fail. If this happens to you, then ask the organization to provide you with feedback on your score and identify the parts of the test that you had problems with. Recall and note down the types of question, how many there were and the level of difficulty. Be honest with yourself and try to assess what it is that you need to do in order to pass next time.

I know candidates who repeatedly failed a test and it was only when they set about a major programme of improving their maths or English or both that they then went on to pass. Others simply needed to get more used to the test and working under pressure of time in an exam-type situation. It is not uncommon for accomplished applicants to fail a test because they think too long about the questions or read the passages too deeply. Their work or study does not prepare them well for a test in which you have to act very quickly to complete all the questions in the given time.

Plan a programme of revision and improvement straight away, concentrating on what you are least good at. Seek out sufficient practice material and get down to some seriously hard work.

Apply again as soon as you are able and, this time, attend fully prepared and confident in your abilities.

It will take courage and determination to try again and to keep working to improve yourself until you pass. But these are qualities of which you can be proud. With the right approach you will address your personal challenges and go on to pass. You will then be able to look back on what you can regard as a significant achievement.

May I take this opportunity to wish you every success in the psychometric test that you face?

3

SITUATIONAL JUDGEMENT AND PERSONALITY QUESTIONNAIRES

Give honest, considered responses in these very common tests whist seeking to present yourself in the best possible light. Find out about the preferred style of working of the organization and stress those parts of your personality over others. Practise on these questions to make a winning impression.

A personality questionnaire often occurs early in an application process and can serve to reject a great many applicants, so take it seriously. It will most likely be completed online. These questionnaires comprise a number of statements or situations and it is your task to, for example, rank them or say whether you agree or disagree with the sentiment or situation described. They include lots of statements such as:

'If colleagues will not listen then it is sometimes necessary to raise your voice.'
'I prefer a working environment where everyone knows their role and responsibilities.'

The test might require you to indicate whether you agree or disagree with the statement, neither agree nor disagree or strongly agree or disagree. Otherwise they may describe a hypothetical situation and it is your task to provide an answer assuming that situation to be true or say which of a list of suggested answers is the most appropriate and which the least appropriate.

Often there is no strictly right or wrong answer as your answer will depend on the role and preferred working style of the organization and on your preferences and personality.

Take the first example. Most employers would find raising your voice in the suggested situation an inappropriate way to act at work, so we should almost certainly disagree with this statement. However, how you answer the second example is completely dependent on your and the organization's preferred way of working and the vacant role. Some companies prefer not to work in such a defined way and would prefer not to recruit people who like that style of organization.

In a questionnaire it is best not to make too many responses that suggest you neither agree nor disagree as this may be taken to mean that you find it difficult to commit yourself or to make up your mind. Another general point worth remembering is that you should avoid too many agree or disagree strongly responses as this might risk the impression that you have too many strongly held opinions.

This chapter comprises questions typical of those found in real personality questionnaires and situational judgement exercises. They are organized under nine headings typical of key categories of behaviour at work investigated by personality questionnaires. These are:

Customer care

communicating with others;

your approach to decision making;

your approach to planning;

managing people and resources;

motivating yourself;

features of your ideal role;

your attitude towards risk;

appropriate responses in work;

situational awareness.

Use these practice questions to practise for a real test. Keep at the forefront of your mind the position for which you are looking and the likely culture of the company and industry of your choice. Always answer the question in the context of how you would act if you were working for the company in the vacant role.

There is no conflict between giving an honest response and presenting yourself in the best possible light. It is perfectly reasonable that you should stress some parts of your personality over others in response to your understanding of the organization's culture and preferred way of working.

Be prepared to make a number of responses that you know will not support your application but to do otherwise would involve making a misleading response. Everyone will answer some questions with low-scoring responses and it is rare for a few responses to determine the overall result.

Most personality questionnaires do not have a time limit so take as long as you like over these practice questions. No answers to most of these practice questions are given in chapter 7, as how you respond will usually depend on your personality and the job and company in question. However, explanations are offered of the likely way in which the question may be interpreted.

Customer care

In these questions it is your task to decide which is the most and least appropriate suggested response to the hypothetical situation described. Each question has a new hypothetical situation. You record your answers in the answer box provided. Explanations are provided in chapter 7.

1   Which of the suggested answers is the most and which the least appropriate response to the following situation.

Situation

You work in a large grocery store and are busy replenishing shelves when a customer asks where the can find the fresh milk.

Suggested answers

A   Give them clear directions to where the milk is found.
B   Stop your work and walk the customer to the section containing milk.
C   Direct them to customer services who can explain where the milk is.
D   Explain that you're too busy to help.
E   Explain that you're busy and suggest they ask another member of staff.

Answer

Most appropriate	
Least appropriate	

2   Which of the suggested answers is the most and which the least appropriate response to the following situation.

Situation

A customer asks if you sell an item that you know is temporarily out of stock, a delivery of the item is expected early the following week. You would respond to the customer by saying:

Suggested answers

A   Yes we normally do but we're out of stock
B   Sorry we don't have any until next week
C   No we are out of stock but I can get you one early next week
D   Yes but we don't have any until next week.
E   Yes and I can get you one early next week

Answer

Most appropriate	
Least appropriate	

3   Which of the suggested answers is the most and which the least
   appropriate response to the following situation.

Situation

It's obvious that one of your colleagues has made a mistake and the shopper
has returned to complain.

Suggested answers

A   Explain to them that it wasn't your mistake.
B   Take responsibility for the error and put it right.
C   Apologize and go and find who served them.
D   Apologize but explain that it wasn't your mistake.
E   Listen to their complaint and promise to raise it with the person who
   served them.

Answer

Most appropriate	
Least appropriate	

4   Which of the suggested answers is the most and which the least
   appropriate response to the following situation.

Situation

While helping pack someone's shopping they tell you that their mother has a
chronic heath condition that means they must care for her much of the time.
You would:

Suggested answers

A   Ask them about the details of their mother's condition.
B   Tell them about your mother who is in a nursing home and also very frail.
C   Share with them that you're bringing up children alone.
D   Say how you imagine that must be difficult and you hope they too get support.
E   Listen but say nothing about their personal matters.

Answer

Most appropriate	
Least appropriate	

5   Which of the suggested answers is the most and which the least appropriate response to the following situation.

Situation

A customer answers their phone while you are serving them and continues in conversation for several minutes. You would:

Suggested answers

A   Walk away.
B   Politely interrupt them and ask if they could call the person back.
C   Get on with something else.
D   Wait for them to finish the conversation.

Answer

Most appropriate	
Least appropriate	

6   Which of the suggested answers is the most and which the least appropriate response to the following situation.

Situation

A customer tells you at length why they want to buy something and much of what they are saying is unnecessary.

Suggested answers

A   Wait good-naturedly for them to finish.

B   Listen and smile.

C   Pay close attention to what they are saying.

D   Show that you're eager that they finish.

Answer

Most appropriate	
Least appropriate	

7   Which of the suggested answers is the most and which the least appropriate response to the following situation.

Situation

The store is noisy and crowded and a customer tells you that they are feeling anxiety.

Suggested answers

A   Explain that there is nothing you can do.

B   Stay with them for a few minutes.

C   Tell them to calm down.

D   Ask them why they are upset.

E   Ask them if there is some way you can help.

Answer

Most appropriate	
Least appropriate	

8   Which of the suggested answers is the most and which the least appropriate response to the following situation.

Situation

A customer is abusive on the telephone.

Suggested answers

A   Hang up.

B   Tell them you will put them through to a manager.

C   Yell back.

D   Put them on hold so you can tell your supervisor.

E   Tell them to stop being abusive.

Answer

Most appropriate	
Least appropriate	

9 Which of the suggested answers is the most and which the least appropriate response to the following situation.

Situation

A shopper hadn't realized that an offer had ended and wanted to buy at the discounted price.

Suggested answers

A Apologize that it wasn't clear that the offer was finished and ask if they still want the item at the regular price.

B Tell them that the offer had ended and explain that they were mistaken.

C Politely explain that it's company policy that when an offer ends the discounted price is no longer available.

D Explain that the offer has ended and that there is nothing that can be done.

Answer

Most appropriate	
Least appropriate	

10 Which of the suggested answers is the most and which the least appropriate response to the following situation.

Situation

Your line manager asks you to attend a day's training at a store across town.

Suggested answers

A You explain that you've already been on training that covers that subject area.

B You explain that you can't because the longer journey would prevent you collecting your child from school.

C You tell him you're reluctant because it will mean a longer journey from home.

D You ask him for more information about the course so you can decide.

E You explain that you're not willing to learn new things.

Answer

Most appropriate	
Least appropriate	

11 Which of the suggested answers is the most and which the least appropriate response to the following situation.

Situation

There is a new customer at the counter in your store and a regular tries to jump in to be served before them.

Suggested answers

A   You serve the new customer.
B   You ask the regular customer if you may serve the new customer first.
C   You tell the regular customer to please wait their turn.
D   You serve the regular customer.

Answer

Most appropriate	
Least appropriate	

12 Which of the suggested answers is the most and which the least appropriate response to the following situation.

Situation

In the store where you work the rule is that you only approach a customer when they are ready to buy and you know someone is ready to buy when:

Suggested answers

A   They spend time looking at just one type of product.
B   They're observing and touching a range of different items.
C   They start to handle one item and hold onto it.
D   When you look at them they avoid your stare.
E   They are looking around and hold your gaze.

Answer

Most appropriate	
Least appropriate	

Communicating with others

13 Above all else my success to date is due to my ability to build and maintain business relationships.

A. Agree strongly
B. Agree
C. Do not agree or disagree
D. Disagree
E. Disagree strongly

Answer

14 If a colleague is performing below par, then they can expect honest, constructive feedback from me.

A. Agree strongly
B. Agree
C. Do not agree or disagree
D. Disagree
E. Disagree strongly

Answer

15 When all the hard work has been done, the key points identified and the recommendations formulated, then I feel comfortable if others have the job of selling the policy.

A. Agree strongly
B. Agree
C. Do not agree or disagree
D. Disagree
E. Disagree strongly

Answer

16 I pride myself in being able to do a high-pressure job while dealing sensitively with people and issues.

A. Agree strongly
B. Agree
C. Do not agree or disagree
D. Disagree
E. Disagree strongly

Answer [_____]

17 I have a very direct approach.

A. Agree strongly
B. Agree
C. Do not agree or disagree
D. Disagree
E. Disagree strongly

Answer [_____]

18 Knowledge is a commodity and so I prefer to keep it to myself.

A. Agree strongly
B. Agree
C. Do not agree or disagree
D. Disagree
E. Disagree strongly

Answer [_____]

19 I am happiest producing written material and much prefer that role to one that involves presenting an argument orally.

A. Agree strongly
B. Agree
C. Do not agree or disagree
D. Disagree
E. Disagree strongly

Answer [_____]

20 Being opinionated is not always a bad thing.

A. Agree strongly
B. Agree
C. Do not agree or disagree
D. Disagree
E. Disagree strongly

Answer [_____]

21 I am used to presenting recommendations to groups of people drawn from all levels of an institution or organization.

A. Agree strongly
B. Agree
C. Do not agree or disagree
D. Disagree
E. Disagree strongly

Answer

22 I do not consider it a part of my current job to suggest ways in which something could be done more efficiently.

A. Agree strongly
B. Agree
C. Do not agree or disagree
D. Disagree
E. Disagree strongly

Answer

23 Being personable can make up for many potential pitfalls.

A. Agree strongly
B. Agree
C. Do not agree or disagree
D. Disagree
E. Disagree strongly

Answer

24 If you can get people to buy into a set of objectives or targets, then everyone will work that bit harder towards a shared goal.

A. Agree strongly
B. Agree
C. Do not agree or disagree
D. Disagree
E. Disagree strongly

Answer

25 I wish I could more often make novel links between previously unconnected issues.

A. Agree strongly
B. Agree
C. Do not agree or disagree
D. Disagree
E. Disagree strongly

Answer

Your approach to decision making

26   I would not normally expect to be part of the important decision-making process.

A. Agree strongly
B. Agree
C. Do not agree or disagree
D. Disagree
E. Disagree strongly

Answer [   ]

27   I could make recommendations that went against my personal beliefs.

A. Agree strongly
B. Agree
C. Do not agree or disagree
D. Disagree
E. Disagree strongly

Answer [   ]

28   Only those qualified in a subject area should contribute to a debate.

A. Agree strongly
B. Agree
C. Do not agree or disagree
D. Disagree
E. Disagree strongly

Answer [   ]

29   I feel happiest when I can implement defined regulatory processes.

A. Agree strongly
B. Agree
C. Do not agree or disagree
D. Disagree
E. Disagree strongly

Answer [   ]

30   I expect to take joint responsibility for important decisions and am comfortable to provide a justification for the conclusions reached.

A. Agree strongly
B. Agree
C. Do not agree or disagree
D. Disagree
E. Disagree strongly

Answer [   ]

31 I would expect most decisions to be based predominantly on numerical information.

A. Agree strongly
B. Agree
C. Do not agree or disagree
D. Disagree
E. Disagree strongly

Answer [ ]

32 When painful choices have to be made I find it difficult to commit myself.

A. Agree strongly
B. Agree
C. Do not agree or disagree
D. Disagree
E. Disagree strongly

Answer [ ]

33 When information is incomplete a decision is best deferred.

A. Agree strongly
B. Agree
C. Do not agree or disagree
D. Disagree
E. Disagree strongly

Answer [ ]

34 The decisions that really shape an organization or policy are best handed down from senior management.

A. Agree strongly
B. Agree
C. Do not agree or disagree
D. Disagree
E. Disagree strongly

Answer [ ]

35 The views of someone who has been in an organization only a short time are not as valid as those of someone with long service.

A. Agree strongly
B. Agree
C. Do not agree or disagree
D. Disagree
E. Disagree strongly

Answer [ ]

36 If you know something is right, then it is important to keep telling people no matter how repetitive it becomes.

  A. Agree strongly
  B. Agree
  C. Do not agree or disagree
  D. Disagree
  E. Disagree strongly

Answer [   ]

37 A compromise is rarely good for business.

  A. Agree strongly
  B. Agree
  C. Do not agree or disagree
  D. Disagree
  E. Disagree strongly

Answer [   ]

Your approach to planning

38 Always plan for the worst case even if it is very unlikely to happen.

  A. Agree strongly
  B. Agree
  C. Do not agree or disagree
  D. Disagree
  E. Disagree strongly

Answer [   ]

39 My greatest attribute is my ability to think strategically while overseeing day-to-day activities.

  A. Agree strongly
  B. Agree
  C. Do not agree or disagree
  D. Disagree
  E. Disagree strongly

Answer [   ]

40 You have to take stock, be sure that all the financial needs and objectives are served before you press on with new initiatives.

A. Agree strongly
B. Agree
C. Do not agree or disagree
D. Disagree
E. Disagree strongly

Answer

41 Drive and, of course, luck will effect a positive solution to most challenges.

A. Agree strongly
B. Agree
C. Do not agree or disagree
D. Disagree
E. Disagree strongly

Answer

42 Accuracy should never be sacrificed to speed.

A. Agree strongly
B. Agree
C. Do not agree or disagree
D. Disagree
E. Disagree strongly

Answer

43 Leadership is more about leading people through unforeseen challenges than being able to visualize, communicate and deploy strategies.

A. Agree strongly
B. Agree
C. Do not agree or disagree
D. Disagree
E. Disagree strongly

Answer

44 I am 100% customer focused; the rest can look after itself.

A. Agree strongly
B. Agree
C. Do not agree or disagree
D. Disagree
E. Disagree strongly

Answer

45 Every business can benefit from a few regulations and written procedures but very soon you can have too many and they are bad for business.

   A. Agree strongly
   B. Agree
   C. Do not agree or disagree
   D. Disagree
   E. Disagree strongly

Answer

46 I am entirely comfortable with ambiguity.

   A. Agree strongly
   B. Agree
   C. Do not agree or disagree
   D. Disagree
   E. Disagree strongly

Answer

47 I excel when faced with a number of competing and demanding tasks but routine administration is something I find demeaning.

   A. Agree strongly
   B. Agree
   C. Do not agree or disagree
   D. Disagree
   E. Disagree strongly

Answer

48 I like to know what is expected of me and prefer not to have to drop everything to help solve someone else's problems.

   A. Agree strongly
   B. Agree
   C. Do not agree or disagree
   D. Disagree
   E. Disagree strongly

Answer

49 Delegation is something less committed colleagues do.

   A. Agree strongly
   B. Agree
   C. Do not agree or disagree
   D. Disagree
   E. Disagree strongly

Answer

Managing people and resources

50 It is better to focus on selling a few more products rather than worry about how much we are spending on stationery.

A. Agree strongly
B. Agree
C. Do not agree or disagree
D. Disagree
E. Disagree strongly

Answer

51 Everyone makes mistakes, so it is best if we report them immediately.

A. Agree strongly
B. Agree
C. Do not agree or disagree
D. Disagree
E. Disagree strongly

Answer

52 I would feel uncomfortable in a situation where resources were being used that did not represent best value for money.

A. Agree strongly
B. Agree
C. Do not agree or disagree
D. Disagree
E. Disagree strongly

Answer

53 I understand the importance of effective listening.

A. Agree strongly
B. Agree
C. Do not agree or disagree
D. Disagree
E. Disagree strongly

Answer

54 To manage people well you have to get fully involved in the detail.

A. Agree strongly
B. Agree
C. Do not agree or disagree
D. Disagree
E. Disagree strongly

Answer

55 Above all else, good management includes trusting people to do the job.

    A. Agree strongly

    B. Agree

    C. Do not agree or disagree

    D. Disagree

    E. Disagree strongly

Answer [   ]

56 Yes, managing people is important but it must come second to fulfilling the client's expectations.

    A. Agree strongly

    B. Agree

    C. Do not agree or disagree

    D. Disagree

    E. Disagree strongly

Answer [   ]

57 I wish more credit was given to all the positive outcomes that you can't put numbers on.

    A. Agree strongly

    B. Agree

    C. Do not agree or disagree

    D. Disagree

    E. Disagree strongly

Answer [   ]

Motivating yourself

58 I may have some faults but a lack of get up and go is not one of them.

    A. Agree strongly

    B. Agree

    C. Do not agree or disagree

    D. Disagree

    E. Disagree strongly

Answer [   ]

59 I have always considered myself the best qualified in taking charge of my own personal development.

   A. Agree strongly
   B. Agree
   C. Do not agree or disagree
   D. Disagree
   E. Disagree strongly

Answer [ ]

60 In work I prefer to set my own targets and objectives.

   A. Agree strongly
   B. Agree
   C. Do not agree or disagree
   D. Disagree
   E. Disagree strongly

Answer [ ]

61 A target is only a target if it is stretching.

   A. Agree strongly
   B. Agree
   C. Do not agree or disagree
   D. Disagree
   E. Disagree strongly

Answer [ ]

62 If you want to motivate others successfully, you need to make them feel that they can succeed. Success must be demonstrable and that requires measurable, well-defined performance indicators and feedback.

   A. Agree strongly
   B. Agree
   C. Do not agree or disagree
   D. Disagree
   E. Disagree strongly

Answer [ ]

63 Above all else I am motivated by the desire to deliver results.

   A. Agree strongly
   B. Agree
   C. Do not agree or disagree
   D. Disagree
   E. Disagree strongly

Answer [ ]

64 I most want a career in which my contribution will make a difference.

    A. Agree strongly
    B. Agree
    C. Do not agree or disagree
    D. Disagree
    E. Disagree strongly

Answer [ ]

65 There is no better reward in work than a large salary.

    A. Agree strongly
    B. Agree
    C. Do not agree or disagree
    D. Disagree
    E. Disagree strongly

Answer [ ]

66 I am looking for a role without restrictions or barriers.

    A. Agree strongly
    B. Agree
    C. Do not agree or disagree
    D. Disagree
    E. Disagree strongly

Answer [ ]

67 It is important for me that I work in a meritocracy.

    A. Agree strongly
    B. Agree
    C. Do not agree or disagree
    D. Disagree
    E. Disagree strongly

Answer [ ]

68 I am seeking a role where a different perspective will be valued.

    A. Agree strongly
    B. Agree
    C. Do not agree or disagree
    D. Disagree
    E. Disagree strongly

Answer [ ]

Features of your ideal role

Which of the following statements would you like to feature in your next role? What is your approach towards, for example, a demanding role, out-of-hours working, order or chaos? Employers want to know because they want to recruit someone with the right approach for the vacant role.

Consider the following and decide how you would respond to these questions.

69 I want a job where my cool-headed approach will serve me well.

- A. Agree strongly
- B. Agree
- C. Do not agree or disagree
- D. Disagree
- E. Disagree strongly

Answer

70 I like nothing better than to get my teeth into a challenge.

- A. Agree strongly
- B. Agree
- C. Do not agree or disagree
- D. Disagree
- E. Disagree strongly

Answer

71 I work best when I can get on with my job with the minimum of distractions.

- A. Agree strongly
- B. Agree
- C. Do not agree or disagree
- D. Disagree
- E. Disagree strongly

Answer

72 I feel I perform best in a job where I need to be copied into every e-mail.

- A. Agree strongly
- B. Agree
- C. Do not agree or disagree
- D. Disagree
- E. Disagree strongly

Answer

73 My current job is 24/7 and my next one will be – it goes with the territory.

  A. Agree strongly
  B. Agree
  C. Do not agree or disagree
  D. Disagree
  E. Disagree strongly

  Answer [   ]

74 I feel resentment if my working life starts to impinge on my home life.

  A. Agree strongly
  B. Agree
  C. Do not agree or disagree
  D. Disagree
  E. Disagree strongly

  Answer [   ]

75 I prefer a high degree of order and tend to get stressed if things do not go to plan.

  A. Agree strongly
  B. Agree
  C. Do not agree or disagree
  D. Disagree
  E. Disagree strongly

  Answer [   ]

Your attitude towards risk

An important aspect of an organization's culture and working practice is its approach to risk. Some employers are looking for a safe pair of hands while others want to break from the past and accept that this must involve a degree of risk. Many organizations are governed by procedures and are highly regulated and they are looking for people who are comfortable in such a culture.

76 The higher the risk, the higher the potential return.

  A. Agree strongly
  B. Agree
  C. Do not agree or disagree
  D. Disagree
  E. Disagree strongly

  Answer [   ]

77 The importance of avoiding loss is often underestimated.

    A. Agree strongly
    B. Agree
    C. Do not agree or disagree
    D. Disagree
    E. Disagree strongly

Answer

78 Regulations stifle creativity.

    A. Agree strongly
    B. Agree
    C. Do not agree or disagree
    D. Disagree
    E. Disagree strongly

Answer

79 Success belongs to the bold.

    A. Agree strongly
    B. Agree
    C. Do not agree or disagree
    D. Disagree
    E. Disagree strongly

Answer

80 Provided the customer is happy, everything else should bode well.

    A. Agree strongly
    B. Agree
    C. Do not agree or disagree
    D. Disagree
    E. Disagree strongly

Answer

Appropriate responses in work

Employers are increasingly using personality-style tests to try to predict how an applicant, once employed, might conduct themself in the workplace. In this context the employer is trying to identify the potential employee who might have the wrong approach to, for example, health and safety, equal opportunities, the handling of a grievance or someone in a position of authority.

You need to approach these questions slightly differently. In particular, you must avoid the wrong answers. By this I mean answers that could imply that you would act inappropriately in work and so should not be employed.

In your current work you may well have a contract of employment and a number of policy documents that form a part of that contract. Read these before you complete a personality-style test of this sort as they will help you understand the responsibilities of an employee and what is reasonable for an employer to expect of you. For example, the grievance procedure should state that you should at the first opportunity inform your manager of any issue that you are feeling unhappy about. The equal opportunities policy will describe how every employee can expect to work in an environment free of the fear of discrimination on the grounds of race, gender, sexual orientation or disability and that it is every employee's responsibility to help ensure such an environment. The health and safety policy will require all employees to report immediately anything they consider to represent a danger. These conditions of employment are very similar across all employers.

Use the following questions to decide how you would respond to this style of question in a personality test. Think of the questions from the employer's perspective and ask yourself whether or not a particular answer would present you as a suitable employee.

81 A rude customer cannot expect the same level of service as one who is nice.

   A. Agree strongly
   B. Agree
   C. Do not agree or disagree
   D. Disagree
   E. Disagree strongly

   Answer [   ]

82 Sometimes you cannot properly make a point without raising your voice.

   A. Agree strongly
   B. Agree
   C. Do not agree or disagree
   D. Disagree
   E. Disagree strongly

   Answer [   ]

83 In work it is sometimes necessary to tell a little lie.

   A. Agree strongly
   B. Agree
   C. Do not agree or disagree
   D. Disagree
   E. Disagree strongly

   Answer [   ]

84 If a personal problem arose that affected my performance at work I would inform my line manager straight away.

A. Agree strongly
B. Agree
C. Do not agree or disagree
D. Disagree
E. Disagree strongly

Answer [_____]

85 There are some types of people you just know you are not going to get on with.

A. Agree strongly
B. Agree
C. Do not agree or disagree
D. Disagree
E. Disagree strongly

Answer [_____]

86 At work you should avoid upsetting people by telling them something they do not want to hear.

A. Agree strongly
B. Agree
C. Do not agree or disagree
D. Disagree
E. Disagree strongly

Answer [_____]

87 When something goes wrong it is best to put it right and then report it.

A. Agree strongly
B. Agree
C. Do not agree or disagree
D. Disagree
E. Disagree strongly

Answer [_____]

88 I prefer to give orders rather than receive them.

A. Agree strongly
B. Agree
C. Do not agree or disagree
D. Disagree
E. Disagree strongly

Answer [_____]

89 I do not worry too much if a job might be dangerous.

    A. Agree strongly
    B. Agree
    C. Do not agree or disagree
    D. Disagree
    E. Disagree strongly

Answer _____

90 If someone keeps upsetting me, then sooner or later I will get them back.

    A. Agree strongly
    B. Agree
    C. Do not agree or disagree
    D. Disagree
    E. Disagree strongly

Answer _____

91 If I witnessed someone being bullied I would inform my supervisor.

    A. Agree strongly
    B. Agree
    C. Do not agree or disagree
    D. Disagree
    E. Disagree strongly

Answer _____

92 A joke at work is normal but some people can't take them and they need to lighten up a bit.

    A. Agree strongly
    B. Agree
    C. Do not agree or disagree
    D. Disagree
    E. Disagree strongly

Answer _____

93 It's a fact of nature that women do some jobs better than men and men do some better than women.

    A. Agree strongly
    B. Agree
    C. Do not agree or disagree
    D. Disagree
    E. Disagree strongly

Answer _____

94 Taking a few pens or some paper home from work for the children is something everyone does and it is not really stealing.

A. Agree strongly
B. Agree
C. Do not agree or disagree
D. Disagree
E. Disagree strongly

Answer [   ]

95 If someone is not pulling their weight, then they are being unfair to their colleagues.

A. Agree strongly
B. Agree
C. Do not agree or disagree
D. Disagree
E. Disagree strongly

Answer [   ]

96 If a customer was angry and unhappy about the service they had received I would listen carefully to their complaint, tell them what I was going to do and report back to them when I had done what I said.

A. Agree strongly
B. Agree
C. Do not agree or disagree
D. Disagree
E. Disagree strongly

Answer [   ]

97 If I found that I regularly could not complete all my jobs I would stay late to get the job done.

A. Agree strongly
B. Agree
C. Do not agree or disagree
D. Disagree
E. Disagree strongly

Answer [   ]

98 If I found I could complete all my tasks with time to spare I would offer to help a colleague who was busy.

A. Agree strongly
B. Agree
C. Do not agree or disagree
D. Disagree
E. Disagree strongly

Answer [＿＿＿＿]

99 I do not think it is right if I am asked to do something that is not in my job description.

A. Agree strongly
B. Agree
C. Do not agree or disagree
D. Disagree
E. Disagree strongly

Answer [＿＿＿＿]

100 If I choose to have a drink of alcohol at lunchtime it is none of my employer's business.

A. Agree strongly
B. Agree
C. Do not agree or disagree
D. Disagree
E. Disagree strongly

Answer [＿＿＿＿]

101 If I saw something that I considered dangerous I would go out of my way to inform someone in authority.

A. Agree strongly
B. Agree
C. Do not agree or disagree
D. Disagree
E. Disagree strongly

Answer [＿＿＿＿]

102 I am prepared to argue my corner until I am blue in the face.

A. Agree strongly
B. Agree
C. Do not agree or disagree
D. Disagree
E. Disagree strongly

Answer [＿＿＿＿]

Situational awareness

In these questions you are presented with a situation and must decide between the suggested responses. Your task is to rank each of the suggested responses as the most appropriate, acceptable or less than acceptable. However, there are more suggested responses than categories in which you can rank them. This means that you must rank more than one response the same. Enter your rankings in the answer matrix.

Identify as the most appropriate the response that you consider is the best of those suggested. If you consider two or more of the suggested responses the most appropriate, then do not rank any of the answers as A but instead rank them both as B, an acceptable response. It is possible that you do not consider any of the suggested responses the most appropriate or acceptable; then do not rank any of the answers as A or B and instead rank them all as C. The answer and explanation to the first situation and question are provided below as an example.

Situation 1

You are the only black person in the company and you believe you are being treated differently from your colleagues because you are offered only the unpopular shifts and denied the overtime everyone else is offered. Your fears were confirmed when colleagues started calling you names that are obviously a reference to your ethnic origin. Your confidence is low, you felt humiliated and physically sick.

Rate the suggested responses as:

A. The most appropriate response
B. An acceptable response
C. A less than acceptable response

The suggested responses:

1 Say and do nothing, because if you do not react, the name calling will fail in its purpose and people will get bored with it.

2 Talk to colleagues who might be suffering the same problems; if they are, work out together what you can do about it together.

3 Keep a diary of events of who said what, when, circumstances and any witnesses. This will give a vital record of the nature of the racism you are facing.

4 Find out whether your employer has specific rules about racism at work or a grievance procedure you can use to raise the issue and try to solve the problem.

Answer

1	2	3	4
C	C	B	B

Explanation

Race discrimination occurs when a person is treated less favourably on the grounds of race, colour, nationality, ethnic or national origin. It is unlawful to practise racial discrimination. Your employer is responsible for ensuring that there is no racism in the workplace. Colleagues who knowingly discriminate against another employee on the grounds of race, or who aid discriminatory practices, are also acting unlawfully. Suggested response 1 is less than acceptable because it is only concerned with the name calling and not the other forms of discrimination described in the passage. Suggested response 2 is also less than acceptable because in the passage you are described as the only black employee, so you can't talk to colleagues who might be suffering the same problems. Both suggested response 3 and 4 are acceptable because they might end the discrimination. Neither of the responses in isolation is the most appropriate response because it would be better if you did both and kept a record of the instances as well as used an official grievance procedure to give your employer the chance to stop the discrimination.

Situation 2

The work is dirty and the washing facilities are rudimentary and there is nowhere to store your clothes so that you can wear the protective clothing provided. Nor is there an area for rest breaks and eating meals. So you stand around during breaks and eat where you can. When it rains you all get wet. None of your co-workers are women and the general public are not allowed on site, so you don't believe there is any need to provide somewhere private to get changed or suitable facilities for pregnant women or nursing mothers. However, you do believe that your employer should provide better facilities or at least some sort of facilities. You have discussed this with him more than once but you are just dismissed as a troublemaker.

Rate the suggested responses as:

A. The most appropriate response

B. An acceptable response

C. A less than acceptable response

The suggested responses:

1 Try talking informally again with your employer about the inadequate working conditions.

2 Do nothing because only businesses employing five or more people must have facilities for staff to change, rest and eat.

3 Refuse to work until facilities are improved and not worry about being threatened with disciplinary action because an industrial tribunal would be bound to agree that conditions are inadequate.

4 Raise the matter in writing with your employer, outlining your concerns and how you believe things might be arranged differently.

Your answer

1	2	3	4

Situation 3

I have a few strong beliefs, especially when it comes to the welfare of animals but this does not normally affect my working relationship with colleagues. Last week, however, during a tea break I found myself in a heated argument when a colleague said it was OK to drown unwanted kittens in a bucket. Things got a bit out of hand and I guess we all said things we didn't really mean. Except for essential work-related communication we have not spoken since. I feel upset and stressed by the situation and it is affecting my work.

Rate the suggested responses as:

A. The most appropriate response

B. An acceptable response

C. A less than acceptable response

The suggested responses:

1 I would try to resolve things informally with my co-workers and if that did not work, then I would next raise the matter informally with my supervisor to see if she could help resolve matters.

2 The first thing I would do is write a letter to my employer setting out the details of the grievance I have with my co-workers.

3 I would ask my employer if I could be transferred to another section and if this was not possible, I would tender my resignation.

4 I would try talking with my employer informally to see if there was anything they could do to improve the situation. If that did not work, I would raise a formal grievance against my colleagues.

Your answer

1	2	3	4

Situation 4

The only complaint I had about my job was that there was too much of it. I simply couldn't get everything done without overstretching and stressing myself. Things got even worse with the recession. The company undertook a major cost-saving exercise and this meant even more for me to do and less support. I found it harder and harder to keep up with my workload and in the end I went to my doctor and he diagnosed stress-related illness, He signed me off work for a month.

Rate the suggested responses as:

A. The most appropriate response

B. An acceptable response

C. A less than acceptable response

The suggested responses:

1 Before returning to work I would write to my manager, informing him that my illness was stress related and that I believed that it was caused by my workload. I would ask for my job to be changed so that the workload was more reasonable.

2 When I return to work I would take care that I always took lunch breaks and left on time.

3 At the end of my period of sick leave I would go back to my doctor and seek a further period off work.

4 Before returning to work I would write to my manager to inform him that I believe my stress-related illness was caused by the amount of work I was expected to undertake. I would ask to meet with him in order that we might discuss ways in which my job might be reorganized so that the risk of my falling ill again was avoided.

Your answer

1	2	3	4

Situation 5

A bereavement is something we all face at some stage. Even when it is expected after a long period of ill health, it is still a terrible thing to have to deal with. When the person who dies is close to you, then it affects everything. When it is your husband, wife or partner, your private life is obviously turned upside down and how your friends and relatives relate to you is somehow different following the death. Going back to work after such a bereavement often helps: it keeps you busy and helps make things seem more normal. At least, that is what you thought, but in your experience work soon became too much and you found it harder and harder to cope. In the end you felt you really needed to speak to your boss about how you felt and during the conversation you found that you could not hide your feelings any longer and you broke down in tears.

Rate the suggested responses as:

A. The most appropriate response

B. An acceptable response

C. A less than acceptable response

The suggested responses:

1 You would compose yourself as much as possible and continue with the conversation.

2 You would apologize and close the meeting.

3 You would compose yourself, ask your boss to make no allowances for your situation and as much as possible to ensure everything at work is as it was before the bereavement.

4 You would take as much time as is required to compose yourself and then explore practical ways in which you workload might be adjusted to take into account your situation.

Your answer

1	2	3	4

Situation 6

My manager often smells of alcohol and it appears she is drinking during the day, which makes me very uncomfortable. She often does not seem to know what is going on and makes bizarre requests and decisions. She takes a lot of time off work and this puts extra pressure on us all as we end up with a different temporary manager each time. I feel senior management have left us in a chaotic situation and it is unfair to us to have to work in this atmosphere. I am finding it a major source of upset.

Rate the suggested responses as:

A. The most appropriate response

B. An acceptable response

C. A less than acceptable response

The suggested responses:

1 I would go to HR and ask to speak to them anonymously about the situation.

2 She obviously has a major problem, so I would just try to put up with it.

3 I would approach one of our HR representatives and share my concerns in as professional and empathetic manner as I could.

4 I would approach her directly and discuss my suspicions and the upset it is causing with her.

Your answer

1	2	3	4

Situation 7

One of the foremen at your place of work has a terrible reputation when it comes to how he treats his staff. For example, he calls them 'boy', which the black members of his team say they find particularly offensive. He swears at all his team, using really objectionable terms of a sexual nature and which insult their mothers and sisters. Management knows about it but does nothing to stop it. You are so relieved that you do not work for him.

Rate the suggested responses as:

A. The most appropriate response

B. An acceptable response

C. A less than acceptable response

The suggested responses:

1 Support your colleagues by trying to work out with them what they can do about the harassment.

2 Tell friends what is going on.

3 Find out whether your employer has specific rules about harassment at work or a grievance procedure and encourage your colleagues to use these to raise the problem.

4 Offer to support your colleagues in an approach to your employer, at first informally but if this does not work, then through a formal grievance.

Your answer

1	2	3	4

Situation 8

It was the birthday of one of your crew and you agreed to meet at the pub at the end of the shift for a drink. There was the usual banter and jokes going on and it was all light-hearted and fun. However, then you heard someone tease Jane over her sexuality.

Rate the suggested responses as:

A. The most appropriate response

B. An acceptable response

C. A less than acceptable response

The suggested responses:

1 I would call the person who was teasing Jane an idiot and tell Jane to take no notice of the nonsense.

2 I would let Jane deal with it but explain to her afterwards that I witnessed the remark and if she needed me as a witness to make a formal complaint at work the next day she need only ask.

3 If it had been in work, then what was said would have contravened our code of conduct and I would have backed Jane in bringing a grievance against the person if that was what she had wished to do. However, it was outside work, so the code does not apply.

4 Harmless banter outside work is something we have to accept but if it upsets you then you should tell the person that it does and they should refrain from it in the future.

Your answer

1	2	3	4

Situation 9

You work for the regional airport and your employer is quarrying just beside the airport and crushing the recovered rock to form hardcore which is then used to expand the airport apron. The apron is where the jet planes stand when not in use. The airport gets really busy a couple of times a year and the extension of the apron must be finished in time for the next busy time. Key to the whole operation is a giant rock crusher. The crusher is being operated 24/7 to ensure that enough hardcore is produced in time. Your employer has asked if you would operate the crusher for a shift as the usual operator has asked to take a day off. You know the machine is potentially very dangerous.

Rate the suggested responses as:

A. The most appropriate response

B. An acceptable response

C. A less than acceptable response

The suggested responses:

1 I would ask the current operator to show me how to use the machine and once I felt I had got the hang of it I would work the shift.

2 I would operate the machine as asked because while the request is obviously dangerous, only businesses employing five or more people must have plans in place to deal with any risks.

3 I would refuse to work the machine as it is not safe for me to do so. I would not worry about being threatened with disciplinary action because an employer can't make you do something unsafe.

4 I would explain that I was not suitably trained or experienced to work the rock crusher but if they could organize the necessary training I would be happy to operate it.

Your answer

1	2	3	4

Situation 10

This is about an annoying member of your team. Like lots of people, Paul believes that global warming threatens the existence of the human race. He spends a lot of his spare time visiting climate change websites and shares the latest views with the rest of the team. Some of your colleagues agree with him. Others either are not interested or respond negatively sometimes, just to wind him up. However, he rarely talks about anything else and you have all become really fed up with his determination to convert you to his point of view. There have been a few stand-up rows and between you all you tried to agree a ban on all talk of climate change but Paul is as determined as he is dogmatic and he will not let the subject drop. As far as he is concerned, whoever disagrees with him is a denier of the obvious facts.

Rate the suggested responses as:

A. The most appropriate response

B. An acceptable response

C. A less than acceptable response

The suggested responses:

1 I would take the matter up with my immediate manager and ask if he could intervene and try to put a stop to the cause of the bad feeling.

2 I would suggest that we all agree again for there to be no more talk about climate change.

3 I would ask to be transferred to another team.

4 I would go to the personnel officer and ask if there was anything they could do to help.

Your answer

1	2	3	4

Situation 11

Your wife of 12 years has left you and most of your mutual friends found out when, even though you are still man and wife, she posted on Facebook that she is single and had moved out of the family home. She has stopped wearing her wedding ring and is fooling around with other men. As hard as you try, your marriage problems are impacting on your work. Colleagues who had read the Facebook message naturally asked you what was happening, others have started to comment on the change in your approach at work and you know it is only a matter of time before your team leader asks you if everything is OK.

Rate the suggested responses as:

A. The most appropriate response

B. An acceptable response

C. A less than acceptable response

The suggested responses:

1 I would try even harder to ensure that my family problems do not impact on my job.

2 I would tell my co-workers and supervisor nothing; that way, my personal problems can't affect my work.

3 I would tell my supervisor about my problems and ask him not to share them with anyone else and where practical to make allowances for the impact it was having on my work.

4 I would tell my co-workers and supervisor to please help me by keeping my private life separate from work.

Your answer

1	2	3	4

Situation 12

You are entering the building where you work and find a man standing at the door. The door requires a pass to be placed over a pad before it opens and you use your pass to unlock the door. Without thinking you hold the door open for this person, who enters with you and thanks you. He looks smart and business-like but you do not recognize him. This does not mean that he does not work in the building or should not be inside as many people work there and you do not know them all. You decide to ask to see his security pass but he refuses and tells you that he works in security and that he does not have to show his pass.

Rate the suggested responses as:

A. The most appropriate response

B. An acceptable response

C. A less than acceptable response

The suggested responses:

1 Ask his name and go to your office and call security to check if it is true that he works there.

2 Politely insist that he shows you his pass.

3 Offer to accompany him to the office of the security team so that they may confirm he works there.

4 Let the matter drop.

Your answer

1	2	3	4

Situation 13

A colleague complains to you about the body odour of a member of your team. On a few occasions you have noticed the bad odour yourself but decided against saying anything as you are aware of some personal difficulties that the individual faces.

Rate the suggested responses as:

A. The most appropriate response

B. An acceptable response

C. A less than acceptable response

The suggested responses:

1 You would quietly explain to your colleague the nature of the personal problems that the individual faces and ask them to be more understanding.

2 Resolve to raise the matter with the individual at the next team meeting and inform your colleague that you will handle it.

3 Ask your colleague to say no more on the subject and do nothing.

4 Meet privately with the member of your team and ask that they pay more attention to their personal hygiene.

Your answer

1	2	3	4

Situation 14

You overhear a heated conversation between two members of staff, neither of whom is in your team. You are shocked to hear one of the individuals threaten the other with physical violence. You know both the individuals concerned and can't really believe what you are hearing. Soon after the threat the individuals become aware of your presence and the conversation abruptly stops.

Rate the suggested responses as:

A. The most appropriate response

B. An acceptable response

C. A less than acceptable response

The suggested responses:

1 You would act as if you had heard nothing and not get involved.

2 You would take the matter up according to the procedure laid down in the staff handbook.

3 You would approach their respective line managers and report the matter to them.

4 You would speak to the two individuals and explain to them what you heard and that you consider it a very serious matter and something they need to sort out between themselves without resort to threats of violence.

Your answer

1	2	3	4

Situation 15

You criticize a member of your staff for grammatical errors in a report and the individual denies being the author. You realize that you were mistaken but the individual concerned gets extremely angry and starts shouting and using bad language.

Rate the suggested responses as:

A. The most appropriate response

B. An acceptable response

C. A less than acceptable response

The suggested responses:

1 You would interrupt them to instruct them to stop shouting and using bad language and you would tell them that when they have calmed down you wish to speak to them. You would then turn away and leave them.

2 You would let them have their say and then apologize and retract your criticism.

3 You would let them finish and calmly tell them not to shout and swear and then you would apologize and retract your criticism.

4 You would interrupt them to stop them and explain that you wish to apologize for your error but that it is entirely unacceptable for them to shout and use bad language and if they do not stop immediately you will walk away and discuss the matter with them later.

Your answer

1	2	3	4

Situation 16

A visitor to your building reported that their mobile phone and packet of sweets went missing when they left a room that they were working in, to use the toilet facilities. There is a large sign in the room that states that personal belongings should not be left unattended and that the management cannot take any responsibility for any loss of or damage to personal items. The room is covered by a security camera and when you review the footage you observe a member of your staff enter the room and appear to pick something up from the table. You approach the member of staff and they confess to taking the sweets but deny taking the mobile phone.

Rate the suggested responses as:

A. The most appropriate response

B. An acceptable response

C. A less than acceptable response

The suggested responses:

1 You would call the police and report the theft and tell them that you have CCTV footage which appears to identify the thief and that a member of staff has admitted to stealing one of the missing items.

2 You would insist that the individual replace the sweets and apologize to the visitor. You would also explain to the visitor that there was nothing you could do about the phone and remind them of the content of the sign in the room.

3 You would search the individual's desk and pockets to see if you could locate the phone.

4 You would arrange for a meeting between the visitor and the individual so that they could explain that they only took the sweets and apologize.

Your answer

1	2	3	4

Situation 17

A member of your team complains of feeling stressed and apprehensive. You arrange to speak to him in private and he explains that he feels most apprehension whenever anything goes wrong at work and that he then feels helpless and unsure how he can help put things right.

Rate the suggested responses as:

A. The most appropriate response

B. An acceptable response

C. A less than acceptable response

The suggested responses:

1 You would explain his role and the extent of his responsibilities and explain how these fit in with the team overall. You would also say that he should come to speak to you at any time.

2 You would suggest that he goes to see his doctor.

3 You would ask him if there are any changes you could make that would help him feel less stressed and apprehensive.

4 You would tell him to snap out of it and pull himself together.

Your answer

1	2	3	4
		A	C

Situation 18

You are following the usual procedure to induct a new member of your team and are surprised to learn that she is dyslexic.

Rate the suggested responses as:

A. The most appropriate response

B. An acceptable response

C. A less than acceptable response

The suggested responses:

1 You would ask her if there are any special requirements that she needs in order to undertake her role and that should she need things organized differently you would do your best to accommodate her.

2 You would describe your commitment to equality of opportunity and how you believe in treating everyone the same.

3 You would explain that you are concerned that this will mean that you will have to provide her with a great deal of support.

4 You would ask her if this means that she will not be able to undertake some tasks to the high standards expected of your department.

Your answer

1	2	3	4

Situation 19

Part of your responsibilities includes the management of workers in the staff nursery school where there is currently a vacancy for a nursery nurse. You meet with the nursery supervisor to sift applicants for the vacant position. One of the applicants is male and the supervisor explains that you should reject his application because she could not leave a male nursery nurse on his own with the children and he could not be allowed to change nappies on his own.

Rate the suggested responses as:

A. The most appropriate response

B. An acceptable response

C. A less than acceptable response

The suggested responses:

1 You would accept the supervisor's advice and reject the applicant.

2 You would suggest that you stop the sift and resume later after you have had a chance to reread the nursery's policy documents and procedures.

3 You would point out that you would first like to obtain guidance from the human resources department that it is an appropriate thing to do in the circumstances.

4 You would refuse to reject the applicant, pointing out that if you did so, then it would be on the basis of gender, which you believe would be wrong.

Your answer

1	2	3	4

Situation 20

You are really excited about your first day in your dream post. You can't believe your luck in leading a national project of such importance and one that is so topical. You know very well that if you do well in this high-profile role your career could really take off. Your impression of the role is confirmed when a call from a reporter at a national newspaper is put through to you and you are asked to answer some questions and provide comments for an article that will appear in the paper the next morning.

Rate the suggested responses as:

A. The most appropriate response

B. An acceptable response

C. A less than acceptable response

The suggested responses:

1 You would ask the journalist for her telephone number and say that someone will phone her back once you have checked who is the most appropriate person to deal with her request.

2 You would explain that you were new in the post but are happy to provide comments provided that your name does not appear in the article.

3 You would answer the journalist's questions truthfully.

4 You would tell the journalist that you are new in the post and must check what the correct course of action is before you provide any comments.

Your answer

1	2	3	4

Situation 21

It is the first day with your new team and you would organize it so that you:
Rate the suggested responses as:

A. The most appropriate response

B. An acceptable response

C. A less than acceptable response

The suggested responses:

1 Start with an ice-breaker exercise where you and each member of the team take turns to introduce themselves.

2 Meet with the whole team and then meet with each member of the team individually.

3 Start with a series of meetings one after the other with each member of the team and ask staff to bring their project files with them to the meeting so that you can go through them with them.

4 Spend this first day alone, reading all the background papers and files.

Your answer

1	2	3	4

Situation 22

You find the role in which you are currently working very challenging because it is so boring. Initially you were enthusiastic about the new appointment but the role did not turn out to be what you expected and you feel that your development is being held back because you spend your time undertaking simplistic administrative tasks. In your opinion the role could be undertaken by an administrative officer and does not require someone like you in the grade of higher executive officer.

Rate the suggested responses as:

A. The most appropriate response

B. An acceptable response

C. A less than acceptable response

The suggested responses:

1 You would press on regardless and continue to do the best job that you can.

2 You would ask to meet with your line manager and explain to her how you feel.

3 You would wait until your annual review and use that occasion to explain how you feel.

4 You would start looking for another job.

Your answer

1	2	3	4

4

VERBAL REASONING

By building your vocabulary and relearning the rules of usage you can significantly improve your score in these common tests. The practice provided in this chapter will mean that you approach the test on the day with greater confidence, speed and accuracy.

A verbal reasoning test features in most psychometric test batteries. They are used to test your vocabulary, comprehension and command of the rules of usage called grammar.

This chapter includes practice questions on most styles of question. Hundreds of examples are provided, affording many hours of practice. Set aside sufficient time to work through these questions and you will significantly improve your performance in these common tests.

Be prepared for different types of question as you work through the practice material. They are there to keep you on your toes and make sure you are prepared for every eventuality.

If you don't already have one, buy a dictionary and thesaurus and get into the habit of using them on a daily basis. Read a quality paper whenever you can, perhaps when commuting to work or at the weekend.

You can find further practice questions of this sort in other titles in the Kogan Page Testing Series.

At the intermediate level

The Verbal Reasoning Test Workbook (over 700 practice questions)

At a more advanced level

How to Pass Graduate Psychometric Tests, 4th edition

Graduate Psychometric Test Workbook, 2nd edition

How to Pass Advance Verbal Reasoning Tests, 2nd edition

Word link

Find two words, one from each list, closest in meaning or with the strongest connection.

1 A. Bargain   D. Property
    B. Purchase   E. Acquisition
    C. Leverage   F. Positive

Answer ☐

2 A. Recognition   D. Acknowledgement
    B. Denial   E. Reckon
    C. Ignore   F. Acquaintance

Answer ☐

3 A. Fashionable   D. Dejected
    B. Liable   E. Blame
    C. Counsel   F. Accountable

Answer ☐

4 A. Constant   D. Variable
    B. Valuable   E. Ridged
    C. Flexible   F. Flow

Answer ☐

5 A. Resentment   D. Attachment
    B. Embarrassment   E. Argument
    C. Supplement   F. Statement

Answer ☐

6 A. Adapt
  B. Observe
  C. Believe

  D. Obscure
  E. Respect
  F. Disregard

Answer

7 A. Jagged
  B. Justified
  C. Adjoining

  D. Affected
  E. Competing
  F. Juxtaposed

Answer

8 A. Suspension
  B. Hasten
  C. Intentional

  D. Instruction
  E. Disappointment
  F. Deferral

Answer

9 A. Discriminate
  B. Cultivate
  C. Arbitrate

  D. Negotiate
  E. Generate
  F. Initiate

Answer

10 A. Fix
  B. Secure
  C. Expose

  D. Concoct
  E. Rectify
  F. Trouble

Answer

11 A. Governing Body
  B. Counsel
  C. Delegate

  D. Advise
  E. Authority
  F. Advocate

Answer

Note: it is common in this type of question for more than one pair of the suggested answers to have connections; you must select the two words with the closest connection.

12 A. Itemize
  B. Observe
  C. Outline

  D. Glance
  E. Sketch
  F. Explain

Answer

13 A. Serious
   B. Beneficial
   C. Favourite

   D. Expedient
   E. Benevolent
   F. Favourable

Answer [   ]

14 A. Willing
   B. Considerate
   C. Oppressive

   D. Overbearing
   E. Wretched
   F. Immerse

Answer [   ]

15 A. Prime
   B. Pride
   C. Preceding

   D. Prior
   E. Procedure
   F. Subsequent

Answer [   ]

Word link – synonyms

In the following style of word link questions you are again looking for the two words closest in meaning or with the strongest connection. Such words are called synonyms.

16 Corporate is to conglomerate as:
   focus is to

   A. diverge
   B. aim
   C. fringe

Answer [   ]

17 Observant is to vigilant as:
   align is to

   A. disembark
   B. fondness
   C. affiliate

Answer [   ]

18 Symbolic is to metaphorical as:
   all is to

   A. every
   B. the
   C. of

Answer [   ]

19 Alleviate is to mitigate as:
adverse is to

    A. opponent
    B. fortunate
    C. ill-starred

Answer [   ]

20 Nullify is to quash as:
insincerity is to

    A. platitudes
    B. genuine
    C. forthright

Answer [   ]

21 Relent is to acquiesce as:
remiss is to

    A. diligent
    B. sensible
    C. imprudent

Answer [   ]

22 Rebuke is to reprimand as:
contingent is to

    A. fortuitous
    B. deliberate
    C. incidental

Answer [   ]

23 Genre is to class as:
obsolete is to

    A. modern
    B. outmoded
    C. watchful

Answer [   ]

24 Deceit is to fraud as:
decision is to

    A. conclusion
    B. solve
    C. indecision

Answer [   ]

25 Uphold is to sustain as:
magnitude is to

    A. infinitive
    B. charm
    C. proportion

Answer [   ]

26 Announce is to declare as:
characterize is to   A. disposition
                      B. portray
                      C. distinguished

Answer [　　　　　]

27 Objective is to goal as:
judge is to   A. punish
                      B. appraise
                      C. forensic

Answer [　　　　　]

28 Co-ordinate is to harmonize as:
commodity is to   A. primary product
                      B. brown goods
                      C. bonds

Answer [　　　　　]

29 Responsive is to elastic as:
rival is to   A. colleague
                      B. partner
                      C. competitor

Answer [　　　　　]

30 Manufacture is to production as:
lease is to   A. agreement
                      B. ownership
                      C. liberate

Answer [　　　　　]

31 Niche is to segment as:
perks are to   A. deductions
                      B. benefits
                      C. taxation

Answer [　　　　　]

32 Train is to teach as:
services are to   A. utilities
                      B. churches
                      C. commodities

Answer [　　　　　]

33 Amount is to volume as:
   abrupt is to   A. courteous
                         B. private
                         C. brusque

                                          Answer [   ]

34 Get back is to return as:
   distribute is to   A. collect
                         B. allocate
                         C. manage

                                          Answer [   ]

Word link – opposites

This style of word link question requires you to identify the suggested answer that means the opposite of the word on the left.

35 Ascend   A. Surmount
                         B. Escalate
                         C. Descend

                                          Answer [   ]

36 Scornful   A. Jovial
                         B. Mocking
                         C. Sneering

                                          Answer [   ]

37 Warrant   A. Authorize
                         B. Prohibit
                         C. Ratify

                                          Answer [   ]

38 Shrewd   A. Foolish
                         B. Discerning
                         C. Intelligent

                                          Answer [   ]

39 Plummet

    A. Decline
    B. Rise
    C. Falter

Answer

40 Tortuous

    A. Safeguard
    B. Meandering
    C. Direct
    D. Devious

Answer

41 Aggravate

    A. Vex
    B. Annoy
    C. Pacify

Answer

42 Annul

    A. Confirm
    B. Rescind
    C. Cancel

Answer

43 Respect

    A. Admire
    B. Despise
    C. Exalt

Answer

44 Relapse

    A. Recede
    B. Progress
    C. Retreat
    D. Worsen

Answer

45 Arrest

    A. Impede
    B. Hinder
    C. Check
    D. Accelerate

Answer

46 Unfaltering

A. Courageous
B. Irresolute
C. Inflexible
D. Adamant

Answer

47 Replenish

A. Restock
B. Stock
C. Exhaust
D. Provide

Answer

48 Answer

A. Echo
B. Reply
C. Question
D. Respond

Answer

49 Lucrative

A. Unprofitable
B. Unlimited
C. Advantageous

Answer

50 Exact

A. Conscientious
B. Lax
C. Advantageous

Answer

51 Counter

A. Confirm
B. Rebut
C. Deny

Answer

52 Purified

A. Pure
B. Clarified
C. Crude
D. Refined

Answer

53 Right
- A. Amend
- B. Redress
- C. Remedy
- D. Wrong

Answer [ ]

54 Distraction
- A. Amusement
- B. Work
- C. Pastime
- D. Hobby

Answer [ ]

55 Sway
- A. Deter
- B. Entice
- C. Allure
- D. Coax

Answer [ ]

56 Steep is to gradual as:
bicker is to
- A. agree
- B. wrangle
- C. scrap

Answer [ ]

57 Solemn is to frivolous as:
rudimentary is to
- A. basic
- B. sophisticated
- C. fundamental

Answer [ ]

58 Cower is to stand as:
devastating is to
- A. damaging
- B. cataclysmic
- C. beneficial

Answer [ ]

59 Contend is to agree as:
scramble is to
- A. scurry
- B. dawdle
- C. sprint

Answer [ ]

60 Disdain is to respect as:
disseminate is to

    A. collect
    B. broadcast
    C. disperse

Answer

61 Incentive is to deterrent as:
terrific is to

    A. rich
    B. poor
    C. marvellous

Answer

62 Impromptu is to rehearsed as:
audit is to

    A. inspect
    B. scrutinize
    C. ignore

Answer

63 Particular is to general as:
speculation is to

    A. reality
    B. surmise
    C. hypothesis

Answer

64 Alleviate is to irritate as:
disagreeable is to

    A. repulsion
    B. pleasant
    C. nastiness

Answer

65 Complicate is to clarify as:
busy is to

    A. slack
    B. limp
    C. lax

Answer

66 Memorable is to ordinary as:
tortuous is to

    A. devious
    B. meandering
    C. direct

Answer

67 Divulge is to conceal as:
percentage is to

    A. fraction
    B. whole
    C. decimal

Answer _____

68 Savage is to mild as:
tangible is to

    A. insensitive
    B. appreciable
    C. imperceptible

Answer _____

69 Different is to corresponding as:
superior is to

    A. elder
    B. junior
    C. manager

Answer _____

70 Presently is to later as:
infrequently is to

    A. scarcely
    B. seldom
    C. often

Answer _____

71 Captivity is to freedom as:
fit is to

    A. compulsive
    B. competent
    C. incapacitated

Answer _____

72 Disgrace is to honour as:
alarmist is to

    A. optimist
    B. scaremonger
    C. outright

Answer _____

73 Eminent is to unknown as:
descendant is to

    A. accent
    B. ancestor
    C. family

Answer _____

Find the new word

In this type of verbal reasoning test you must find a four-letter word that is made from the end of one of the given words and the beginning of the next. Sometimes more than one answer is possible, though you need give only one. An example has been worked for you.

74 lumpy   sweat   ourselves   *Answer*   [   ]

75 anthropoid   learning   peppery   *Answer*   [   ]

76 welcome   guarantee   muddle   *Answer*   [   ]

77 result   motivation   lyric   *Answer*   [   ]

78 handlebar   identify   succulent   *Answer*   [   ]

79 recharge   nephew   handful   *Answer*   [   ]

80 nature   lyric   composer   *Answer*   [   ]

81 alcohol   swear   charcoal   *Answer*   [   ]

82 glorify   tormentil   tutor   *Answer*   [   ]

83 hour   geology   rescind   *Answer*   [   ]

84 unearth   overhear   library   *Answer*   [   ]

85 offspring   incision   toxic   *Answer*   [   ]

86 gastric   humane   engage   *Answer*   [   ]

87 ashore   airline   archer   *Answer*   [   ]

88 lapse   multi-media   lifeboat   *Answer*   [   ]

89 Hindu   typical   peddle   *Answer*   [   ]

90 reserve   proposal   electricity   *Answer*   [   ]

91 defuse   education   voyage   Answer   [   ]

92 flatter   muscle   scream   *Answer*   [   ]

93 jaded   piano   teaspoon   *Answer*   [   ]

94 jersey   elliptical   monster   *Answer*   [   ]

95 cockroach   aplomb   winkle   *Answer*   [   ]

96 insult   ignore   alternate   *Answer*   [   ]

97 monumental   epidemic   fortify   *Answer*   [   ]

98 taste   arduous   season   *Answer*   [   ]

99 staff   lagoon   scuffle   *Answer*   [   ]

100 contest   scientific   ultimate   *Answer*   [   ]

101 flotsam   epicentre   anonymous   *Answer*   [   ]

102 effigy   enzyme   aluminium   *Answer*   [   ]

103 rumpus   habit   tension   *Answer*   [   ]

104 siphon   lyric   notebook   *Answer*   [   ]

105 wobbly   echo   petrol   *Answer*   [   ]

106 amoeba   nervous   rummage   *Answer*   [   ]

107 conjuror   parabola   stringy   *Answer*   [   ]

108 litmus   throttle   needle   *Answer*   [   ]

109 hypnotize   rough   scribble   *Answer*   [   ]

110 aurora   censure   official   *Answer*   [   ]

111 altogether   momentum   alternate   *Answer*   [   ]

112 ideal   lynch   senior   *Answer*   [   ]

113 windfall   mask   incapable   *Answer*   [   ]

114 into   negotiate   hoist   *Answer* [＿＿＿＿＿＿＿＿]

115 underline   mode   afraid   *Answer* [＿＿＿＿＿＿＿＿]

116 envelop   almighty   rumour   *Answer* [＿＿＿＿＿＿＿＿]

117 island   miscellaneous   thwart   *Answer* [＿＿＿＿＿＿＿＿]

118 physical   American   inedible   *Answer* [＿＿＿＿＿＿＿＿]

119 helmet   charcoal   selfish   *Answer* [＿＿＿＿＿＿＿＿]

120 normal   prig   asphalt   *Answer* [＿＿＿＿＿＿＿＿]

121 international   usherette   apartment   *Answer* [＿＿＿＿＿＿＿＿]

122 wrestle   maybe   statute   *Answer* [＿＿＿＿＿＿＿＿]

123 commonwealth   athletic   nonsense   *Answer* [＿＿＿＿＿＿＿＿]

124 also   urgent   inventor   *Answer* [＿＿＿＿＿＿＿＿]

Word swap

Each of the following questions comprises a sentence in which two words need to be interchanged to make it read sensibly. Swap only two words so that one replaces the other.

125 Don't try to be yourself else, be someone.

Answer [＿＿＿＿＿＿＿＿＿＿＿＿＿]

126 Breaking up to hard is do.

Answer [＿＿＿＿＿＿＿＿＿＿＿＿＿]

127 Squabbles is so often the root of family money.

Answer [＿＿＿＿＿＿＿＿＿＿＿＿＿]

128 Every Americans of generation has thought itself more stressed out than the last.

Answer [＿＿＿＿＿＿＿＿＿＿＿＿＿]

129 Sometimes these remedies can result remarkably quickly, with a positive work occurring within hours.

Answer

130 As steady she goes.

Answer

131 We met in a city in the heart of the café of Milan.

Answer

132 Book publishing is big business – the industry is worth £4 billion and more than 12,000 books are published in the UK a year, each third of which are exported.

Answer

133 The spokeswoman for the company 'Archrival' said it would give a board and shareholders of 'Goodbuy' the further two weeks to consider its improved takeover bid.

Answer

134 A two-hour drive of 200 kilometres from the motorway on Milan would bring you to the Mediterranean Sea.

Answer

135 Reporting to the Chief Accountant, the challenging candidate will work in a successful environment providing high-level economic analysis on diverse, key industrial issues.

Answer

136 Good employees establish unity of purpose and direction among the leaders of an organization.

Answer

137 We know evolution happens because of a convergence of evidence from developed fields of science, together they reveal that life diverse driven by the process of natural selection.

Answer

138 People will be better motivated and understand the organization goals and objectives if miscommunication between the levels of an organization's are avoided.

Answer [   ]

139 The distances to remote galaxies are increasing and this inflation can be explained with an analogy of the expansion of a balloon.

Answer [   ]

140 A fuel cell powered car is an electric supplied vehicle with effectively a refuelable battery that keeps generating electricity so long as hydrogen and oxygen are powered.

Answer [   ]

141 A new hypothesis puts forward the human view that global warming in fact started thousands of years before the industrial revolution caused by unfashionable deforestation and farming.

Answer [   ]

142 The scene of the rich at play could be played out anywhere in the world, the vase of orchids, a man in a bar speaking into a mobile phone, laughter from the suit and an elegantly dressed woman checking in at reception.

Answer [   ]

143 Paula wrote that American bull markets were long overdue a correction as they were in her opinion greatly overvalued after the longest financial market in economic history.

Answer [   ]

144 As far as economic management is concerned he was very lucky to inherit what he did, growth had already fallen and inflation had returned, importantly, the lessons of the deep recession had been learnt.

Answer [   ]

145 France's National Assembly approved a constitutional treaty to allow for the referendum on the European Union's constitutional change and a date for the referendum was set for 2005.

Answer [   ]

146 Last year's records from England and Wales suggest that marriage is still more popular than divorce as 57,000 couples were married against 150,000 divorced.

Answer

147 Drive into Liverpool from Manchester and the route of economic dereliction that once dominated the signs are now almost all gone.

Answer

148 Speaking on his mobile phone he would argue, pour and romantic secrets out talk so loudly that everyone on the bus would find it hard not to listen.

Answer

149 The most important tenet of foreign policy for America is to maintain good relations with its powerful neighbour and most dominant trading partner Mexico.

Answer

150 Comparisons between India and China are tempting because they are both large agricultural societies that are undergoing economic development at a fantastic rate but China is fundamentally an open society while India is still intolerant of dissent.

Answer

151 Manufacturing has spread from its origins of setting up and running a company's IT systems and now provides a multitude of services including finance, accounting, human resources, design and even outsourcing.

Answer

Sentence sequencing

Your task in this style of question is to reorganize the sentences into the order in which they were originally written.

152 A. Pluto is the ninth and the most distant from the sun. B. It is tiny compared with the giants Jupiter, Saturn, Neptune and Uranus which have massive, dense, gaseous atmospheres. C. Our solar system has nine planets formed from gas and dust left over after the sun was formed.

Answer

153 A. The best farmland and industries are concentrated in the north which is mountainous and has a cool wet climate. B. The mainland peninsula and the island of Sicily and Sardinia make up the country. C. The dryer, hotter south relies more on farming and tourism than industry and has active volcanoes.

Answer

154 A. This is pollution. B. It can be small-scale or global and most plants and animals suffer its effects. C. Harmful by-products of industry and agriculture enter the environment.

Answer

155 A. Large buildings have foundations which form the base on which they are constructed. B. They all tend to have a roof, walls and a floor. C. Buildings come in a huge variety of sizes and shapes from tower blocks and supermarkets to garden sheds. D. Despite the differences they all serve the same purpose of providing shelter for us and our belongings.

Answer

156 A. Food is important in other ways too. B. Anything that we can digest is food. C. We get our energy and essential bodily nourishment from what we eat. D. Because not having enough, the right sort or eating too much leads to bad health.

Answer

157 A. The rapid growth in urban living has been largely unplanned. B. By contrast, today half the world's population lives in cities. C. As a consequence, inadequate housing and an absence of essential amenities are common. D. Two hundred years ago most people lived in villages or small towns.

Answer

158 A. It protects us from the most harmful of the sun's rays and retains the sun's heat. B. The earth is surrounded by colourless and odourless gases. C. They are mainly nitrogen and oxygen but also carbon dioxide and a gas called argon. D. Without this atmosphere life on the planet would not be possible.

Answer

159 A. Plastics have become the most used material in the world. B. The exception is rubber, a naturally occurring plastic extracted from trees. C. Their molecules are made up of very long chains of atoms. D. Most are synthetic, made from chemicals extracted from oil.

Answer

160 A. However, while muscles can pull they cannot push; for this reason most movements rely on a pair of muscles pulling in opposite directions. B. One end is connected to a bone that does not move and the other to one that does. C. We can move because our muscles contract. D. When the muscle contracts it pulls the moving bone.

Answer [   ]

161 A. It is readily exchanged for goods as long as the buyer and seller both accept its value. B. They may only be made from common metals and paper but they are accepted as valuable because of what they represent. C. Money works as a 'standard of value'. D. The most familiar forms of money are coins and banknotes.

Answer [   ]

162 A. It is produced by vibrations that travel by moving molecules which bump into one another. B. In air sound travels at over 300 metres per second. C. Sound is a form of energy. D. These vibrations are called sound waves.

Answer [   ]

163 A. Frames are constructed rising from the foundations. B. The building site is cleared and levelled. C. The interior is decorated. D. Foundations are built by pouring concrete into the holes. E. Services are installed on each floor. F. Excavations are made for foundations and basements.

Answer [   ]

164 A. The findings of a study concluded that three-quarters of taxpayers pay too much tax. B. It was claimed that taxpayers will pay more than £5 billion in unnecessary taxes next year. C. Their investigations found that the vast majority of taxpayers take no action to reduce the amount of tax that they pay. D. The authors urged taxpayers to take the trouble to claim refunds and reliefs to which they are entitled.

Answer [   ]

165 A. Iron is by far the most used by mankind. B. To produce iron its ore is mixed with coal and limestone and heated to high temperatures in a furnace. C. There are more than 50 metals found naturally as ores. D. This produces pig iron which is further refined to make steel.

Answer [   ]

166 A. The system is interactive. B. A travel agency illustrates well how telecommunications and computers are used to improve customer service. C. This means that when an employee wants to access the system he or she enters data and the system replies with further screens until the desired outcome is realized. D. The agency uses an online enquiry and booking service from a terminal in the office that is connected to a remote server by a telecommunications link.

Answer [   ]

167 A. The home page is usually the first thing that you will see when you first access a site. B. Each website has its own unique address which is called its uniform resource locator. C. It is divided into millions of sites which are files made up of pages of information. D. Perhaps the most significant service available on the internet is the World Wide Web.

Answer [   ]

168 A. There are thought to be billions of them. B. Perhaps the most common objects in the universe are stars. C. It includes everything visible, invisible, known and not yet known. D. The universe is made up of everything that exists.

Answer [   ]

169 A. It involves the temporary, voluntary movement of people. B. It is estimated that one in ten of the working population is engaged in the industry. C. Affected are the places and people through which they pass and the people who make the trip possible. D. Tourism is the fasting-growing industry in the world today.

Answer [   ]

170 A. But most of the population live in the much milder south. B. It occupies the Scandinavian peninsular with Norway. C. Twenty-five per cent of the country lies within the bitterly cold Arctic circle. D. Sweden is the fifth largest country in Europe.

Answer [   ]

171 A. Reformers want new laws that will make the owners of casinos act in socially responsible ways. B. These tricks might include removing clocks from the gambling floor, simulating daylight and making the exit hard to find. C. The new super casinos will be something completely new and some fear that they will deploy psychological techniques to maximize gambling. D. In particular, they want regulations that ban the casino operators from encouraging people to gamble or that increase the risk of problem gambling.

Answer [   ]

172 A. 'It is a great disappointment to find young employees so deficient in their command of English,' wrote one. B. Reading is one of the most important keys to success. C. But what is happening to standards? D. Employers are critical.

Answer [   ]

173 A. From the road you just glimpse the tops of the houses with names such as Sweet View and Ocean Swell. B. It boasts a cinema, tennis court, two pools and elegant but informal gardens and terraces that all look out to sea. C. Inside the high walls and closed gates of the two-and-a-half hectare site you begin to appreciate the extent to which it caters for the lifestyle of the extremely wealthy.

Answer [   ]

174 A. The very hot coolant is used to generate steam to drive turbines and produce electricity. B. A nuclear power station uses the energy produced by a controlled nuclear reaction. C. A series of chain reactions occurs inside the core and produce heat. D. The heat is carried away by a coolant circulating the core.

Answer [   ]

175 A. The fairy-tale writer is its most famous adopted daughter. B. She gave the world classics such as *The Lost Teddy Bear* and *The Adventures of Young Tom*. C. The centenary of Lisa Smith approaches and the city of Leeds plans many celebrations. D. Adopted because she was not born there but made it her home for over three decades.

Answer [   ]

176 A. Therefore keeping the walls warm can save heat. B. Office managers who leave the heating on over weekends report lower annual fuel bills than if they turn the heating off at these times. C. This has been proven in several academic studies and is supported by considerable anecdotal evidence. D. When heating is turned on in a cold building a lot of heat is first used to evaporate condensed moisture in the walls.

Answer [   ]

Best word(s) to complete a sentence

These questions comprise a sentence with one or more pairs of suggested words from which you must choose the one that correctly completes the sentence.

177 If the courts make insurance companies pay liabilities/compensation on claims for asymptomatic conditions then premiums must be expected to rise sharply.

Answer [   ]

178 According to industrial sources Castle Cole, the property company, is performing/perfume in line with expectations at the operating level/cycle.

Answer [   ]

179 Macleans, the London insurer, was on tract/track to meet full-year expectations the/with future performance underpinned by its successful new savings product.

Answer [   ]

180 A rescue plan for Village Leisure, the failing/falling media company, was agreed by shareholders at an extraordinary meeting/moratorium.

Answer [   ]

181 A/The biggest utility company in the new EU member countries reported that its recent perpetuity/promotional activities had failed to have the desired impact.

Answer [   ]

182 Strikes escalated as/at the Guy company yesterday after a third round of negotiations with unions failed to reach a commodity/compromise.

Answer [   ]

183 The chancellor faced revenue/renewed demands to avoid further increases for/in the tax burden on companies in the forthcoming budget report.

Answer [   ]

184 Output in Britain's factories rallied/depreciated as strong demand from/to China and South East Asia boosted exports.

Answer [   ]

185 Manufacturing growth of/in the Eurozone dwindled to its lowest level in 12 months as a result of high oil prices and a slowing/deprecating global economy.

Answer [   ]

186 Continuing price competition and higher utility and labour costs resulted in/ from a second-quarter decline in the group's net operating margins/accruals.

Answer

187 British firms have failed to/in implement government recommendations about investing in and managing their workforces because they have been busy responding/adjusting to unprecedented regulatory changes.

Answer

188 Forty per cent of the total cost base is commissions or bonuses, making it frequently/comparatively easy for costs to be slashed when/if demand shrinks; offices are on short-term leases, again giving flexibility to cut back at short notice.

Answer

189 The litigation/strategy fits with the practice of mining a diversified set of related revenue seams, hopefully giving the business a broader and more solid form/from from/form which to build profits.

Answer

190 The company is in the midst of a growth spurt/opportunity cost, funded through a reversible/convertible bond, to expand and diversify its portfolio of business activities.

Answer

191 Based on/in new data collected last year, the actuarial/actors profession estimates hundreds of thousands more asbestos-related insurance/malicious claims over the next 30 years.

Answer

192 The miscellaneous/media regulator has decreed that advertisements must not link alcohol with sexual attractiveness or success or imply that alcohol can enhance attractiveness, or/nor may the commercial/memorandum refer to daring tough or unruly behaviour.

Answer

193 Flotation/cautious trading ahead of the imminent election meant that markets were especially quiet. Volumes were more akin/like to those at Christmas with investors reluctant to take up large positions/permutations ahead of the outcome of the ballot.

Answer

194 Europe's ageing population will be able/unable to sustain the cost of maintaining pensions for its growing number of pensioners because economic growth will stagnate and institutions will be faced with contraction/contradictions and decline/abatement.

Answer

195 Eurozone GDP growth is/while still weak, which is discouraging for UK exporters to the region, but US GDP growth/market is stronger than has been expected and UK interest rates/fluctuations are likely to increase only slowly.

Answer

196 Results/measures of companies' expectations of orders, sales and profitability show the extremely/theoretical sharp drop in confidence in the wake of the terrorist attacks in the United States followed by the strong return of confidence last June and then a trailing off during the remaining/previous months.

Answer

English usage

This style of question comprises a sentence with some words missing and suggested lists from which you must choose the answer that correctly completes the sentence.

197 __A___ the animals in the park while we were ___B___ behind the tree.

A	B
1. We saw	1. sitting
2. We see	2. sit
3. Seeing	3. sat

Answer

198 Which of the following words can be a preposition?

A. location
B. no
C. in
D. position

Answer

199 I __A__ call because I had __B__ my telephone.

A
1. can't
2. couldn't
3. could
4. can

B
1. forgotten
2. forget
3. forgetting

Answer

200 Which of the following is a superlative?

A. large
B. larger
C. largest

Answer

201 Children, please don't make so much noise. __A__.

A
1. I am concentrating.
2. I concentrate.
3. While I concentrate

Answer

202 Which word is the past participle?

The broken marriage was a great disappointment to all.

Answer

203 My mother is in hospital. I went to __A__ to visit her. My brother is at __B__ now.

A
1. the hospital
2. hospital

B
1. hospital
2. the hospital

Answer

204 As I get __A__ I find myself getting ___B___.

A
1. more old
2. older

B
1. seriouser
2. more serious

Answer

205 When I __A__ Sam last night he was out __B__ in the park.

A   B
1. call   1. run
2. calling   2. ran
3. called   3. running

Answer

206 Which word is the noun?

'Good ideas sometimes occur slowly.'

Answer

207 Two thousand euros __A__ found in the waste paper bin.

A. is
B. was
C. were
D. are

Answer

208 Which adjective is the comparative?

A. late
B. later
C. latest

Answer

209 The apartment was expensive but not __A__ expensive __B__ the first one we viewed.

A   B
1. so   1. as
2. as   2. so

Answer

210 The oldest person __A__ the world also lives the __B__ from a doctor.

A   B
1. of   1. most far
2. in   2. furthest
3. farthest

Answer

211 You __A__ earn a fortune to __B__ such an expensive house.

A	B
1. mustn't	1. live in
2. might	2. lived
3. can't	3. living
4. must	4. lived in
5. can	

Answer [   ]

212 Which is the verb?

Cleaning the bookshelves was done every Tuesday.

Answer [   ]

213 I __A__ animals __B__ I prefer them to people.

A	B
1. like very much	1. very much and
2. like	2. and
3. very much	

Answer [   ]

214 With the cancellation the exhibition would __A__ longer be sold out but anyway it is not on ___B___ longer.

A	B
1. any	1. no
2. no	2. any

Answer [   ]

215 I __A__ a lot of films when I __B__ a teenager.

A	B
1. watched	1. wasn't
2. have watched	2. am
3. watching	3. was

Answer [   ]

216 He left late yet __A__ the fact that it was very cold and in __B__ the snow he still got there early.

A	B
1. despite of	1. spite of
2. despite	2. spite

Answer [   ]

217 I hope to visit the church __A__.

A
1. while I am there
2. while I will be there
3. while I am their

Answer [ ]

218 I was given __A__ ten __B__ notes for my three __C__ work.

A	B	C
1. a	1. pound	1. hour
2. one	2. pounds	2. hours'
3. two		

Answer [ ]

219 My wife will be away __A__ Sunday __B__ which time we will have finished the work.

A	B
1. until	1. by
2. by	2. until

Answer [ ]

220 Neil Armstrong walked on the moon __A__ 3 am __B__ a Saturday __C__ July 1969.

A	B	C
1. at	1. in	1. on
2. on	2. on	2. in
3. in	3. at	3. at

Answer [ ]

221 When we saw him, we __A__ for __B__ so much noise.

A	B
1. apologize	1. make
2. apology	2. making
3. apologized	3. made

Answer [ ]

222 The __A__ was in the __B__.

A	B
1. childs bag	1. back of the car
2. child's bag	2. car's back
3. bag of the child	3. car back

Answer [   ]

223 The journey to the party involved getting __A__ a plane, __B__ a car, __C__ a bicycle and at last I arrived __D__ the party.

A	B	C	D
1. on	1. on	1. on	1. on
2. in	2. in	2. in	2. in
3. at	3. at	3. at	3. at

Answer [   ]

Identify the correct sentence or word(s)

What follows is a mix of question styles, including questions that offer a number of sentences, of which only one or none is correct in terms of English usage.

224 Which sentence if any contains an error?

A. Before the meeting he greeted both the Company Secretary and the Finance Director.

B. Before the meeting he greeted the Company Secretary and Finance Director.

C. Neither is correct.

Answer [   ]

225 Which sentences if any contain an error?

A. Bart usually drove real careful but the police officer was unimpressed that he had both broken the speed limit and jumped the red light.

B. Bart usually drove really carefully but the police officer was both unimpressed that he had broken the speed limit and jumped the red light.

C. Bart usually drove really carefully but the police officer was unimpressed that he had broken the speed limit and jumped a red light.

D. None is correct.

Answer [   ]

226   __A__ friend is a friend of __B__.

A	B
1. You	1. mine
2. Yours	2. me
3. Your	

Answer [   ]

227   Indicate which if any of the following sentences contain an error.

A. The five children really enjoyed the show and was happy to share the sweets among them.

B. The five children really enjoyed the show and were happy to share the sweets between them.

C. The five children really enjoyed the show and were happy to share the sweets among them.

D. None is correct.

Answer [   ]

228   I saw them __A__ to the kitchen just before I __B__ something burning in the kitchen.

A	B
1. to go	1. smelt
2. going	2. smell
3. smelling	

Answer [   ]

229   We had a lovely holiday __A__ Sardinia and spent the last day __B__ the beach.

A	B
1. in	1. in
2. on	2. on
3. at	3. at

Answer [   ]

230   Which is the adjective?

The slow car stopped.

Answer [   ]

231 My sister and I have three brothers; two of __A__ are left-handed.

A
1. them
2. they
3. which

Answer [   ]

232 He could not decide if he was __A__ experienced or if he wasn't experienced __B__ .

A	B
1. enough	1. too
2. to	2. to
3. too	3. enough

Answer [   ]

233 I was sitting __A__ the bus when we saw David __B__ the back of the
building.

A	B
1. in	1. in
2. at	2. at
3. on	3. on

Answer [   ]

234 Which part of the sentence is the continuous present tense?

I am doing my best.

Answer [   ]

235 They __A__ Italy on time but did not __B__ Rome until late and __C__
home in the early hours.

A	B	C
1. arrived	1. got to	1. arrived in
2. arrived to	2. get	2. arrived to
3. arrived in	3. get to	3. arrived

Answer [   ]

236 We drove there __A__ car. Can you remember whether or not we paid
__B__ cheque or __C__ cash?

A	B	C
1. in my	1. by	1. by
2. by my	2. in	2. in

Answer [   ]

237 How many adjectives are in the sentence:

The beautiful young woman was wearing a blue and green dress.

Answer _____

238 How many of the following sentences contain an error?

    A. The design was one of the most unique.
    B. The design was the most unique.
    C. The design was unique.
    D. None.

Answer _____

239 It rained __A__ much and for __B__ long time.

A	B
1. such	1. such
2. so	2. so
	3. such a

Answer _____

240 The man was wearing a __A__ coat.

A
1. long and red   2. red and long
3. long, red   4. long red

Answer _____

241 Peter is a good friend __A__ lives in Italy, a country __B__ I have never visited.

A	B
1. who	1. what
2. that	2. whom
3. and	3. which
4. whom	

Answer _____

242 Which is a plural reflexive pronoun?

    A. myself
    B. my
    C. ours
    D. mine
    E. yourself
    F. themselves

Answer _____

243 __A__ rugby team scored three kick goals.

According to the timetable the train runs __B__ day twice __C__ hour.

A	B	C
1. Every	1. each	1. every
2. Each	2. every	2. each

Answer [   ]

244 With little money but __A__ time you can visit a __B__ museums.

A	B
1. little	1. little
2. much	2. much
3. few	3. few

Answer [   ]

245 Tom is lazy and never has __A__ work while Joe always has __B__ work to do.

A	B
1. some	1. any
2. any	2. some

Answer [   ]

246 __A__ a new cinema opened in town but when I went __B__ was closed.

A	B
1. It	1. there
2. There	2. there's
3. Their	3. it
4. There's	4. their

Answer [   ]

Read a passage and evaluate a statement

These questions provide a series of passages and statements that relate to them. It is your task to read the passage and decide if the statements are true, false or that you cannot tell if they are true or false. It is important to remember that in your decision you should rely only on the information provided in the passage.

If you find these questions easy, then you may be allowing yourself too leisurely a read and too much time to answer the questions. In a real test situation you really only have time for one fast, careful read and you will have to work through the question very quickly; also, you may have to turn the page and so not have the passage to hand for cross-referencing. You may well also be suffering from anxiety. For realistic practice set yourself a strict time constraint and work quickly, to the point where you risk getting some questions wrong. That way you will develop a winning exam technique.

Passage 1

Light is made up of electromagnetic waves. These vary in length and it is these differences that we perceive as different colours. White light has all the wavelengths of the light spectrum mixed up together. An object looks coloured because light falls on it and it reflects only certain parts of the spectrum. The rest of the spectrum is absorbed by the object. An object that looks white reflects all the light that falls on it. An object that looks red reflects the red part of the spectrum and absorbs the rest. Our eyes detect these different reflected waves and we see them as different colours.

247 Without colours we would consider the world a dull and less beautiful place.

A. True   B. False   C. Cannot tell

Answer   C.

248 White light is an amalgam of all the wavelengths of light.

A. True   B. False   C. Cannot tell

Answer   A.

249 The passage states that an object that looks blue absorbs all but the blue wavelengths of light.

A. True   B. False   C. Cannot tell

Answer   B.

250 The colour we perceive an object to be is determined by the electromagnetic waves that it absorbs or reflects.

A. True   B. False   C. Cannot tell

Answer   A.

251 White paint reflects more light than red paint.

A. True   B. False   C. Cannot tell

Answer   A.

Passage 2

Between 1797 and 1815 Europe went through the Napoleonic wars. This period saw France at war with the kingdoms of Prussia, Russia, Austria, Spain and Britain. At that time the French army was the most powerful in Europe. By 1808 France had conquered much of the continent and had created the largest European empire since the Romans two thousand years before. Napoleon Bonaparte was its emperor and the military leader who oversaw the many major victories. However, a disastrous campaign in Russia, retreat from the Spanish peninsular and British supremacy at sea eventually allowed a combined European force to defeat Napoleon's army at Waterloo.

252 The Napoleonic wars lasted 18 years.

   A. True   B. False   C. Cannot tell

Answer A.

253 By 1808 Napoleon headed an empire that controlled most of the continent of Europe.

   A. True   B. False   C. Cannot tell

Answer A.

254 At the height of Napoleon's victories the French army was the largest in Europe.

   A. True   B. False   C. Cannot tell

Answer C.

255 France won battles against Prussia, Russia, Austria and Britain.

   A. True   B. False   C. Cannot tell

Answer C.

256 The passage states that the battle of Waterloo took place in 1815.

   A. True   B. False   C. Cannot tell

Answer B.

Passage 3

Traditionally medicine was the science of curing illness with treatments. For thousands of years people would have used plants and would have turned to priests for cures. In more recent times illness has been attributed less to the intervention of gods or magic and instead to natural causes. Medicine today is as much concerned with prevention as cure. Doctors use treatments of many types, including radiation and vaccination, both of which were unknown until very recent times. Other treatments have been known about and practised for centuries. Muslim doctors were skilled surgeons and treated pain with opium. When Europeans first reached the Americas they found healers who used many plants to cure illnesses. The Europeans adopted many of these treatments and some are still effective and in use today.

257 Modern medicine is the science of curing illness.

A. True   B. False   C. Cannot tell

Answer   B.

258 Medicine is a science that owes its success to modern treatments.

A. True   B. False   C. Cannot tell

Answer   B.

259 Vaccination is a relatively recent discovery.

A. True   B. False   C. Cannot tell

Answer   A.

260 The author of the passage believes that prevention is better than cure.

A. True   B. False   C. Cannot tell

Answer   C.

261 Practitioners of modern medicine make use of many techniques and technologies.

A. True   B. False   C. Cannot tell

Answer   A.

Passage 4

Asia is the world's largest continent and stretches from the Baring Sea in the east to Turkey and Europe in the west. Its southern border comprises many islands, including those that make up Indonesia. Since independence of colonial powers, Asian economies have boomed. First were Japan, Singapore, Taiwan and South Korea and later Malaysia, Thailand and Indonesia. More recently China and India have enjoyed rapid economic growth. The south-west and central parts of the continent are deserts. The Himalayan mountains divide the cold north from the tropical south. The people of Asia make up over two-thirds of the world's population and they live in the birthplace of the world's earliest civilizations.

262 Civilization began in the continent of Asia.

    A. True   B. False   C. Cannot tell

Answer | A.

263 The colonial era was a disaster for Asia.

    A. True   B. False   C. Cannot tell

Answer | C.

264 More of the world's population live in Asia than in any other continent.

    A. True   B. False   C. Cannot tell

Answer | A.

265 Post-colonial growth first occurred in Singapore.

    A. True   B. False   C. Cannot tell

Answer | C.

266 The continent of Antarctica is smaller than Asia.

    A. True   B. False   C. Cannot tell

Answer | A.

Passage 5

In tropical rainforests the climate remains hot and damp all the year round. In the Arctic it is cold all year, and high up in mountain ranges the climate is much colder than in nearby low-lying lands. Climate is not the same as weather. The weather can change quickly whereas the climate describes the likely weather conditions over a much longer period of time. The world is divided into five climate zones. Polar is the only zone where it is always cold, tropical where it is hot all year round, temperate where there are warm summers and cold winters, desert where it is dry and cool, and forest where the summers are cool and short. Great climate changes have occurred, an example of which is the last ice age. Mankind can affect climate when, for example, he causes great forest fires that create so much smoke that the sun is obscured for months, cooling a region. More recently man has affected the climate as a result of pollution from industry, causing the earth to warm through what is called the greenhouse effect.

267 The passage states that the weather in high mountain ranges is cooler than in nearby low-lying areas.

    A. True   B. False   C. Cannot tell

Answer | A.

268 The passage describes how climate can change.

   A. True   B. False   C. Cannot tell

   Answer   B.

269 In a tropical rainforest the climate is the same winter and summer.

   A. True   B. False   C. Cannot tell

   Answer

270 In deserts the winter is cooler than the summer.

   A. True   B. False   C. Cannot tell

   Answer

271 You can infer from the passage that the Arctic is a polar climate zone.

   A. True   B. False   C. Cannot tell

   Answer

Passage 6

The theory goes that everything around us is built up of tiny particles called atoms. Some materials are made up of only one type of atom; these are called elements. An example is hydrogen. Others are made up of different sorts of atom bonded together into molecules. These are called compounds. Water, for example, is a compound made up of molecules that contain two hydrogen atoms and one oxygen atom. The force which holds atoms together is called bonds. Atoms are made up of even smaller particles such as neutrons, electrons and protons. Neutrons and protons are made up of even smaller particles. These have been called quarks and gluons. The search is on for the particles that make up quarks.

272 The atom is the smallest particle of matter.

   A. True   B. False   C. Cannot tell

   Answer

273 All substances are made up of elements.

   A. True   B. False   C. Cannot tell

   Answer

274 A molecule is a cluster of atoms held together by bonds.

   A. True   B. False   C. Cannot tell

   Answer

275 Neutrons are made up of quarks and gluons.

A. True   B. False   C. Cannot tell

Answer _____

276 It can be inferred from the passage that molecules are made up of neutrons, electrons and protons.

A. True   B. False   C. Cannot tell

Answer _____

Passage 7

Credit card fraud has reached £500 million despite the introduction of new controls. Figures show that losses to fraud rose by 20 per cent last year. Most frauds result from cards intercepted in the post. One hundred thousand cards were posted to customers every day last year. This represents rich pickings for fraudsters. The banks knew the year would be difficult because it was thought that fraudsters would try to commit as many crimes as possible before new controls were introduced. It is hoped that this time next year the effect of the new measures will be known and that the level of fraud will have fallen considerably.

277 Top of the table of types of fraud are those committed with credit cards stolen from people's post.

A. True   B. False   C. Cannot tell

Answer _____

278 The new measures are sophisticated anti-fraud strategies.

A. True   B. False   C. Cannot tell

Answer _____

279 The new measures are already in place.

A. True   B. False   C. Cannot tell

Answer _____

280 Credit card fraud committed as a result of cards intercepted through the post has reached £500 million.

A. True   B. False   C. Cannot tell

Answer _____

281 The level of losses to overall credit card fraud rose by 20 per cent.

A. True   B. False   C. Cannot tell

Answer [   ]

Passage 8

The ambulance service estimates that as many as 500 lives are lost because of the slower emergency response times caused by road humps. Some claim that road humps, or sleeping policemen as they are sometimes called, cost more lives than are saved as a result of the traffic being slowed. Critics of road humps also claim that they cause more pollution as drivers repeatedly slow down and speed up and that they cause more congestion by disrupting the flow of traffic. Residents complain of the noise of cars crossing them and accelerating away from them. Some of these claims run counter to published research which shows that road humps cause average speeds to drop by 10 mph and as a result save lives. Since 1980 and the widespread introduction of road humps, figures show that the level of deaths and serious injury fell by 60 per cent.

282 Delays to the ambulance service and environmental concerns are raised as objections to road humps.

A. True   B. False   C. Cannot tell

Answer [   ]

283 It is fair to say that road humps can save lives and injuries but at a price.

A. True   B. False   C. Cannot tell

Answer [   ]

284 Drivers find road humps annoying.

A. True   B. False   C. Cannot tell

Answer [   ]

285 Critics believe that traffic would flow more smoothly if road humps were removed.

A. True   B. False   C. Cannot tell

Answer [   ]

286 The passage states that it is true that the repeated slowing and accelerating of cars over road humps causes more pollution.

A. True   B. False   C. Cannot tell

Answer [   ]

Passage 9

People assume that they go to hospital to get well. However, in the past few years this perception has been challenged by the real risk of acquiring a deadly infection while in hospital. As a consequence, public confidence in the health service has suffered. An antibiotic-resistant strain of bacteria was first identified in the 1950s. It was a staphylococcus common in abscesses and bloodstream infections and it had become resistant to the antibiotic penicillin. Since then the bacteria have become resistant to a second antibiotic and have become established as a source of infection in many nursing homes and hospitals. Today they are believed to cause about 1,000 deaths each year as a result of hospital-acquired infections. Action that can beat this 'superbug' is simple but expensive. It requires very high levels of hygiene and cleanliness and a programme of testing so that infected patients can be isolated and treated.

287 Staphylococcus infections kill around 1,000 people a year.

A. True   B. False   C. Cannot tell

Answer

288 If clean hospitals had been a priority in the 1950s we would not face this threat today.

A. True   B. False   C. Cannot tell

Answer

289 Staphylococcus became established as a source of infection in many nursing homes and hospitals in the 1950s.

A. True   B. False   C. Cannot tell

Answer

290 Staphylococcus has become a 'superbug'.

A. True   B. False   C. Cannot tell

Answer

291 Infections of the bloodstream are more serious than abscesses.

A. True   B. False   C. Cannot tell

Answer

Passage 10

Recent changes to the postal voting system are considered by election officials to significantly increase the risk of electoral fraud. If it were to become wide-spread, such fraud could discredit the whole electoral process. Greatest concerns centre around the very limited time the new system allows electoral administrators to check that requests for postal ballots are genuine. The government is keen to increase the number of people who cast a vote and believe that people should not be denied a vote simply because they do not apply in good time. Fraud is currently rare and there is so far no evidence of postal votes leading to widespread fraud.

292 The government was warned by electoral administrators that the risk of fraud is now much higher.

   A. True   B. False   C. Cannot tell

   Answer [   ]

293 There is currently insufficient fraud to bring the electoral system into disrepute.

   A. True   B. False   C. Cannot tell

   Answer [   ]

294 The previous system of postal voting was considered by election administrators to be less open to fraud.

   A. True   B. False   C. Cannot tell

   Answer [   ]

295 There is a process for checking the validity of applications for postal votes.

   A. True   B. False   C. Cannot tell

   Answer [   ]

296 It is clear that the author of the passage agrees with the concerns raised by the administrators.

   A. True   B. False   C. Cannot tell

   Answer [   ]

Passage 11

Oil prices have been at record levels and are currently at around $45 a barrel. In the most efficient oilfields it costs only 80 to 90 cents to extract a barrel. Most producing countries want greater oil price stability and fear for the effect on their economies and on world demand when, as in recent years, oil prices have fluctuated between $20 and $50 a barrel. In response, some producers are expanding production capacity in order that they can respond more flexibly to demand and rising prices with greater production. Exploration and research into extraction techniques have been commissioned to investigate ways in which production can be expanded. This exploration and research brought unexpected results. Oil analysts have concluded that there is much more oil in the world than current estimates assume and that new techniques make it possible to extract much more of the known reserves economically than previously thought.

297 The record price for crude oil is $50 a barrel.

    A. True   B. False   C. Cannot tell

    Answer [   ]

298 New extraction techniques allow oil to be extracted at a price of between 80 and 90 cents a barrel.

    A. True   B. False   C. Cannot tell

    Answer [   ]

299 It is reasonable to assume that greater capacity at times of high demand will help stabilize prices.

    A. True   B. False   C. Cannot tell

    Answer [   ]

300 The passage states that the recent exploration has found new reserves.

    A. True   B. False   C. Cannot tell

    Answer [   ]

301 It would be reasonable to infer from the passage that oil analysts were impressed by the findings of the exploration and research.

    A. True   B. False   C. Cannot tell

    Answer [   ]

Passage 12

Solicitors, doctors and priests have all traditionally kept in strict confidence information they hold about or are told by their clients. A doctor will not disclose a patient's illness to anyone but the patient or next of kin. Priests have sought to keep secret the content of what they learn in the confessional and solicitors have guarded carefully the confidentiality of the client–lawyer relationship.

However, under certain circumstances all these professions make exceptions and will break confidences. A doctor must by law report injuries they believe are the result of gunshots and conditions that represent serious threats to public health. Priests have provided information to the police in relation to child abuse cases and murder. Solicitors are required to report only suspicions they have of money laundering. Journalists also adopt a code of confidentiality to protect their sources. They have a reputation for being a profession far less likely to break their code even when ordered by the courts. In a number of high-profile cases journalists have chosen to go to jail for contempt of court rather than reveal the source of a story.

302 The passage mentions priests, doctors and solicitors as professions with a confidentiality ethic.

A. True   B. False   C. Cannot tell

Answer

303 Solicitors are obliged to report a client to the authorities if they suspect them of tax evasion.

A. True   B. False   C. Cannot tell

Answer

304 The passage details circumstances where a client's confidentiality might be broken by all the mentioned professions.

A. True   B. False   C. Cannot tell

Answer

305 All professions have a confidentiality code but some are stricter than others.

A. True   B. False   C. Cannot tell

Answer

306 The passage states that a doctor can be prosecuted if he or she does not report a patient who has suffered gunshot wounds.

A. True   B. False   C. Cannot tell

Answer

Passage 13

In the past 12 months benefit fraud has fallen by £½ billion to its lowest level for over a decade. The fall is equivalent to a 25 per cent drop to 1.5 per cent of the total £100 billion benefit bill. This spectacular fall follows permission for the benefit office to access Inland Revenue taxation data. Benefit officers can now immediately check to see if a claimant is working and claiming benefits intended only for those out of work. This new measure has led to over 80,000 people being caught making false claims. A similar initiative has also succeeded in a substantial cut in the level of fraud committed by claimants of housing benefit. Local authorities are responsible for the administration of this allowance, which is awarded to the unemployed and low paid to help with housing costs. Until recently local authority staff had been unable to access central government records to check the information provided by claimants. These checks have so far identified 44,000 claimants who have provided false information in order to make claims for allowances for which they are not eligible.

307 By making it possible to share information, over 120,000 cases of fraud have been detected.

A. True   B. False   C. Cannot tell

Answer

308 Ten years ago the level of benefit fraud was higher.

A. True   B. False   C. Cannot tell

Answer

309 Only the unemployed should legitimately claim these benefits.

A. True   B. False   C. Cannot tell

Answer

310 The tone of the passage suggests that these reductions in fraud are a good thing.

A. True   B. False   C. Cannot tell

Answer

311 A year ago the level of benefit fraud totalled £2 billion.

A. True   B. False   C. Cannot tell

Answer

Passage 14

In most parts of the developed world many middle-class people ask themselves over and over again whether they should buy or rent a house. If they live in the United States, Spain, Ireland or the UK, then in a loud chorus they answer 'Buy'. In these countries house prices have almost doubled over the past seven years.

Other parts of the developed world have not seen such house price inflation and anyway, is it realistic to assume that prices will always continue to rise?

Some people argue that paying rent is like throwing money away and it is better to repay a mortgage and build some equity. But what if house prices fall? A really quite minor adjustment would quickly wipe out the equity of many home owners. If house price inflation is something of the past, then home ownership becomes less attractive. Renting too has some advantages. In particular, people who rent find it far easier to move for their work.

312 The passage raises the spectre that homeowners may not always be able to rely on capital growth.

A. True   B. False   C. Cannot tell

Answer _____

313 Most middle-class people in the developed world prefer to own their own home.

A. True   B. False   C. Cannot tell

Answer _____

314 It is reasonable to infer that fewer people will rent if house prices stop going up in value.

A. True   B. False   C. Cannot tell

Answer _____

315 Spaniards have seen their homes more than double in value.

A. True   B. False   C. Cannot tell

Answer _____

316 The passage is written from the standpoint that buying may not always be better than renting.

A. True   B. False   C. Cannot tell

Answer _____

Passage 15

For most of the last two decades of the previous century the economy of the city of Liverpool was mostly stagnant and far behind that of the rest of the UK. But as other cities have become more expensive, Liverpool has become a more popular place in which to invest and live. Liverpool's population dropped from 800,000 after the war to less than 500,000 at the turn of the century. The process of depopulation has now reduced to a trickle and for the first time in decades the working population has grown. The level of unemployment, which once stood at 20 per cent, is down to under 5 per cent. Construction of office space is booming and currently being built are conference complexes, a series of department stores and two 50-floor tower blocks. It is not surprising, therefore, that the working population is expected to grow further still. Low living and housing costs have attracted many public sector organizations to relocate to the city. Forty per cent of the workforce of Liverpool work in this sector and it seems that this trend will continue as over half of the new jobs created are public appointments. Subsidy has played a significant part in attracting jobs and investment. Over £4 billion has been spent in the regeneration of the region and the lion's share of this has been committed to the city of Liverpool itself.

317 The city of Liverpool is no longer a net exporter of people.

    A. True   B. False   C. Cannot tell

                                      Answer [   ]

318 Forty per cent of the new jobs are public appointments.

    A. True   B. False   C. Cannot tell

                                      Answer [   ]

319 During the 1990s the economy of the region fell far behind that of the rest of the UK.

    A. True   B. False   C. Cannot tell

                                      Answer [   ]

320 Without the subsidy fewer jobs would have been attracted to the region.

    A. True   B. False   C. Cannot tell

                                      Answer [   ]

321 Much of Liverpool's recent success is owed to the fact that the costs of living and housing there are less than in other cities in the UK.

    A. True   B. False   C. Cannot tell

                                      Answer [   ]

5

NUMERICAL REASONING

Psychometric tests of your numeracy skills are by far the most common type. There are few if any tests that do not include a sub-test of these skills and it is crazy to be judged as a great candidate except for the maths! So get down to some serious score-improving practice now. If you are already good at maths, then use these questions to build up your speed and attend ready to press home your advantage to the full.

Everyone can master these questions – it is just that some of us have to practise more than others. If you have to pass such a test to realize your career or educational dream and you hate maths, then it is time to get down to some serious work and rise to the challenge.

I have known many candidates who have done just this and you can too. I remember one candidate who wanted to be an airline pilot. He had to pass a test for only a few places against many candidates and he was poor at maths. His prospects looked bad but he did it and he is now flying. The secret to his success was his sheer determination and hard work. He used to go for a run every morning and every car he passed he started to add up the numbers of their number plates. Once he had mastered addition he began to multiply the numbers and then divided them. He did this every day for weeks until the day of the test. By this time his command of mental arithmetic was up there with the very best. You don't have to take up running to succeed in this common area of weakness but you do need to let it take over a bit of your life for a while and to really go for it.

This chapter will prepare you for the different types of question that can appear. Further practice at both an intermediate and advanced level is available in the Kogan Page Testing Series.

Intermediate

The Numeracy Test Workbook, 2nd edition, contains over 1,000 practice questions.

Advanced

How to Pass Advanced Numeracy Tests, 2nd edition
Advanced Numeracy Test Workbook, 2nd edition

The key operations

Mental arithmetic

It is common for a test to include a section on mental arithmetic. You are required to work the sums in your head without a calculator or doing any working out on paper. These are easy marks for the well-practised candidate. Sharpening your skills is boring, painful even, but everyone can do it. It is simply a matter of practice. Be sure that you attend for a test confident, fast and accurate in these essential operations. Even if the test you face allows you to use a calculator, you should still attend being able to do these calculations in your head. You will save time if you do.

Below are 100 practice questions for your command of multiplication. I have not provided practice for addition and subtraction as you can devise your own questions for these key operations if necessary (you might change the sign of the following sums to make them, for example, addition instead of multiplication). Even if the test that you face does not include questions of this style, they are essential skills – and skills that you must command if you are to triumph in any numeracy test.

Work out the following in your head as quickly as possible. Do not stop practising until you are really quick and accurate. Answers are provided on page 244. Explanations are not provided for the first 64 questions.

1 $? \times 5 = 15$ *Answer*

2 $7 \times ? = 49$ *Answer*

3 $? \times 4 = 24$ *Answer*

4 $11 \times 7 = ?$ *Answer*

5 $4 \times ? = 24$ *Answer*

6 $6 \times ? = 54$ *Answer*

7 $3 \times ? = 36$ *Answer*

8 $12 \times 12 = ?$ *Answer*

9 $6 \times ? = 48$ *Answer*

10 $? \times 4 = 16$ *Answer*

11 $7 \times 12 = ?$ *Answer*

12 $? \times 7 = 21$ *Answer*

13 $9 \times ? = 45$ *Answer*

14 $? \times 8 = 88$ *Answer*

15 $7 \times ? = 28$ *Answer*

16 $3 \times 11 = ?$ *Answer*

17 $9 \times ? = 63$ *Answer*

18 $4 \times ? = 360$ *Answer*

19 $11 \times ? = 121$ *Answer*

20 $? \times 12 = 60$ *Answer*

21 $? \times 9 = 54$ *Answer*

22 $7 \times ? = 63$ *Answer*

23 $9 \times ? = 90$ *Answer*

24 $? \times 3 = 99$ *Answer*

25 $8 \times ? = 32$ *Answer*

26 $12 \times ? = 60$ *Answer*

27 $? \times 9 = 99$ *Answer*

28 $3 \times ? = 21$ *Answer*

29 $6 \times 7 = ?$ *Answer*

30 $9 \times ? = 81$ *Answer*

31 $4 \times ? = 100$ *Answer*

32 $? \times 9 = 99$ *Answer*

33 $? \times 6 = 48$ *Answer*

34 $9 \times 12 = ?$ *Answer*

35 $? \times 5 = 55$ *Answer*

36 $4 \times ? = 32$ *Answer*

37 $6 \times ? = 42$ *Answer*

38 $5 \times ? = 100$ *Answer*

39 $9 \times ? = 72$ *Answer*

40 $? \times 5 = 20$ *Answer*

41 $15 \times ? = 90$ *Answer*

42 $11 \times ? = 44$ *Answer*

43 $? \times 5 = 30$ *Answer*

44   ? × 8 = 64   Answer [   ]

45   ? × 12 = 48   Answer [   ]

46   3 × 6 = ?   Answer [   ]

47   ? × 6 = 66   Answer [   ]

48   4 × ? = 36   Answer [   ]

49   ? × 9 = 72   Answer [   ]

50   4 × 8 = ?   Answer [   ]

51   7 × ? = 42   Answer [   ]

52   ? × 4 = 36   Answer [   ]

53   8 × 8 = ?   Answer [   ]

54   6 × ? = 66   Answer [   ]

55   ? × 8 = 56   Answer [   ]

56   6 × 5 = ?   Answer [   ]

57   3 × ? = 27   Answer [   ]

58   ? × 12 = 132   Answer [   ]

59   8 × 6 = ?   Answer [   ]

60   ? × 9 = 81   Answer [   ]

61   4 × ? = 28   Answer [   ]

62   6 × 6 = ?   Answer [   ]

63   8 × ? = 96   Answer [   ]

64   ? × 4 = 12   Answer [   ]

65   List the factors of 18.   Answer [   ]

Tip: factors are the numbers that divide exactly into a number. For example, the factors of 12 are 1, 2, 3, 4, 6, 12.

66   List the factors of 27.   *Answer* [   ]

67   List the factors of 11.   *Answer* [   ]

68   List the factors of 22.   *Answer* [   ]

69   List the factors of 36.   *Answer* [   ]

70   How many factors does 20 have?   *Answer* [   ]

71   How many factors does 56 have?   *Answer* [   ]

72   How many factors does 19 have?   *Answer* [   ]

73   List the factors of 60.   *Answer* [   ]

74   How many factors does 14 have?   *Answer* [   ]

75   List the factors of 42.   *Answer* [   ]

76   How many factors does 37 have?   *Answer* [   ]

77   List the factors of 16.   *Answer* [   ]

78   How many factors does 48 have?   *Answer* [   ]

79   List the factors of 24.   *Answer* [   ]

80   How many factors does 32 have?   *Answer* [   ]

81   How many factors does 34 have?   *Answer* [   ]

82   What is the highest common factor of 8 and 20?   *Answer* [   ]

83   How many common factors do 12 and 18 have?   *Answer* [   ]

84   What is the highest common factor of 21 and 49?   *Answer* [   ]

85   How many common factors do 12 and 16 have?   *Answer* [   ]

86 $12.7 \times 100 = ?$ *Answer*

87 $16.3 \times 10 = ?$ *Answer*

88 $376 \div 100 = ?$ *Answer*

89 $90.6 \times 1{,}000$ *Answer*

90 $2.4 \div 100 = ?$ *Answer*

91 $96 \div 10 = ?$ *Answer*

92 $15.02 \div 1{,}000 = ?$ *Answer*

93 $3.002 \times 1{,}000 = ?$ *Answer*

94 $0.07 \div 10 = ?$ *Answer*

95 $0.03 \times 100 = ?$ *Answer*

96   Multiply 20 by 920.   *Answer*

97   Divide 1,200 by 400.   *Answer*

98   Multiply 3,000 by 70.   *Answer*

99   Divide 48,000 by 60.   *Answer*

100 Multiply 600 by 300.   *Answer*

Percentages

After mental arithmetic and multiplication the next most essential skill demanded by psychometric tests is percentages. Do these questions to revise your ability in these essential operations. Keep practising until you are confident, fast and accurate. Remember not to use a calculator but feel free to use some scrap paper to do some working.

 If the answer is recurring, then work the sum to only one decimal place.

Changing fractions to decimals

Tip: divide 100 by the bottom value of the fraction and then multiply the result by the top value.

Worked example: Find 1/2 as a percentage

Answer | 50% |

Explanation: 100 ÷ 2 = 50 × 1 = 50

101 Find 1/5 as a percentage. *Answer*

102 Find 1/4 as a percentage. *Answer*

103 Find 1/9 as a percentage. *Answer*

104 Find 1/12 as a percentage. *Answer*

105 Find 1/8 as a percentage. *Answer*

106 Find 1/16 as a percentage. *Answer*

107 Find 2/3 as a percentage. *Answer*

108 Find 3/5 as a percentage. *Answer*

109 Find 6/16 as a percentage. *Answer*

110 Find 5/8 as a percentage. *Answer*

111 Find 4/6 as a percentage. *Answer*

112 Find 6/8 as a percentage. *Answer*

113 Find 12/15 as a percentage. *Answer*

114 Find 4/20 as a percentage. *Answer*

115 Find 9/24 as a percentage. *Answer*

116 Find 8/20 as a percentage. *Answer*

117 Find 6/32 as a percentage. *Answer*

118 Find 21/28 as a percentage. *Answer*

119 Find 25/80 as a percentage. *Answer*

Changing between decimals and percentages

Tip: multiply a decimal by 100 to get the equivalent percentage or divide the percentage by 100 to get the equivalent decimal. The first one is done for you as a worked example.

120 Convert 0.5 into a percentage.   *Answer* | 50% |
Explanation: 0.5 × 100 = 50

121 Convert 0.2 to a percentage.   *Answer*

122 Convert 0.6 to a percentage.   *Answer*

123 Convert 25% to a decimal.   *Answer*

124 Convert 0.4 to a percentage.   *Answer*

125 Convert 90% to a decimal.   *Answer*

126 Convert 0.35 to a percentage.   *Answer*

127 Convert 5% to a decimal.   *Answer*

128 Convert 0.72 to a percentage.   *Answer*

129 Convert 2.4% to a decimal.   *Answer*

130 Convert 0.425 to a percentage.   *Answer*

131 Convert 1.6% to a percentage.   *Answer*

132 Convert 0.333 to a percentage.   *Answer*

133 Convert 120% to a decimal.   *Answer*

134 Convert 0.5% to a decimal.   *Answer*

Expressing values as percentage

Tip: make the first value a fraction of the second, reduce the fraction to its simplest term and then convert the fraction into a percentage. The first one is done for you.

135 Find 30 as a percentage of 50.   *Answer*   60%

Explanation: 30/50 = 3/5, 100 ÷ 5 = 20 × 3 = 60

136 Find 10 as a percentage of 40.   *Answer*

137 Find 2 as a percentage of 5.   *Answer*

138 Find 3 as a percentage of 27.   *Answer*

139 Find 12 as a percentage of 80.   *Answer*

140 Find 4 as a percentage of 16.   *Answer*

141 Find 12 as a percentage of 40.   *Answer*

142 Find 14 as a percentage of 35.   *Answer*

143 Find 25 as a percentage of 30.   *Answer*

144 Find 10 as a percentage of 12.5.   *Answer*

145 Find 0.5 as a percentage of 3.   *Answer*

146 Find 0.3 as a percentage of 0.9.   *Answer*

147 Find 0.2 as a percentage of 80.   *Answer*

148 Find 3.3 as a percentage of 3.   *Answer*

149 Find 6 as a percentage of 32.   *Answer*

Percentages of quantities

Tip: convert the percentage to a decimal and then multiply by the quantity but take care that you treat all the values equally and express your answer in the appropriate unit. The first one is done for you.

150 Find 12.5% of £80.   *Answer*   £10

Explanation: 12.5 ÷ 100 = 0.125, 80 × 0.125 = 10.

151 Find 25% of 5 hours.   *Answer*

152 Find 25% of 16 metres.   *Answer*

153 Find 5% of £5.   *Answer* [   ]

154 Find 20% of 55 metres.   *Answer* [   ]

155 Find 15% of 1 hour 20 minutes.   *Answer* [   ]

156 Find 12% of £360.   *Answer* [   ]

157 Find 12.5% of 3 hours and 40 minutes.   *Answer* [   ]

158 Find 45% of 70 metres.   *Answer* [   ]

159 Find 45% of £20.40.   *Answer* [   ]

160 Find 15% of 3 metres (express your answer in cm).
                                                                       Answer [   ]

161 Find 30% of 24 hours (express your answer in hours and minutes).
                                                                       Answer [   ]

162 Find 12% of 250 metres.   *Answer* [   ]

163 Find 17.5% of £1,550.   *Answer* [   ]

164 Find 3% of 72 hours.   *Answer* [   ]

Percentage increase

Tip: divide the increase by the original amount and multiply the answer by 100.
The first one is done for you.

165 What is the percentage increase between 20 and 30?
                                                                       Answer [50%   ]
         Explanation: increase = 10, 10 ÷ 20 = 0.5 × 100 = 50

166 What is the percentage increase between 20 and 24?
                                                                       Answer [   ]

167 What is the percentage increase between 40 and 56
                                                                       Answer [   ]

168 What is the percentage increase between 8 and 9?

Answer [   ]

169 What is the percentage increase between 5 and 8?

Answer [   ]

170 What is the percentage increase between 16 and 20?

Answer [   ]

Quantities and conversions

171 1 mile equals 1.6 kilometres, so how many kilometres do 4 miles equal?

Answer [   ]

172 1 litre is equal to 1.75 pints (UK), so how many pints do 5 litres equal?

Answer [   ]

173 If $3US are worth $12AU, how many $AU are $7US worth?

Answer [   ]

174 1 kilogram is equal to 35 oz, so how many ounces do 3 kilograms equal?

Answer [   ]

175 1 litre is equal to 35 fluid ounces, so how many fluid ounces are equal to 5 litres?

Answer [   ]

176 If $2US are worth $5AU, how many $AU are $10US worth?

Answer [   ]

177 1 kilometre equals 1,000 metres, so how many metres are equal to 3.75 kilometres?

Answer [   ]

178 A drum holds 120 litres, so how many do you need to store 700 litres?

Answer [   ]

179 How many 4-metre lengths of timber are required to extend end to end a total of 1/20 of a kilometre?

Answer [   ]

180 1 inch is equal to 25.4 mm, so how many millimetres are equal to 5 inches?

Answer

181 If today is Saturday the 15th of March, what was the date Thursday last?

Answer

182 1 kilogram is equal to 2.2 pounds, so how many pounds are equal to 8 kilograms?

Answer

183 If $2.5US are worth $5AU, how many $AU are $15US worth?

Answer

184 1 kilometre is equal to 1093 yards, so how many yards are equal to 1.1 kilometres?

Answer

185 1 metre is equal to 1,000 mm, so how many millimetres are equal to 7.02 metres?

Answer

186 1 litre is equal to 1.75 pints (UK), so how many pints do 1.2 litres equal?

Answer

187 1 kilometre is equal to 1093 yards, so how many yards are equal to 2 kilometres?

Answer

188 Which is fastest, 0.3 km/s or 20 km/minute?

Answer

189 1 inch is equal to 25.4 mm, so how many millimetres are equal to 4 inches?

Answer

190 How far will you travel in 5 minutes at a speed of 180 km/hr?

Answer

191 If $1US are worth $1.75AU, how many $AU are $6US worth?

Answer

192 1 mile equals 1.6 kilometres, so how many kilometres do 7 miles equal?

Answer

Conversions

193 If $4EC = $16T, how many $EC = $20T? *Answer*

194 If $6EC = $13.5T, how many $EC = $9T? *Answer*

195 If $1HC = $2.5AU, how many $HC = $20AU? *Answer*

196 If $1HC = $1.8 AU, how many $HC = $9AU? *Answer*

197 If $1HC = $4.5AU, how many $HC = $18AU? *Answer*

198 If $1HC = $1.6AU, how many $HC = $8AU? *Answer*

199 If $1HC = $1.1AU, how many $HC = $55AU? *Answer*

200 If $2.5EC = $5T, how many $EC = $10T? *Answer*

201 If $1.5EC = $6T, how many $EC = $1T? *Answer*

202 If $1EC = $3.2T, how many $EC = $48T? *Answer*

203 If $2EC = $8T, how many $EC = $26T? *Answer*

204 If $2EC = $6T, how many $EC = $24T? *Answer*

205 If $3EC = $3.6T, how many $EC = $6T? *Answer*

206 If $2EC = $2.5T, how many $EC = $15T? *Answer*

207 If $9.5EC = $1T, how many $EC = $114T? *Answer*

208 If $2EC = $3.5T, how many $EC = $7T? *Answer*

209 If $3EC = $6T, how many $EC = $22T? *Answer*

210 If $5EC = $15T, how many $EC = $18T? *Answer*

Sequencing

This was once a very fashionable style of question in tests used by employers but today it is less common in employment-related jobs and more likely to be found in IQ tests.

If you find this style of question a complete enigma, then take heart, because practice and taking the time to review the explanations of the answers will lead to considerable improvements in your score.

There are only a certain number of principles that these questions are based on and once you have realized most of them you know what to look for and can get these questions right very quickly.

211

?	17	22	27	32	37

Answer [   ]

212

42	?	26	18	10	2

Answer [   ]

213

?	6	36	216	1296	7776

Answer [   ]

214

20	25	30	?	40	45

Answer [   ]

215

6561	2187	729	243	81	?

Answer [   ]

216

?	75	150	300	600	1,200

Answer [   ]

217

23	19	15	?	7	3

Answer [   ]

218

1	3	9	?	81	243

Answer [   ]

219

435	?	609	696	783	870

Answer [   ]

220

607.5	202.5	?	22.5	7.5	2.5

Answer [   ]

221

7	9	16	?	41	66

Answer [   ]

222

125	142	?	176	193	210

Answer [   ]

223

381	355	329	303	277	?

Answer [   ]

224 | 250 | ? | 40 | 16 | 6.4 | 2.56 | Answer

225 | 28 | 42 | 56 | ? | 84 | 98 | Answer

226 | ? | 2 | 2.5 | 4.5 | 7 | 11.5 | Answer

227 | 1201 | 1302 | 1403 | ? | 1605 | 1706 | Answer

228 | 100 | 10 | ? | 0.1 | 0.01 | 0.001 | Answer

229 | 200 | 129 | 58 | ? | −84 | −155 | Answer

230 | 18 | 21 | 39 | ? | 99 | | Answer

231 | 25 | 10 | ? | 1.6 | 0.64 | 0.256 | Answer

232 | −12 | −34 | ? | −78 | −100 | −122 | Answer

233 | 0.1 | 0.5 | 2.5 | ? | 62.5 | 312.5 | Answer

234 | 15 | 8 | 23 | ? | 54 | 85 | Answer

235 | 10 | ? | 41 | 17 | 52 | 09 | Answer

236 | 2 | 3 | 6 | ? | 108 | 1944 | Answer

237 | 40 | ? | 90 | 135 | 202.5 | | Answer

238 | ? | 1332 | 1665 | 1998 | 2331 | 2664 | Answer

239 | 70 | 11 | 81 | 92 | ? | 265 | Answer

240 | 19 | 81 | 86 | 17 | 41 | ? | Answer

241 | 1 | 3 | ? | 9 | 27 | 243 | Answer

242

| 12 | 2.4 | ? | 0.096 | 0.0192 | |

Answer

243

| 91 | 12 | 01 | 49 | ? | 8207 |

Answer

244

| 1 | 4 | 9 | 16 | ? | 36 |

Answer

245

| 2 | 3 | 5 | 7 | 11 | ? | 17 | 19 |

Answer

246

| 80 | 07 | ? | 76 | 07 | 40 |

Answer

247

| 3:4 | 6:8 | 9:12 | 12:16 | ? |

Answer

248

| 2 | ? | 8 | 32 | 256 |

Answer

249

| 0.5 | 3 | 18 | ? | 648 |

Answer

250

| 14 | 91 | 62 | ? | 6 |

Answer

251

| 15 | ? | 70 | 18 | 52 | 00 |

Answer

252

| 24 | 17 | 41 | 58 | ? |

Answer

253

| 3 | 8 | 24 | ? | 4608 |

Answer

254

| 2401 | 343 | ? | 7 | 1 |

Answer

255

| 36 | ? | 64 | 81 | 100 | 121 |

Answer

256

| ? | 2 | 3 | 4 | 6 | 12 |

Answer

257

| 104 | ? | 130 | 143 | 156 |

Answer

258

| 67.24 | 8.2 | 9 | ? | 3.24 | 1.8 |

Answer

259

| 4 | 8 | 16 | ? | 64 | 128 |

Answer

260 | 11 | 38 | ? | 87 | 136 | 223 | *Answer*

261 | 1:2 | 2:4 | 3:6 | ? | 5:10 | *Answer*

262 | 1 | ? | 5 | 15 | *Answer*

263 | 216 | 343 | 512 | 729 | ? | *Answer*

264 | 0.75 | 3 | ? | 48 | 192 | 768 | *Answer*

265 | ? | 126 | 140 | 154 | 168 | *Answer*

266 | 222 | 426 | ? | 032 | *Answer*

267 | 9 | 27 | ? | 243 | 729 | *Answer*

268 | 12.5 | 2.5 | 0.5 | ? | 0.02 | *Answer*

269 | 7 | 11 | 18 | ? | 47 | 76 | *Answer*

270 | 144 | 121 | ? | 81 | 64 | *Answer*

271 | 1 | 2 | ? | 14 | *Answer*

272 | 2 | 4 | 8 | 32 | ? | *Answer*

273 | 16 | 64 | ? | 1024 | *Answer*

274 | 324 | ? | 36 | 12 | 4 | *Answer*

275 | 192 | ? | 252 | 729 | *Answer*

276 | ? | 3 | 36 | 432 | 5184 | *Answer*

277 | 510 | 152 | ? | 303 | 540 | *Answer*

278 | 1 | 2 | ? | 8 | 16 | *Answer* [　　　　]

279 | 320 | ? | 20 | 5 | 1.25 | *Answer* [　　　　]

280 | 25 | ? | 625 | 3125 | *Answer* [　　　　]

281 | 32 | 40 | 48 | 56 | ? | *Answer* [　　　　]

282 | 0.5 | 0.25 | ? | 0.125 | 0.1 | *Answer* [　　　　]

283 | 1 | 2 | ? | 6 | 9 | 18 | *Answer* [　　　　]

284 | 369 | ? | 518 | 212 | 427 | *Answer* [　　　　]

285 | 19 | 17 | 13 | ? | 7 | *Answer* [　　　　]

Number problems

If you face a psychometric test that comprises this style of question, then do not stop practising until you are really quick and get them all right. Other candidates will be doing just that, so you risk coming a poor second unless you do some serious score-improving practice. All the following 59 questions test your command of multiplication and percentages.

More material of this type is available in the Kogan Page titles *How to Pass Selection Tests* and *How to Pass Graduate Psychometric Tests*. More difficult material is available in *How to Pass Advanced Numeracy Tests* and *Advanced Numeracy Test Workbook*.

Remember not to use a calculator and instead practise at working the sums manually. You will soon find short cuts and faster methods; some are illustrated in the explanations.

286 If your daily newspaper costs 55p during the week and £1.10 on Saturday and Sunday, how much is your weekly paper bill?

    A. £4.80
    B. £4.85
    C. £4.90
    D. £4.95

                     Answer [　　　　]

287 If a tub of ice cream costs £1.20, how much would 6 tubs cost?

A. £7.00

B. £7.20

C. £7.40

D. £7.60

Answer

288 If a printer produces 30 pages a minute, how many can it print in an hour?

A. 18

B. 180

C. 1,800

D. 18,000

Answer

289 If 40 people each donated £6 a month to a charity for one year, how much would be collected?

A. £288

B. £2,880

C. £28,800

D. none of these

Answer

290 If the utility bill with company A is £18 a month and company B offers the same service for £200 a year, how much if anything can you save in a year?

A. £16

B. £17

C. £18

D. £19

Answer

291 If 200 airline passengers bring 15 kg of hand luggage each, what is the total weight of hand luggage?

A. 300 kg

B. 600 kg

C. 3,000 kg

D. 6,000 kg

Answer

292 A fabric shop buys 15 metres of material at 75 pence a metre. How much does it pay for the order?

A. £11.25
B. £11.50
C. £11.75
D. £12.00

Answer

293 If 9 boxes of chocolates weigh 2.7 kg, how much would 4 boxes weigh?

A. 0.9 kg
B. 1.2 kg
C. 1.5 kg
D. 1.8 kg

Answer

294 If a pump lifts 2,000 litres of water in 8 minutes, how many will it lift in 9 minutes?

A. 2,500 litres
B. 2,400 litres
C. 2,350 litres
D. 2,250 litres

Answer

295 If you can buy a 300 gm jar of coffee for £7.50 or a 1 kg jar for £26, which purchase represents better value?

A. 300 gm jar
B. 1 kg jar
C. they are the same

Answer

296 If a box holds 8 pairs of shoes and there are a total of 192 shoes to pack away, how many boxes are required?

A. 8
B. 10
C. 12
D. 24

Answer

297 If a drum holds 40 litres of fuel and there are 15 drums, how much fuel do they contain?

A. 60 litres
B. 300 litres
C. 600 litres
D. 900 litres

Answer [　　　　　]

298 If 50 pencils cost £1.80, how much would 70 cost?

A. £2.52
B. £2.53
C. £2.54
D. £2.55

Answer [　　　　　]

299 If 6 trays contain 132 eggs, how many do 4 contain?

A. 85
B. 86
C. 87
D. 88

Answer [　　　　　]

300 If 30 households produce 6,000 bags of rubbish, how many would you expect 5 to produce?

A. 600
B. 800
C. 1,000
D. 1,200

Answer [　　　　　]

301 If your monthly phone bill is always £14 and it includes a quarterly rental of £9.00, how much would you spend in a year on the cost of calls (total cost minus rental)?

A. £200
B. £185
C. £143
D. £132

Answer [　　　　　]

302 If the monthly premium of a life insurance policy costs 70p per £1,000 of insurance cover and a company insures its key staff for a total of £250,000, how much is the cost of the insurance annually?

A. £2,000
B. £2,100
C. £2,200
D. £2,300

Answer

303 If a worker was paid £5.20 an hour for a 35-hour week and time and a half for any extra hours, how much would he earn if he worked 40 hours?

A. £218
B. £219
C. £220
D. £221

Answer

304 A computer can be purchased for a deposit of £29 and 18 monthly payments of £16. How much is the total cost of the computer?

A. £317
B. £318
C. £319
D. £320

Answer

305 If a household uses £1.20 worth of gas every 5 days and the utility company charges 9p standing charge per day, what would you expect the total charge by the utility company for gas to the household to be over a 60-day period?

A. £19.00
B. £19.80
C. £20.00
D. £20.80

Answer

306 A quality control process results in 30 parts in every 500 being rejected as below standard; express this failure rate as a percentage.

A. 3%
B. 6%
C. 9%
D. 12%

Answer

307 In his end-of-year exams Orlando obtained 52 out of 80; express this score as a percentage.

A. 62%
B. 63%
C. 64%
D. 65%

Answer

308 A survey found that 18 out of 60 respondents preferred dark chocolate to white. What percentage of respondents preferred dark chocolate?

A. 28%
B. 29%
C. 30%
D. 31%

Answer

309 An employment agency paid its staff £4.32 and charged the client £7.20. What percentage of the charge rate is received by the staff?

A. 57%
B. 58%
C. 59%
D. 60%

Answer

310 Ella paid £9.68 tax on her earnings of £88; what percentage tax did Ella pay?

A. 9%
B. 10%
C. 11%
D. 12%

Answer

311 A driver saved £487.50 on his car insurance bill of £650 as a result of his no-claims bonus; what percentage discount does this represent?

A. 60%
B. 65%
C. 70%
D. 75%

Answer

312 A bank charged £120 as an arrangement fee for a personal loan of £4,000;
how much did the fee represent as a percentage of the loan?

A. 3%
B. 4%
C. 5%
D. 6%

Answer _____

313 A die is thrown 420 times and the number 6 is obtained 63 times; express
the frequency of obtaining the number 6 as a percentage.

A. 13%
B. 14%
C. 15%
D. 16%

Answer _____

314 A cold-calling advertising campaign results in 126 orders from a total of
6,300 calls; express this rate of success as a percentage.

A. 0.5%
B. 1%
C. 1.2%
D. 2%

Answer _____

315 A savings account pays 4% interest; how much would be paid on a deposit of £750?

A. £29
B. £30
C. £31
D. £32

Answer _____

316 A train is timetabled to take 3 hours but it is delayed by 15%; how late will
the train be?

A. 25 minutes
B. 26 minutes
C. 27 minutes
D. 28 minutes

Answer _____

317 A 600 gm box of cereal comes with 12.5% extra; how much extra cereal does the purchaser receive?

A. 60 gm
B. 65 gm
C. 70 gm
D. 75 gm

Answer

318 A 400-metre length of rope at full stretch becomes 9% longer; how much longer can the rope become?

A. 36 m
B. 37 m
C. 38 m
D. 39 m

Answer

319 A pump can lift 2,400 litres an hour and its replacement model can lift 2.5% more; how many litres an hour can the new model lift?

A. 2,440 litres
B. 2,450 litres
C. 2,460 litres
D. 2,470 litres

Answer

320 On the flat a cyclist can average 14 mph but downhill his average speed increases by 40%; what speed does the cyclist average downhill?

A. 19.5 mph
B. 19.6 mph
C. 19.7 mph
D. 19.8 mph

Answer

321 The minimum payment of a credit card balance is 3%; how much would you have to pay if the card balance stood at £620?

A. £16.60
B. £17.60
C. £18.60
D. £19.60

Answer

322 On setting A, a motor rotates 3,550 revolutions per minute, and on setting B the motor rotates 20% slower; how many revolutions per minute does the motor make on setting B?

A. 4,260
B. 3,850
C. 2,840
D. 710

Answer [   ]

323 A marathon runner beats her personal best time of 4 hours 30 minutes by 5%; what is her new best time?

A. 4 hours 16 minutes 30 seconds
B. 4 hours 17 minutes
C. 4 hours 17 minutes and 30 seconds
D. 4 hours 18 minutes

Answer [   ]

324 A village population has increased by 3% to 3,605 people; what was the original population?

A. 3,460
B. 3,480
C. 3,500
D. 3,510

Answer [   ]

325 Buying a car with credit is 8% more expensive than the cash price of £7,000; for how much is the car sold if the purchaser is paying with credit?

A. £7,560
B. £7,570
C. £7,580
D. £7,590

Answer [   ]

326 A village population fell over a five-year period by 4% from the original population size of 4,300. How many people now live in the village?

A. 4,126
B. 4,128
C. 4,130
D. 4,132

Answer [   ]

327 The blue party received 8% more votes than the green party's 30,000; how many votes did the blue party receive?

A. 32,000
B. 32,400
C. 32,800
D. 33,200

Answer

328 The yellow party received 18% fewer votes than the red party's 22,000; how many votes did the yellow party obtain?

A. 17,920
B. 17,960
C. 18,000
D. 18,040

Answer

329 After a discount of 8% a computer is advertised for sale at £552; what was the price of the computer before the reduction?

A. £550
B. £600
C. £654
D. £656

Answer

330 When cooled, a length of metal contracts by 2% to a new length of 3 metres; what was the length of the metal before it was cooled?

A. 306 cm
B. 296 cm
C. 276 cm
D. 266 cm

Answer

331 Under load a rope stretches 25% and is now 300 metres long; how long was the rope before the load was applied?

A. 240 m
B. 230 m
C. 220 m
D. 210 m

Answer

332 After an 8% increase Lola's hourly wage is £6.75; what was her hourly wage before the increase?

A. £6.20
B. £6.25
C. £6.30
D. £6.35

Answer

333 If the value of a car, £6,000, depreciates by 12% a year, how much is it worth after two years?

A. £4,246.40
B. £4,446.40
C. £4,646.40
D. £4,846.40

Answer

334 If a population increases from 18,000 each year by 5%, what is the population after two years?

A. 16,245
B. 17,600
C. 18,900
D. 19,845

Answer

335 The time taken to complete an order decreases by 8 seconds to 12 seconds; what is this decrease expressed as an improvement in the efficiency of fulfilling the order?

A. 16%
B. 20%
C. 40%
D. 60%

Answer

336 If an investment increases from £800 to £1,100, what is the percentage increase?

A. 37.5%
B. 39%
C. 40.5%
D. 42%

Answer

337 A car was bought for £8,000 and sold for £6,000; what was the percentage loss?

A. 10%
B. 15%
C. 20%
D. 25%

Answer [   ]

338 A watch was bought for £25 and sold for 8% more than the buying price; what was the price it was sold for?

A. £25
B. £26
C. £27
D. £28

Answer [   ]

339 A house was sold for £120,000 at a 4% loss on the purchase price; what was the purchase price?

A. £115,200
B. £124,800
C. £129,600
D. £132,800

Answer [   ]

340 A box of 12 eggs is bought for £1.50 and each egg is sold for 15p; what is the percentage profit?

A. 20%
B. 18%
C. 15%
D. 13%

Answer [   ]

341 Sweets are purchased at £3.00 per kilo and sold for 60p per 100 gm; what is the percentage profit? (Calculate the percentage on the cost or buying price.)

A. 1,000%
B. 200%
C. 100%
D. 10%

Answer [   ]

342 20 shares were purchased at £2.50 each and sold for a total of £42; what was the percentage profit or loss? (Calculate the percentage on the cost or buying price.)

A. 13% profit
B. 14% loss
C. 15% profit
D. 16% loss

Answer [＿＿＿＿＿]

343 A company's turnover for a year was £500,000 against total costs of £515,000; what was the percentage loss made by the company that year? (Calculate the percentage on the cost or buying price.)

A. 0.3%
B. 1%
C. 2%
D. 3%

Answer [＿＿＿＿＿]

344 A Gino Grosso ice-cream machine makes each ice cream from ingredients that cost only 10p and the ice creams are then sold for £1.20 each; what is the percentage profit? (Calculate the percentage on the cost or buying price.)

A. 110%
B. 220%
C. 660%
D. 1,100%

Answer [＿＿＿＿＿]

NON-VERBAL REASONING, MECHANICAL COMPREHENSION AND DATA INTERPRETATION

If you have been searching for help to prepare for this type of test, then you have found it. All you have to do now is settle down somewhere quiet and get practising. Very soon you will be much faster at answering these questions and achieving a much higher score.

There is little practice material generally available for non-verbal and mechanical comprehension tests, so this chapter should prove useful to candidates who face these styles of test. You will find over 300 further practice diagrammatic and abstract questions in *How to Pass Diagrammatic Reasoning Tests*, published by Kogan Page. This chapter also contains 50 data interpretation questions.

These styles of question are common, especially in selection for graduate management programmes and courses of study. In these tests, like all sorts of psychometric tests, practice can mean the difference between pass and fail. If you face a test that includes this sort of question, then set about a programme of practice, using the questions provided in this chapter.

Non-verbal reasoning

Below are 100 practice questions for non-verbal reasoning tests. Included are three styles of question: identify the feature in common; complete the non-verbal series; and complete the non-verbal matrix. Use them to become more confident, fast and accurate. In many tests the questions are based on rotation (where a shape is turned), alternation (where a shape changes into something else and is then changed back), consistency (where a change is made and is then consistently applied), replacement (where a shape or shapes are replaced by others), and attention to detail.

The first 30 examples require you to identify from sample shapes the feature they have in common and then select from suggested answer shapes the answer that shares that feature.

The next 50 questions present a series of shapes and you must decide which of the suggested answers is the next step or the missing step in the series.

The last 20 examples involve rows and columns of shapes, and it is your task to identify the missing shape from suggested answer shapes.

As with most tests, the examples start easy and get harder. Answers and explanations are provided.

Features in common

1   Identify the suggested answer shape that shares a feature in common
     with the question shapes.

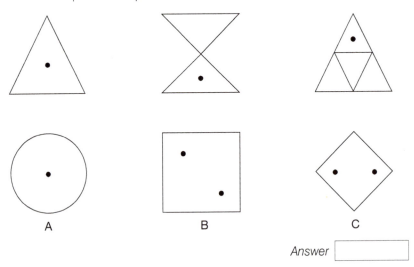

Answer [   ]

2   Identify the suggested answer shape that shares a feature in common with the question shapes.

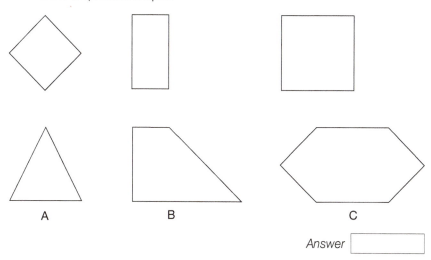

Answer [   ]

3   Identify the suggested answer shape that shares a feature in common with the question shapes (the third shape is a triangular-shaped pyramid).

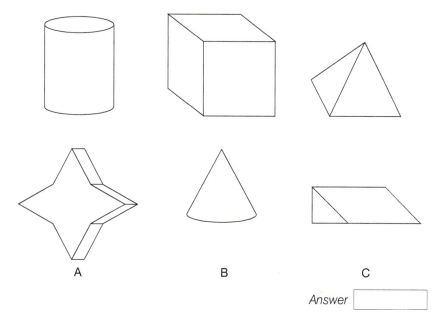

Answer [   ]

4   Identify the suggested answer shape that shares a feature in common
with the question shapes.

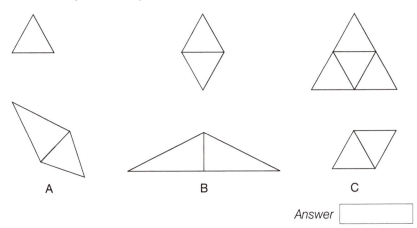

A   B   C

Answer

5   Identify the suggested answer shape that shares a feature in common
with the question shapes.

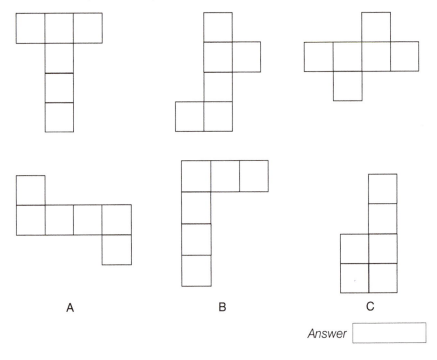

A   B   C

Answer

6   Identify the suggested answer shape that shares a feature in common
with the question shapes.

A

B

C

Answer _____

7   Identify the suggested answer shape that shares a feature in common
with the question shapes.

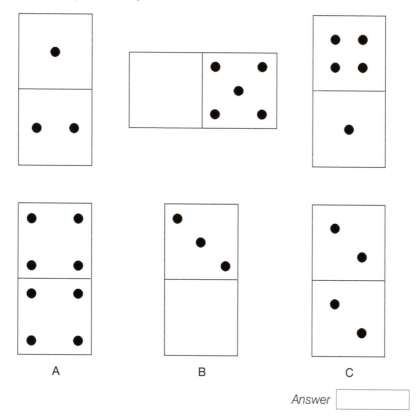

A

B

C

Answer _____

8   Identify the suggested answer shape that shares a feature in common
     with the question shapes.

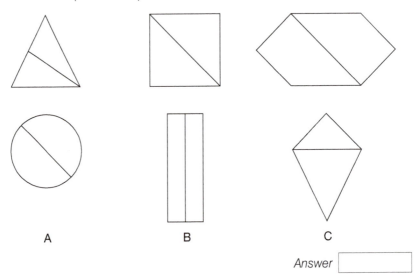

A   B   C

Answer

9   Identify the suggested answer shape that shares a feature in common
     with the question shapes.

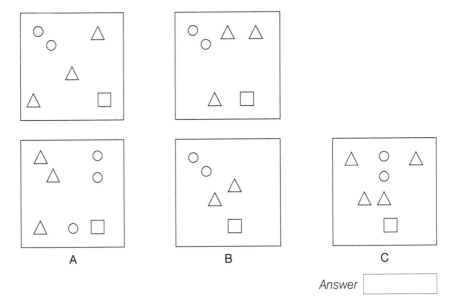

A   B   C

Answer

10 Identify the suggested answer shape that shares a feature in common with the question shapes.

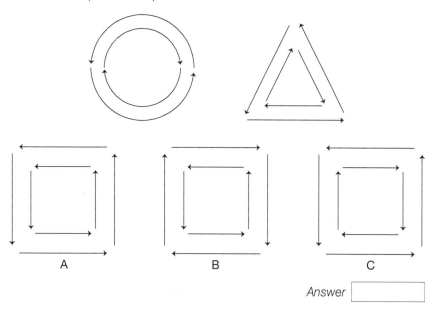

Answer [   ]

11 Identify the suggested answer shape that shares a feature in common with the question shapes.

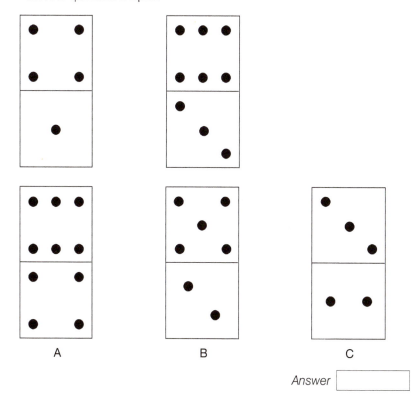

Answer [   ]

12 Identify the suggested answer shape that shares a feature in common with the question shapes.

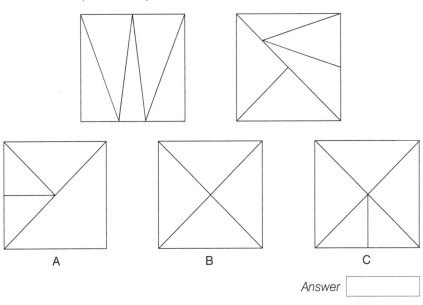

Answer

13 Identify the suggested answer shape that shares a feature in common with the question shapes.

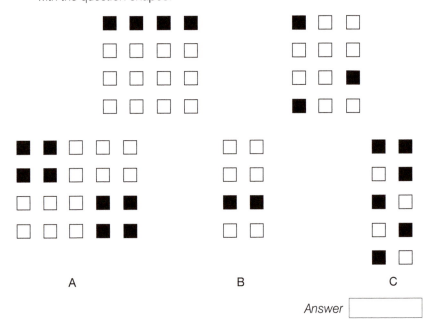

Answer

14   Identify the suggested answer shape that shares a feature in common
with the question shapes.

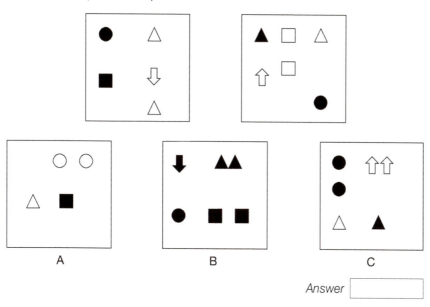

Answer [   ]

15   Identify the suggested answer shape that shares a feature in common
with the question shapes.

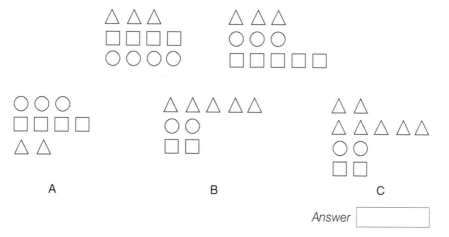

Answer [   ]

16   Identify the suggested answer shape that shares a feature in common
with the question shapes.

●●○○●●   ●●○○○●

○○●●○○   ●○○○○●   ●○●○●○
　　A　　　　　　　　　B　　　　　　　　　C

Answer

17   Identify the suggested answer shape that shares a feature in common
with the question shapes.

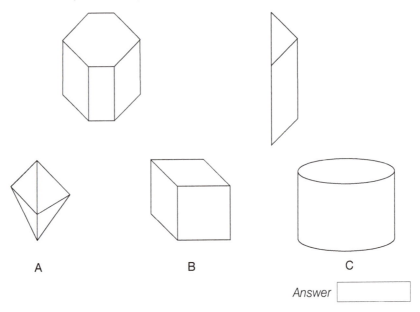

A   B   C

Answer

18 Identify the suggested answer shape that shares a feature in common with the question shapes.

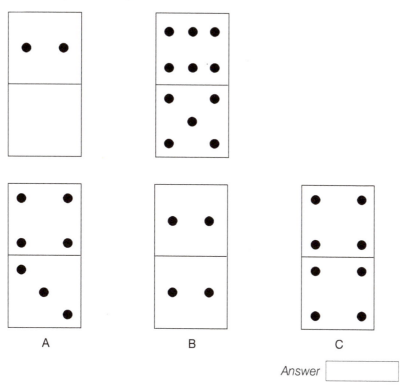

A B C

Answer

19 Identify the suggested answer shape that shares a feature in common with the question shapes.

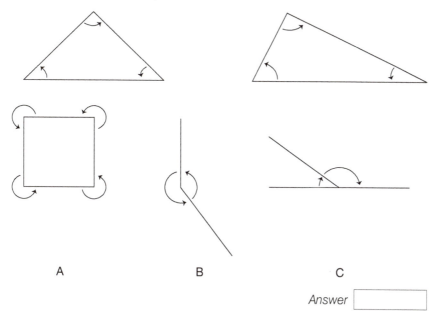

A B C

Answer

20   Identify the suggested answer shape that shares a feature in common with the question shapes.

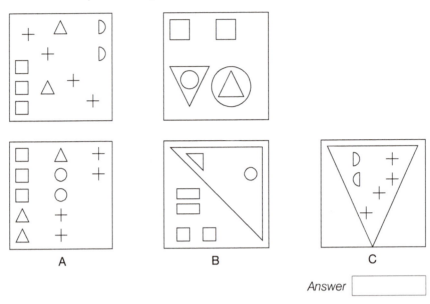

Answer [   ]

21   Identify the suggested answer shape that shares a feature in common with the question shapes.

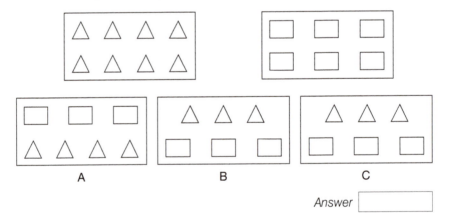

Answer [   ]

22   Identify the suggested answer shape that shares a feature in common with the question shapes.

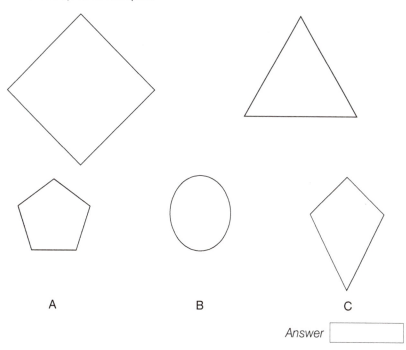

A   B   C

Answer [   ]

23   Identify the suggested answer shape that shares a feature in common with the question shapes.

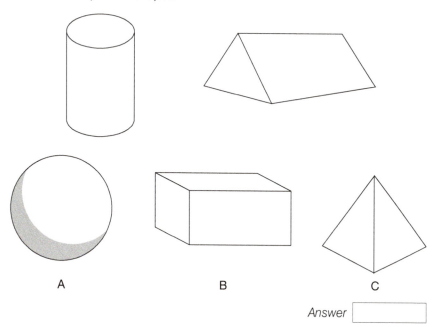

A   B   C

Answer [   ]

24   Identify the suggested answer shape that shares a feature in common
      with the question shapes.

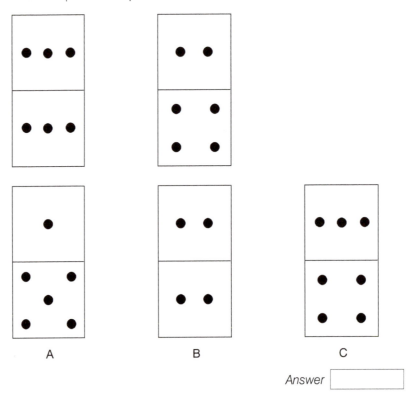

A   B   C

Answer

25   Identify the suggested answer shape that shares a feature in common
      with the question shapes.

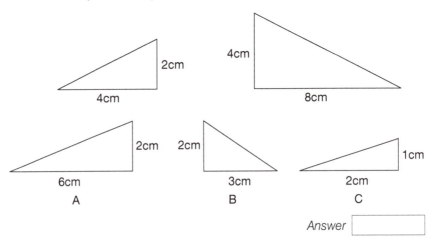

A   B   C

Answer

26 Identify the suggested answer shape that shares a feature in common with the question shapes.

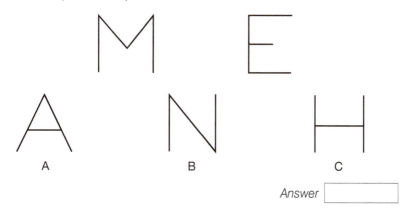

A B C

Answer

27 Identify the suggested answer shape that shares a feature in common with the question shapes.

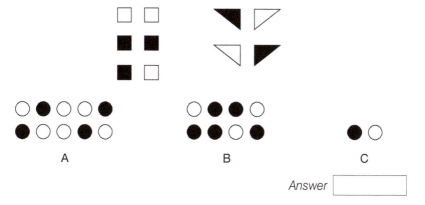

A B C

Answer

28 Identify the suggested answer shape that shares a feature in common with the question shapes.

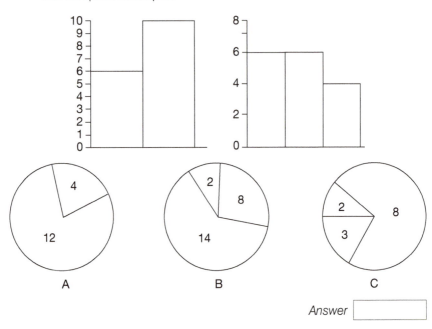

A   B   C

Answer [   ]

29 Identify the suggested answer shape that shares a feature in common with the question shapes.

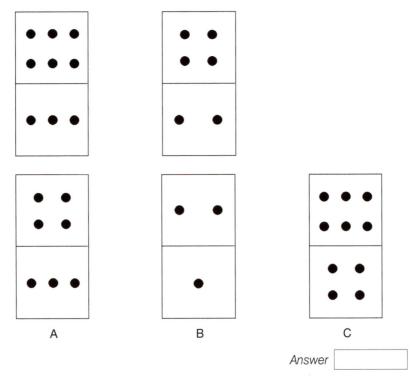

A   B   C

Answer [   ]

30   Identify the suggested answer shape that shares a feature in common
with the question shapes.

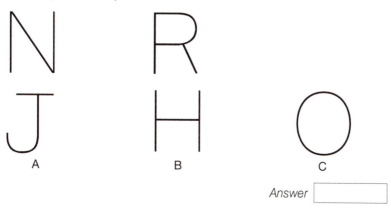

Answer [   ]

Find the shape that completes the series

The next 50 questions are non-verbal questions where the shape or shapes
form a series. It is your task to identify one of the suggested answers as the
missing part of the series or the next step in it.

31   Which of the suggested answers is the next step or the missing step in the
series?

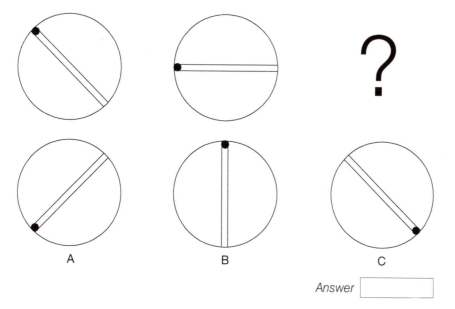

Answer [   ]

32   Which of the suggested answers is the next step or the missing step in the series?

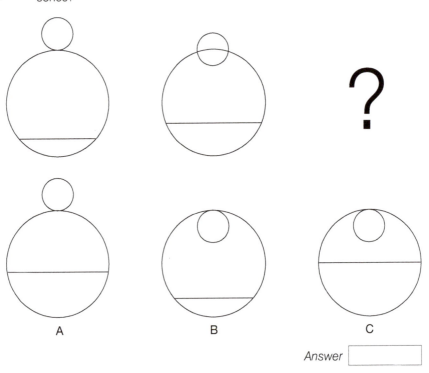

Answer [   ]

33   Which of the suggested answers is the next step or the missing step in the series?

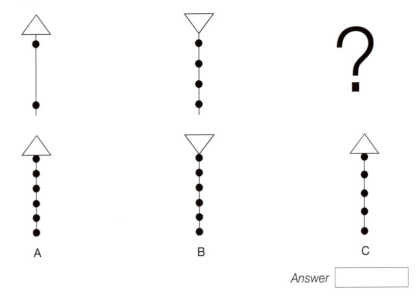

Answer [   ]

34 Which of the suggested answers is the next step or the missing step in the series?

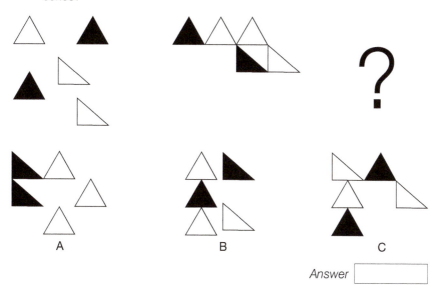

Answer [   ]

35 Which of the suggested answers is the next step or the missing step in the series?

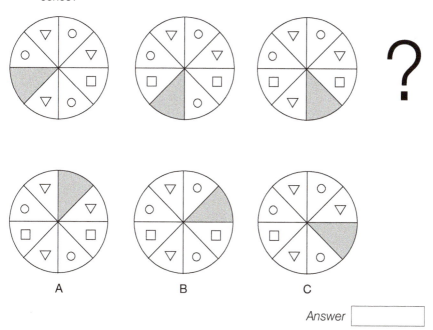

Answer [   ]

36   Which of the suggested answers is the next step or the missing step in the series?

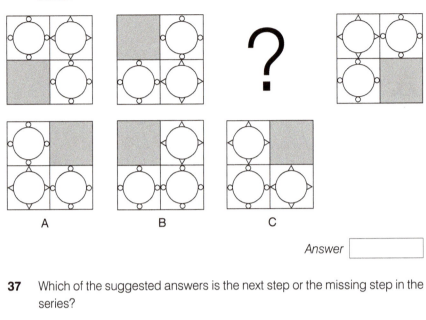

A   B   C

Answer [   ]

37   Which of the suggested answers is the next step or the missing step in the series?

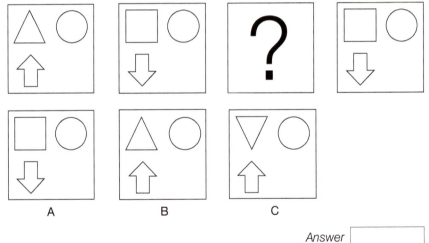

A   B   C

Answer [   ]

38 Which of the suggested answers is the next step or the missing step in the series?

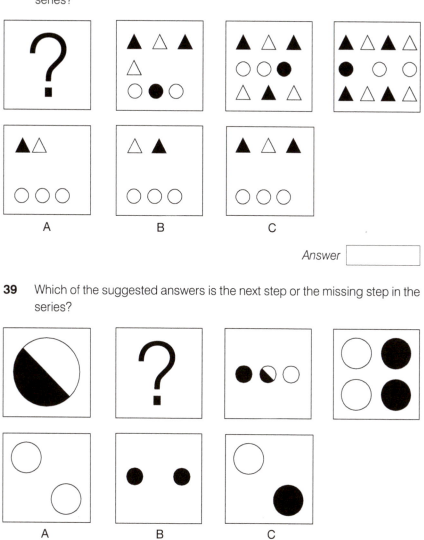

Answer

39 Which of the suggested answers is the next step or the missing step in the series?

Answer

40 Which of the suggested answers is the next step or the missing step in the series?

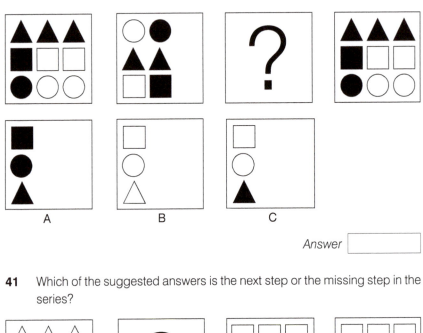

Answer [   ]

41 Which of the suggested answers is the next step or the missing step in the series?

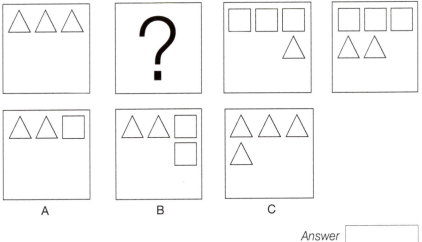

Answer [   ]

42   Which of the suggested answers is the next step or the missing step in the series?

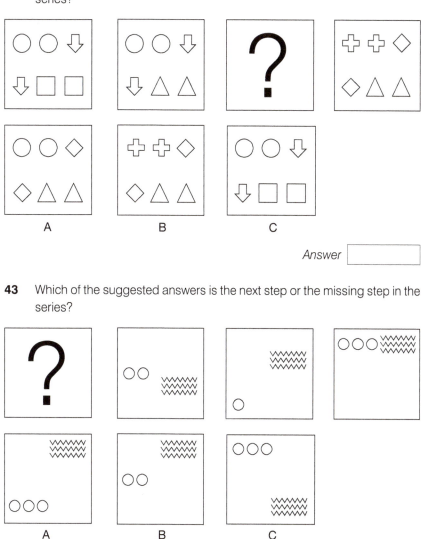

Answer [   ]

43   Which of the suggested answers is the next step or the missing step in the series?

Answer [   ]

44   Which of the suggested answers is the next step or the missing step in the series?

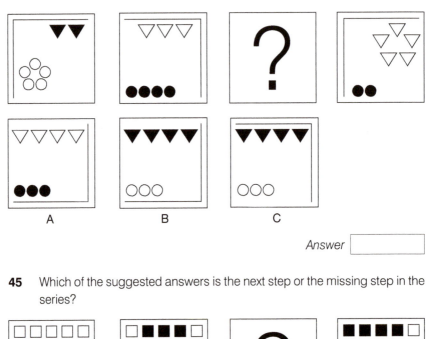

Answer [   ]

45   Which of the suggested answers is the next step or the missing step in the series?

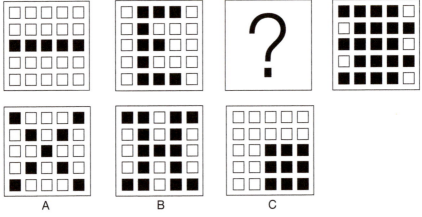

Answer [   ]

46   Which of the suggested answers is the next step or the missing step in the series?

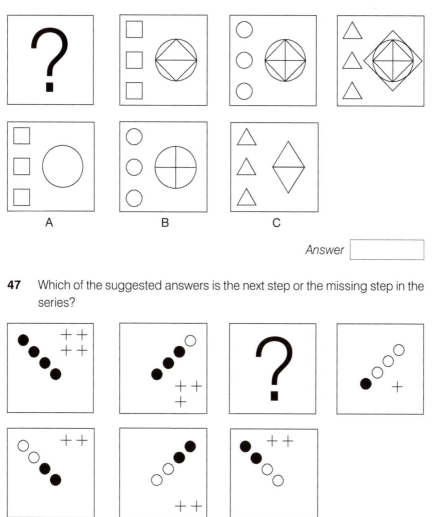

Answer [   ]

47   Which of the suggested answers is the next step or the missing step in the series?

48   Which of the suggested answers is the next step or the missing step in the
series?

Answer

49   Which of the suggested answers is the next step or the missing step in the
series?

Answer

50   Which of the suggested answers is the next step or the missing step in the series?

Answer [   ]

51   Which of the suggested answers is the next step or the missing step in the series?

Answer [   ]

52   Which of the suggested answers is the next step or the missing step in the series?

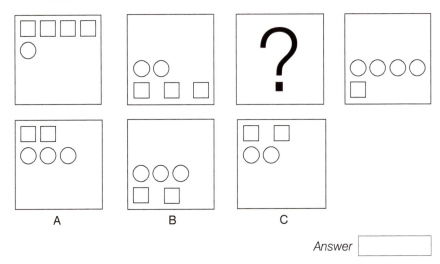

Answer

53   Which of the suggested answers is the next step or the missing step in the series?

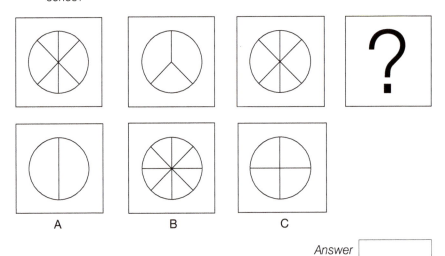

Answer

54   Which of the suggested answers is the next step or the missing step in the series?

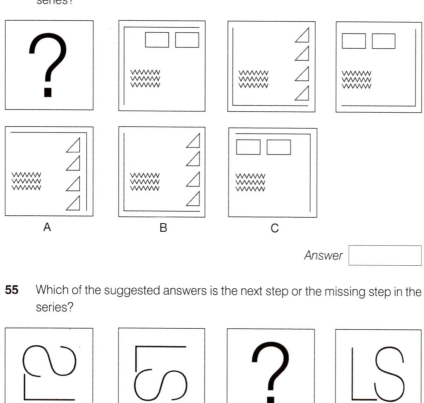

Answer [   ]

55   Which of the suggested answers is the next step or the missing step in the series?

Answer [   ]

56 Which of the suggested answers is the next step or the missing step in the series?

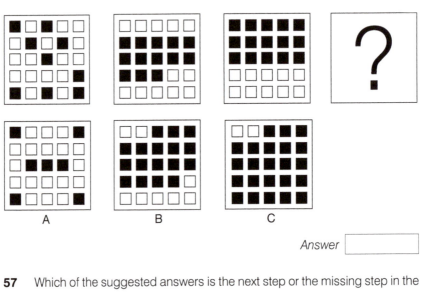

A   B   C

Answer [   ]

57 Which of the suggested answers is the next step or the missing step in the series?

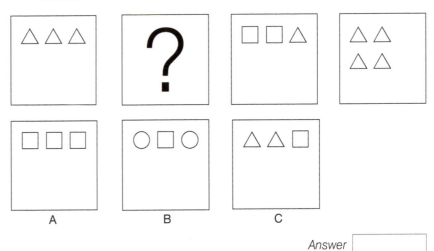

A   B   C

Answer [   ]

58 Which of the suggested answers is the next step or the missing step in the series?

Answer [   ]

59 Which of the suggested answers is the next step or the missing step in the series?

Answer [   ]

60   Which of the suggested answers is the next step or the missing step in the series?

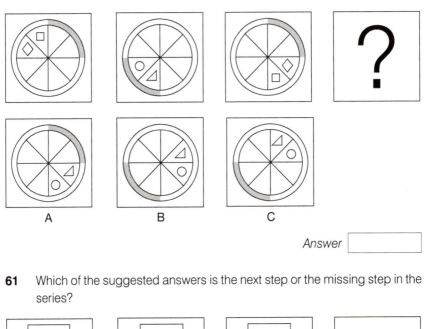

Answer

61   Which of the suggested answers is the next step or the missing step in the series?

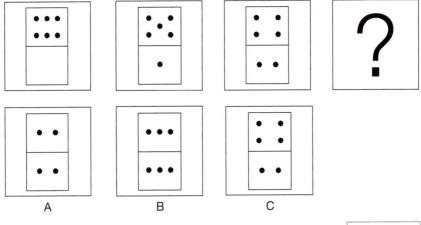

Answer

62   Which of the suggested answers is the next step or the missing step in the series?

63   Which of the suggested answers is the next step or the missing step in the series?

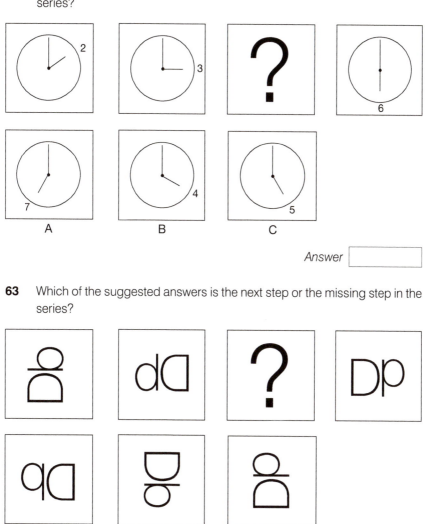

Answer [   ]

64 Which of the suggested answers is the next step or the missing step in the series?

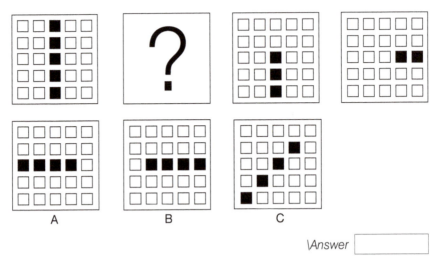

\Answer

65 Which of the suggested answers is the next step or the missing step in the series?

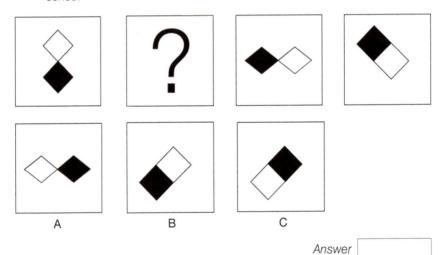

Answer

66 Which of the suggested answers is the next step or the missing step in the series?

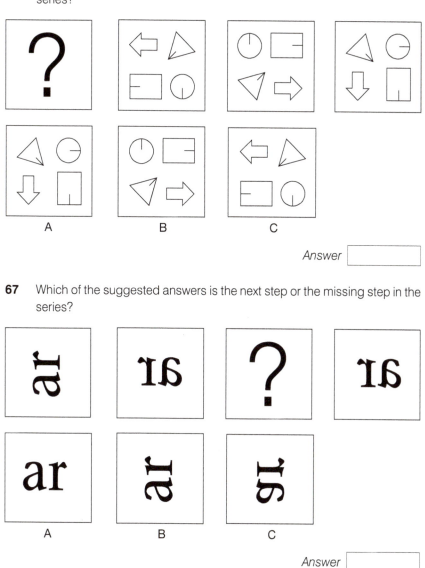

Answer

67 Which of the suggested answers is the next step or the missing step in the series?

Answer

68   Which of the suggested answers is the next step or the missing step in the series?

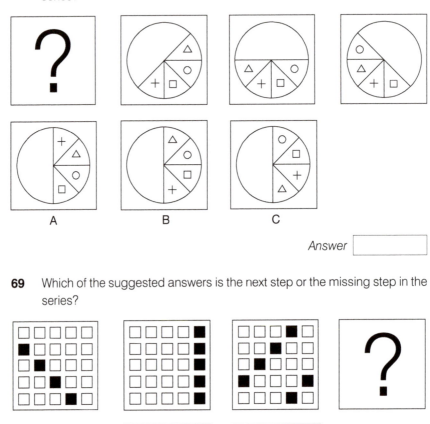

Answer [   ]

69   Which of the suggested answers is the next step or the missing step in the series?

Answer [   ]

70   Which of the suggested answers is the next step or the missing step in the series?

71   Which of the suggested answers is the next step or the missing step in the series?

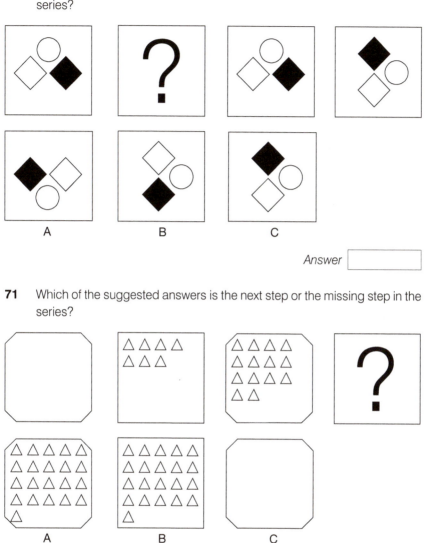

Answer

72 Which of the suggested answers is the next step or the missing step in the series?

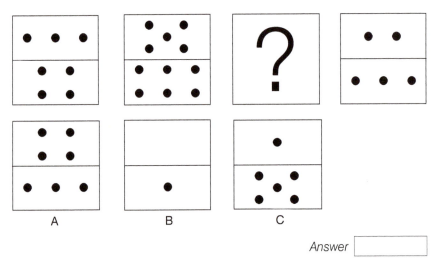

A B C

Answer

73 Which of the suggested answers is the next step or the missing step in the series?

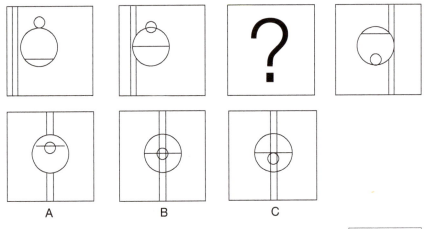

A B C

Answer

74 Which of the suggested answers is the next step or the missing step in the series?

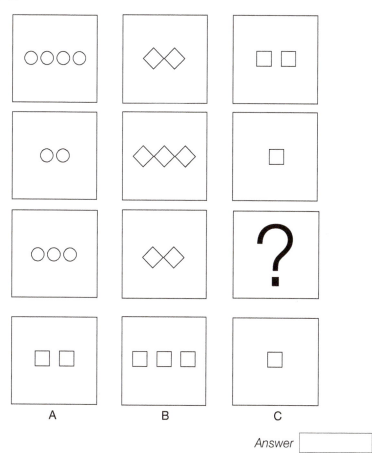

Answer [   ]

75 Which of the suggested answers is the next step or the missing step in the series?

A   B   C

Answer [   ]

76   Which of the suggested answers is the next step or the missing step in the series?

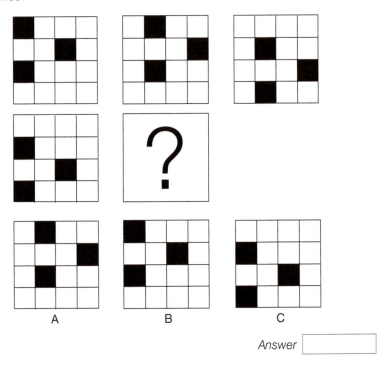

A   B   C

Answer

77   Which of the suggested answers is the next step or the missing step in the series?

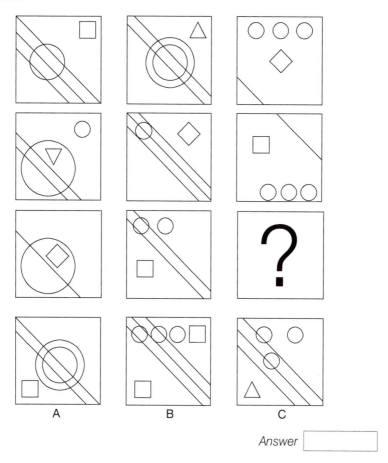

Answer [＿＿＿＿＿＿＿]

78   Which of the suggested answers is the next step or the missing step in the series?

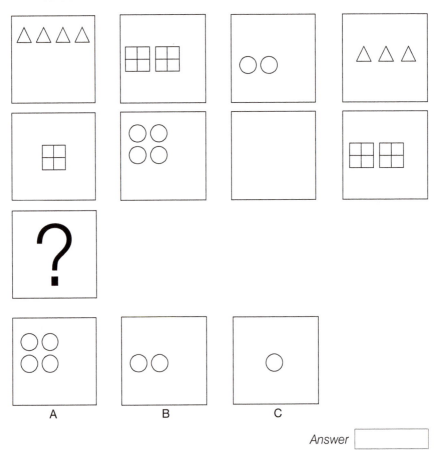

Answer [   ]

79   Which of the suggested answers is the next step or the missing step in the series?

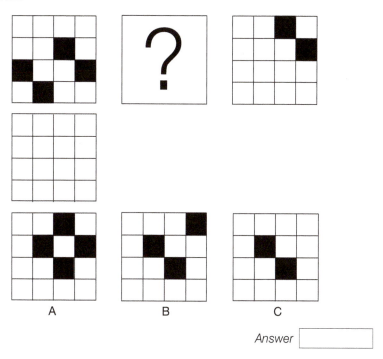

Answer

80   Which of the suggested answers is the next step or the missing step in the series?

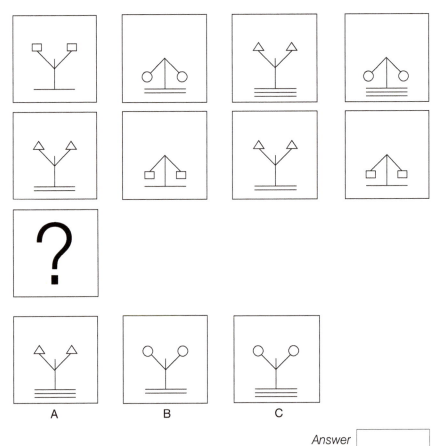

A   B   C

Answer

Completing the series in columns and rows

This style of question requires the series to be continued either horizontally or vertically or both. There are 20 examples with answers and explanations.

81   Identify the suggested answer that correctly completes the series.

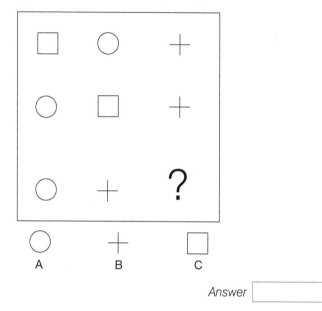

Answer [   ]

82   Identify the suggested answer that correctly completes the series.

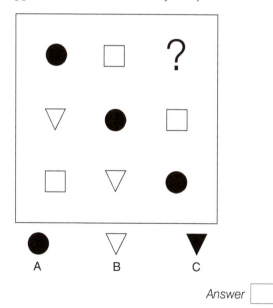

Answer [   ]

83 Identify the suggested answer that correctly completes the series.

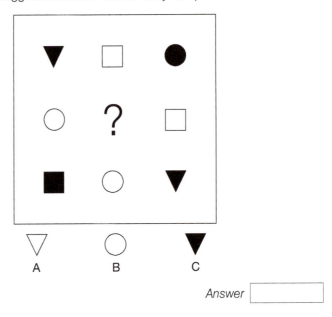

Answer

84 Identify the suggested answer that correctly completes the series.

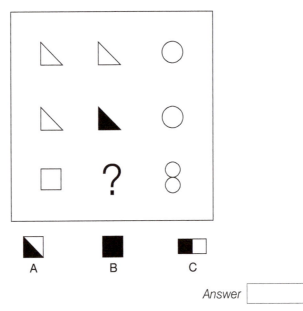

Answer

85 Identify the suggested answer that correctly completes the series.

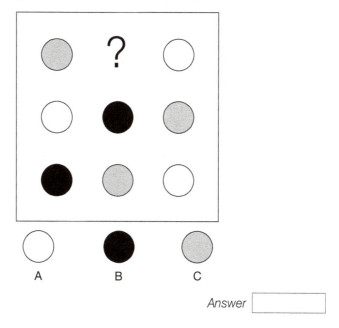

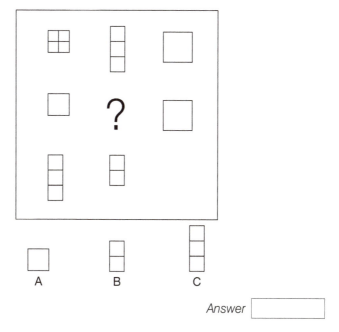

Answer [   ]

86 Identify the suggested answer that correctly completes the series.

Answer [   ]

87 Identify the suggested answer that correctly completes the series.

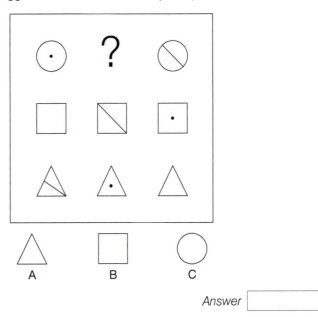

A   B   C

Answer

88 Identify the suggested answer that correctly completes the series.

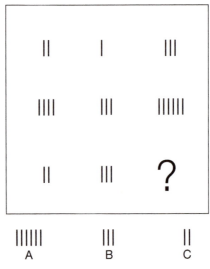

A   B   C

Answer

89 Identify the suggested answer that correctly completes the series.

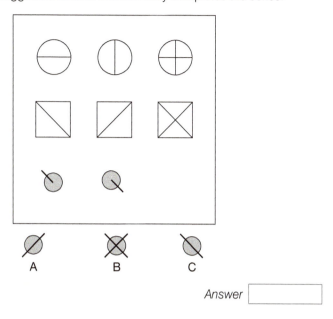

Answer ▭

90 Identify the suggested answer that correctly completes the series.

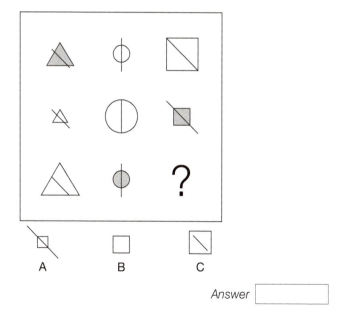

Answer ▭

91 Identify the suggested answer that correctly completes the series.

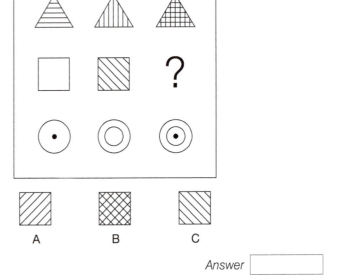

Answer [   ]

92 Identify the suggested answer that correctly completes the series.

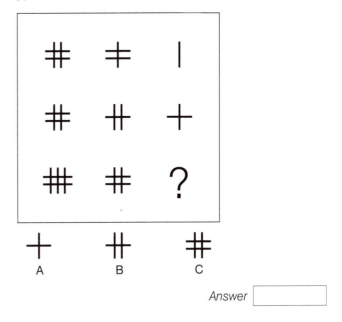

Answer [   ]

93 Identify the suggested answer that correctly completes the series.

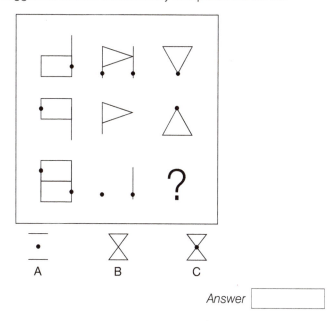

Answer

94 Identify the suggested answer that correctly completes the series.

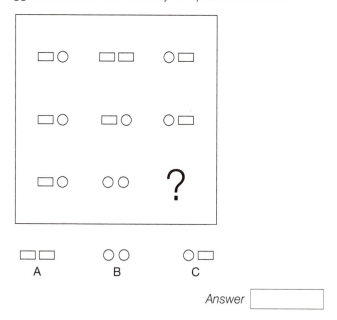

Answer

95   Identify the suggested answer that correctly completes the series.

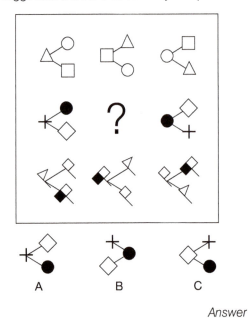

A   B   C

Answer

96   Identify the suggested answer that correctly completes the series.

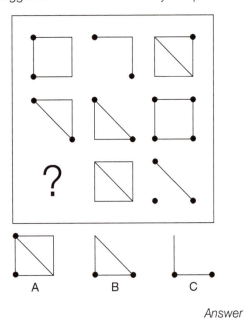

A   B   C

Answer

97   Identify the suggested answer that correctly completes the series.

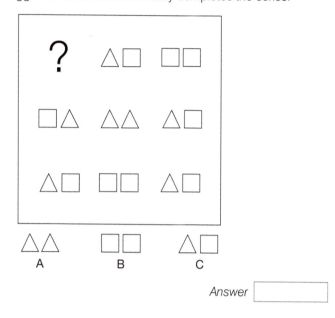

Answer [   ]

98   Identify the suggested answer that correctly completes the series.

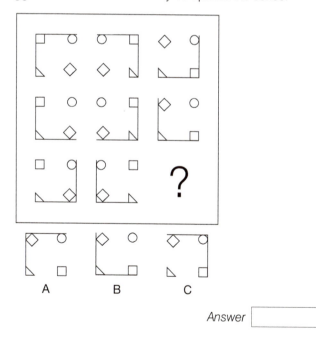

Answer [   ]

99 Identify the suggested answer that correctly completes the series.

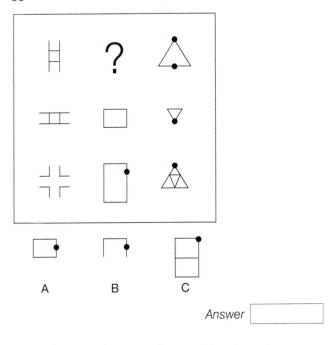

A   B   C

Answer [   ]

100 Identify the suggested answer that correctly completes the series.

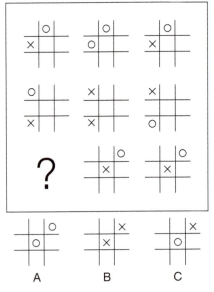

A   B   C

Answer [   ]

Mechanical comprehension

These questions allow you to practise your command of the principles of basic physics and mechanics. Many but not all include a diagram. This style of question is used to select between candidates for positions on apprenticeships and in trainability tests to select for places on craft courses at colleges.

101 Which viewpoint would be least prone to error?

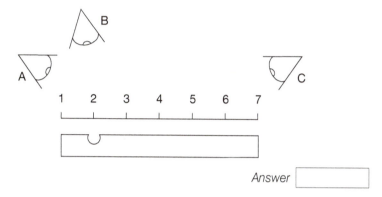

Answer [   ]

102 Which forms of energy does the radio produce?

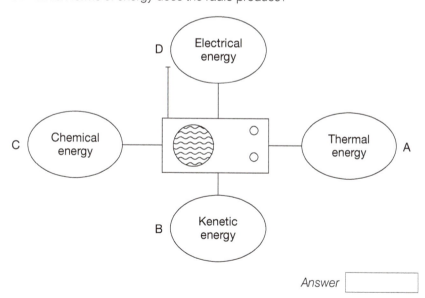

Answer [   ]

103 Which transfer of energy occurs when a firework is lit?

Chemical to   A. Elastic
                     B. Kinetic
                     C. Thermal
                     D. Electromagnetic
                     E. Gravitational

                                                      Answer [   ]

104 Are the forces between molecules stronger in ice or water?

                                                      Answer [   ]

105 Which shape has the smallest surface area for a given volume?

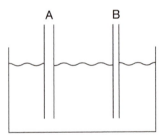

          A   B   C

                                                      Answer [   ]

106 In which clean tube will the water rise higher?

              A   B

A.
B.
C. The liquid will rise to the same level
D. The liquid will not rise at all

                                                      Answer [   ]

107 and 108   Which way does a mercury meniscus curve, if at all?
What is the shape of the meniscus of water?

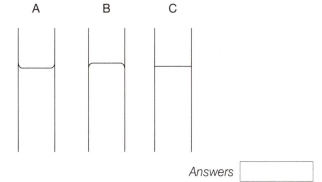

Answers

109   The split pins A and B hold the iron bar tightly against the blocks C and D; what will happen when the iron bar is heated?

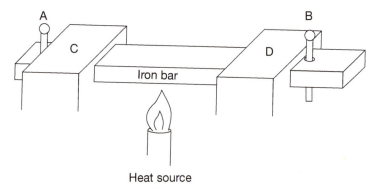

Heat source

A. The pins will be bent
B. A gap will appear between the pins and the blocks
C. Nothing

Answer

110   Are these telephone wires drawn as they appear in the summer or winter?

Answer

111 Which glass beaker is more likely to crack when filled with hot water?

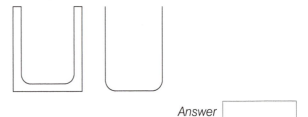

Answer

112 Which way would the bimetallic strip bend if heat were applied to it; or would it stay straight?

Brass

Iron

A. Bend upwards
B. Bend downwards
C. Stay straight

Answer

113 Which liquid is represented by the density curve?

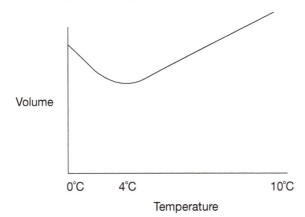

A. Water
B. Oil
C. Petrol

Answer

114 What will happen to the water level in the beaker if the heat source is removed and the air in the glass balloon cools?

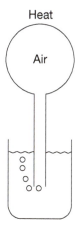

A. Rises
B. Falls
C. Stays the same

Answer [   ]

115 and 116 What will happen when the switch is closed?
What will happen once the bimetallic strip gets hot?

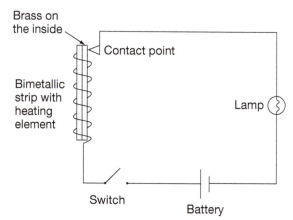

A. The lamp will come on
B. The heating element will warm
C. Both A and B
D. Neither A nor B
E. Contact will remain once the bimetallic strip gets hot
F. Contact will be broken once the bimetallic strip gets hot

Answers [   ]

117 If the temperature remains constant, what will happen to the volume of trapped gas if the pressure is doubled?

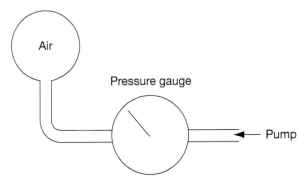

A. The volume it occupies will reduce by a third
B. The volume will double
C. The volume will reduce by a quarter
D. The volume will reduce by half

Answer

118 Which point A on these bars of equal length and thickness would get hottest first?

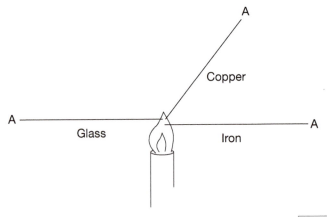

Answer

119 Which liquid would boil last?

A. Water
B. Mercury
C. Alcohol

Answer

120   If a flag was raised on the pole, on which side would it fly?

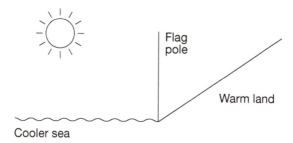

A. The sea side
B. The land side
C. You cannot tell

Answer

121   If left in the sun, in which can will water take longer to warm?

A. Shiny tin can
B. Matt black painted tin can

Answer

122   If a solar panel were located in the northern hemisphere, which way would you expect it to be facing?

A. North
B. South
C. East
D. West
E. Cannot tell

Answer

123   Which way is east?

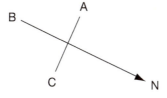

Answer

124 What temperature will the water be?

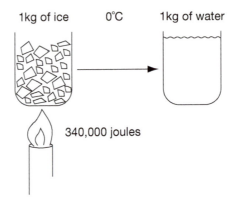

1kg of ice   0°C   1kg of water

340,000 joules

A. Cannot tell
B. Warmer than 0°C
C. 0°C

Answer

125 What will be the temperature of ice made from mineral water?

A. 0°C
B. Lower than 0°C
C. Higher than 0°C

Answer

126 What will happen?

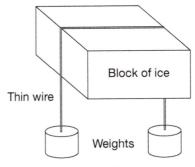

Block of ice

Thin wire

Weights

A. The block of ice will be cut in half
B. Nothing
C. The wire will eventually drop out of the bottom of the block

Answer

127 What happens when salt is added to boiling water?

    A. The water will boil more vigorously

    B. The temperature of the water will fall

    C. The water will stop boiling

    D. The temperature of the water will begin to rise

Answer

128 At what temperature does water boil at altitude?

    A. 100°C

    B. Below 100°C

    C. Above 100°C

Answer

129 If a package weighed 80 kg in New York, how much would it weigh at the North Pole?

    A. The same

    B. Slightly more

    C. Slightly less

Answer

130 Which shape is the most rigid?

    A   B   C

Answer

131 Which is the least and which the most dense?

    A. Ice

    B. Water

    C. Oil

Answer

132 Where is the pressure greatest, at the top, bottom or middle of a drum of water?

Answer

133 In which direction is the pressure greatest?

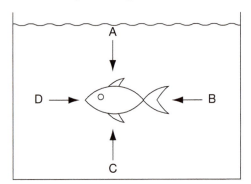

A
B
C
D
All equal

Answer

134 Which is petrol and which is ice?

A

B

A. Petrol
B. Petrol
A. Ice
B. Ice

Answer

135 Which barometric reading would you expect on a rainy day?

A. 970 mbar
B. 1,010 mbar
C. Cannot tell

Answer

136 What force holds a nail in a piece of wood?

    A. Molecular expansion

    B. Friction

    C. Molecular bonding

    D. Conduction

Answer [   ]

137 Which force cannot act remotely?

    A. Electrical force

    B. Magnetic force

    C. Gravity

    D. Frictional force

Answer [   ]

138 When did the vehicle reach a constant speed?

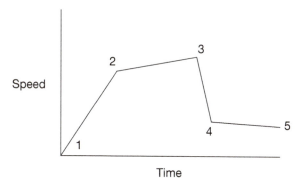

Answer [   ]

139 Which shape is in equilibrium?

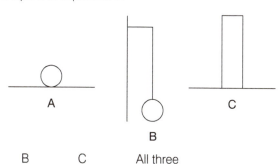

A   B   C   All three

Answer [   ]

140 Which line is most likely to represent the centre of gravity of the shape?

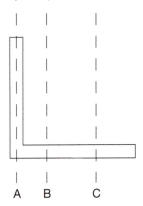

A B   C

Answer [   ]

141 When a gun is discharged the potential energy of the chemical charge is transferred to what?

A. Actual chemical energy
B. Electrical energy
C. Kinetic energy
D. Elastic energy
E. Gravitational energy
F. Heat and light

Answer [   ]

142 Will gear A magnify the force, the distance or both?

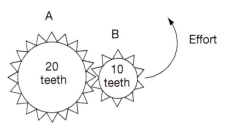

Answer [   ]

143 Which line shows a plane accelerating to take off?

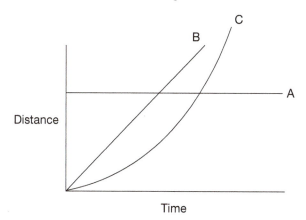

Answer ⬚

144 Where is the smaller effort?

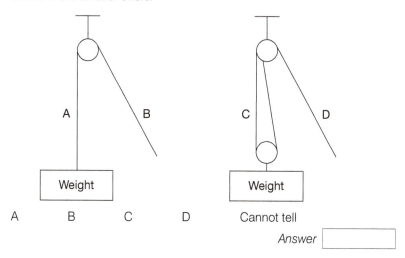

A   B   C   D   Cannot tell

Answer ⬚

145 Which gear is rotating in an anticlockwise direction at 30 revolutions a second?

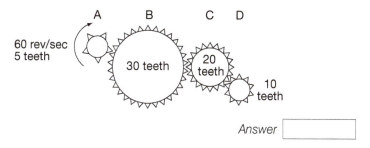

Answer ⬚

146 Is this shape concave or convex?

    A. Concave
    B. Convex
    C. Both
    D. Neither

Answer ⬚

147 Which magnets will repel?

N	N	A
N	S	B
S	S	C

Answer ⬚

148 How many colours are there in a rainbow?

    5   6   7   8

Answer ⬚

149 Does A, B or C indicate the correct direction of the electric current?

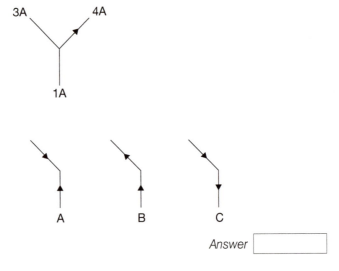

Answer ⬚

150 At which electrode would more bubbles be produced?

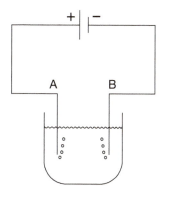

Answer [   ]

151 Match the circuit to the appropriate table.

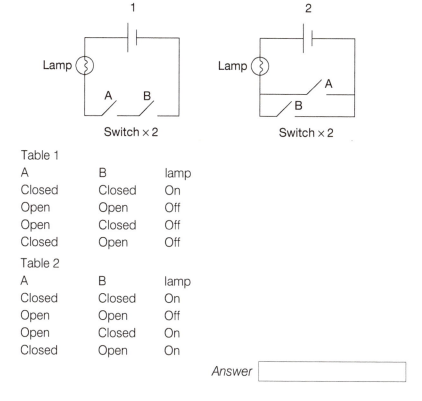

Table 1

A	B	lamp
Closed	Closed	On
Open	Open	Off
Open	Closed	Off
Closed	Open	Off

Table 2

A	B	lamp
Closed	Closed	On
Open	Open	Off
Open	Closed	On
Closed	Open	On

Answer [   ]

152 At what point if any will the rays be stopped?

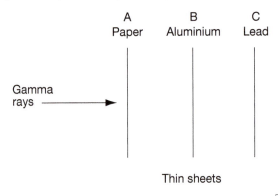

Answer [   ]

153 At which point if any will the rays be stopped?

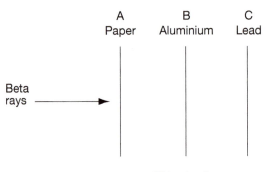

Answer [   ]

154 At which point if any will the rays be stopped?

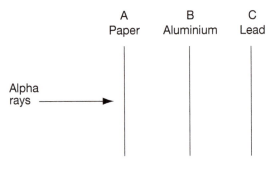

Answer [   ]

155 Best complete the energy transfers in this description of a hydroelectric power station.

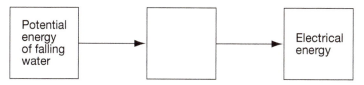

A. Energy in the wires
B. Heat and light
C. Kinetic energy of turbine
D. Chemical energy

Answer

156 If the two identical balls started their descent simultaneously, which would hit the ground first?

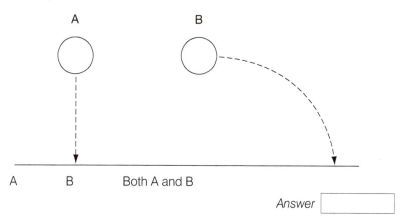

A   B   Both A and B

Answer

157 Which of the tyres is fitted to the vehicle carrying the greater load?

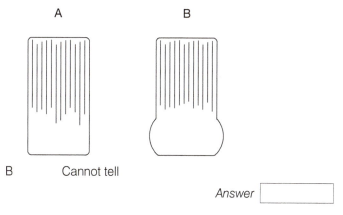

A   B   Cannot tell

Answer

158 If the piston is depressed, at which point is the oil subjected to the greater pressure?

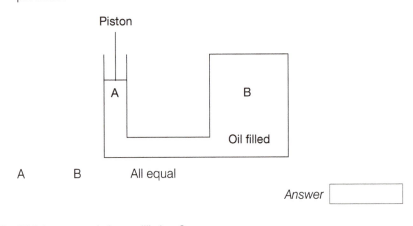

A   B   All equal

Answer ⬚

159 Which seesaw is in equilibrium?

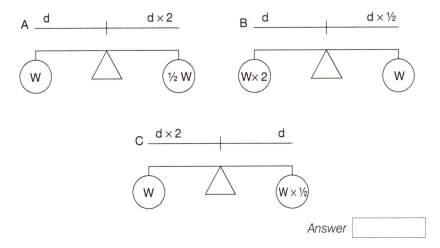

Answer ⬚

Data interpretation

Tests of data interpretation are fast becoming one of the most common types of psychometric tests. They feature in the recruitment process for many positions in, for example, professional services, finance, accountancy and graduate train-eeships. They comprise a series of numeric questions which relate to a set of data. It is your task to extract the appropriate data, demonstrate good judge-ment and undertake any necessary calculations in order to select the correct answer from the list of suggested answers. You will find over a hundred more examples of these questions in *How to Pass Data Interpretation Tests* where these questions are also printed.

Data Set 1: The web-building company

The web-building company plans an aggressive programme of expansion in output and has produced the table below to summarize four scenarios for growth from revenue from sales

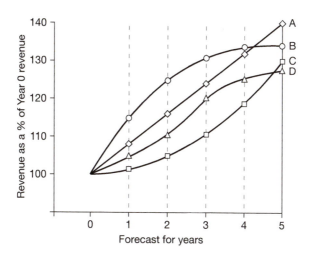

Yr 0 revenue = $26 million

160 How many years of data are detailed in the graph?

    A. 21

    B. 6

    C. 5

    D. 4

                                 Answer

161 In Yr 3, what percentage of Yr 0 revenue is forecast in scenario D?

    A. 130%

    B. 122%

    C. 120%

    D. 110%

                                 Answer

162 Which scenario best fits the following figures:

Yr 1 $30m, Yr 2 $32.5m, Yr 3 $33.8m, Yr 4 $34.5m, Yr 5 $34.7m?

A. Scenario A
B. Scenario B
C. Scenario C
D. Scenario D

Answer

163 Which scenario shows the least variation (change) over the 5 years?

A. Scenario A
B. Scenario B
C. Scenario C
D. Scenario D

Answer

164 Assuming that revenue continues to increase by the same extent, how much more revenue as a percentage of Yr 0 revenue would you expect scenario A to realize in Yr 6?

A. 147–148%
B. 146–147%
C. 145–146%
D. 144–145%

Answer

165 Calculate the $ forecast for revenue for scenario A in Yr 5?

A. 36.1m
B. 36.2m
C. 36.3m
D. 36.4m

Answer

166 Which of the following could help realize the planned aggressive pro-gramme of expansion in output?

A. More production facilities
B. Lowering the unit price
C. Extending the project range
D. Better distribution

Answer

167 Which is the best estimate of how much more revenue over Yr 0 scenario D will generate over Yr 1 and Yr 2 combined (take the scenario D forecast for Yr 1 to be 105%)?

A. 28m
B. 29m
C. 30m
D. 31m

Answer

168 The president of the web-building company sets as a revenue target for Yr 5 the sum of $35m. Estimate how many, if any, of the scenarios can deliver this ambitious target.

A. None of the scenarios
B. Only scenario A
C. Scenarios A and B
D. Scenarios A, B and C

Answer

169 Which scenario best fits the following figures?

A. Yr 1 $26m, Yr 2 $27m, Yr 3 $28.5m, Yr 4 $31m, Yr 5 $34m
B. Yr 1 $28.5m, Yr 2 $30m, Yr 3 $32m, Yr 4 $34m, Yr 5 $39m
C. Yr 1 $27m, Yr 2 $28.5m, Yr 3 $30m, Yr 4 $31.5m, Yr 5 $30m
D. Cannot tell

Answer

Data set 2: The mail order company

The flow diagram below illustrates the delivery options and charging policy for a US-based mail order company. Refer to the diagram to answer the questions that follow.

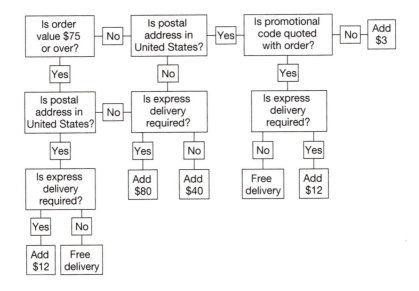

170 How much is added to an order (without a promotional code) valued at $25 with a postal address not in the United States and not requiring express delivery?

A. $40
B. $65
C. $80
D. None of these

Answer _____

171 How much less is added to an order with a US postal address that requires express delivery than to an order with a non-US address that does not require express delivery if the order value is $75?

A. $68
B. $40
C. $28
D. $12

Answer _____

172 How much MORE is added to an order from a non-US postal address if the order is valued at $70 and requires express delivery but does not have a promotional code, compared with an order with a US postal address with a value of $80 that does not have a promotional code and does not require express delivery?

A. $26
B. $40
C. $68
D. $80

Answer [   ]

173 Express delivery is an option for which of the following orders (note more than one suggested answer is correct)?

A. One with a US postal address without a promotional code and with a value under $75
B. One with a value over $75 with a non-US postal address
C. One with a value under $75 with a non-US postal address
D. One with a US postal address with a promotional code and with a value over $75

Answer [   ]

174 Which of the following are always a requirement if an order is to qualify for free   delivery (note that more than one suggested answer is correct)?

A. Value over $75
B. A promotional code
C. Decline express delivery
D. A US postal address

Answer [   ]

Data set 3: Analysis of a population by economic activity and district

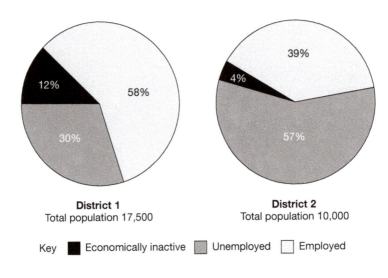

District 1
Total population 17,500

District 2
Total population 10,000

Key ■ Economically inactive ▨ Unemployed □ Employed

175 How many people in district 1 are unemployed?

    A. 5,700
    B. 3,900
    C. 5,250
    D. 10,150

                                                                                                                                    Answer

176 How many people across both districts are employed?

    A. 14,050
    B. 14,060
    C. 14,070
    D. 14,080

             Answer

177 Are more people unemployed in district 1 or in district 2?

    A. District 1
    B. District 2
    C. They are the same

             Answer

178 Express in its simplest form the ratio between economically inactive people and people not economically inactive (those unemployed or employed) in districts 1 and 2 combined

A. 1 : 7
B. 3 : 11
C. 3 : 22
D. 1 : 10

Answer [   ]

179 What percentage of people economically inactive across both districts are resident in district 2?

A. 16%
B. 17%
C. 18%
D. 19%

Answer [   ]

Data set 4: What young people find most and least interesting

A group of young people were presented with four issues and each asked to indicate which they were most and least interested in. All of the group completed the survey and the results are presented in the two graphs below.

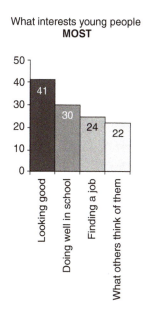

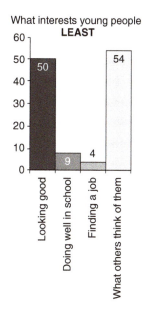

180   How many young people took part in the survey?

    A. 54
    B. 97
    C. 117
    D. 234

Answer

181   How many more young people were most interested in looking good and about what others think of them combined than doing well in school?

    A. 33
    B. 54
    C. 76
    D. 95

Answer

182   Exactly 1/3 of the young people who took part in the survey responded to one of the four issues (ie they indicated that it was the issue that most or least interested them). Which issue was it?

    A. Looking good
    B. Doing well in school
    C. Getting a job
    D. What others think of them

Answer

183   How many times more did young people indicate that they were most interested in finding a job compared with those who indicated that they were least interested in finding a job?

    A. ×3
    B. ×4
    C. ×5
    D. ×6

Answer

184 What is the ratio between young people most interested in looking good and what others think of them combined to the young people most interested in doing well in school and finding a job combined?

A. 9 : 7
B. 7 : 6
C. 8 : 9
D. 6 : 5

Answer

Data set 5: Global sales by world regions

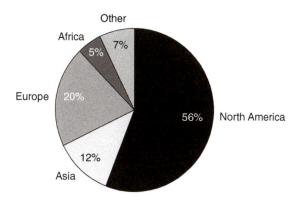

The other category comprises:

Brazil	30%
Mexico	40%
Argentina	20%

The value of the global market in 2008 (actual) was $260m. The global value (forecast) in 2009 is $500m.

185 How many times is the value of the European sales bigger than the value of sales in Africa?

A. ×4
B. ×5
C. ×6
D. ×7

Answer

186 Express in its simplest form the ratio between the comparative sizes of the US market and the segment of the pie chart labelled 'Other'

    A. 6 : 1
    B. 7 : 1
    C. 8 : 1
    D. 9 : 1

                                                        Answer

187 In 2008 the US share of sales was worth $224m. What was the value of all sales that year?

    A. $380m
    B. $400m
    C. $420m
    D. $440m

                                                         Answer

188 In 2008, what was the value of sales in Argentina?

    A. $3.62m
    B. $3.63m
    C. $3.64m
    D. $3.65m

                                                          Answer

189 In 2009, the value of the European market is forecast to contract by $7m of its 2008 value. What percentage of the value of global sales in 2009 is the European market predicted to fall to?

    A. 18%
    B. 15%
    C. 11%
    D. 9%

                                                          Answer

Data set 6: The recruitment agency

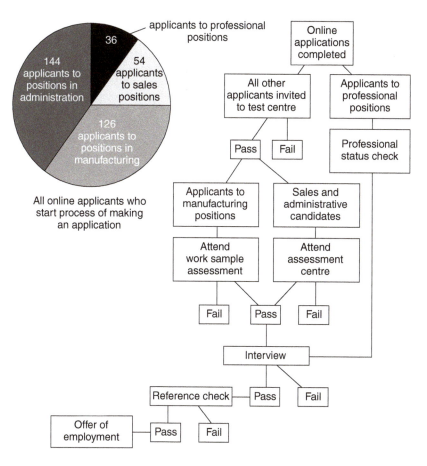

All online applicants who start process of making an application

Note:
75% of online candidates to professional services complete online applications.
50% of online candidates to manufacturing, sales and administrative positions complete online applications.
Percentage of remaining applicants who pass stages of the recruitment process

	Applicants to positions in		
	Manufacturing	**Sales and administration**	**Professional**
Pass test centre	71.5%	66%	–
Pass work sample	60%	–	–
Pass assessment centre	–	55%	–
Pass interview	75%	50%	33%
Pass reference check	60%	70%	80%

190 How many sales and administrative applicants were invited to attend the test centre?

    A. 198
    B. 244
    C. 99
    D. 54

    Answer

191 What is the ratio between the number of online applications made for professional and sales positions?

    A. 4 : 6
    B. 5 : 6
    C. 3 : 5
    D. 4 : 5   *Answer*

192 Assuming that none were rejected at the professional status check, how many   applicants to professional services failed at interview?

    A. 27
    B. 18
    C. 9
    D. 3

    Answer

193 How many manufacturing candidates passed the work sample stage?

    A. 27
    B. 18
    C. 9
    D. 3

    Answer

194 Half of all candidates made an offer of employment accept it and start work. If overall 1/18 candidates who the process of making an application are made an offer of employment, how many start work?

A. 20
B. 15
C. 10
D. 5   *Answer*

Data set 7: Population growth

In 2008 the United Nations projected that by 2050 the world's population would increase by 37 per cent. That same year (2008) the US population was found to be 305 million and growing at an annual rate of 0.88 per cent. The US population was projected to continue to grow until 2050 by when it would reach 439 million. In 2008 the US Census Board found that people under 18 years of age made up a quarter of the population and people 65 or more years of age represented 1/8 of the population. They also found that 80.8 per cent of the population of America lived in urban centres and the most populous states were Texas and California. These trends are expected to continue to a point when 28 per cent of the population is expected to be resident in the two states.

195 How many Americans did the Census Board find in 2008 to be aged 65 or more?

A. 38,125,000
B. 50,330,000
C. 57,187,000
D. 76,250,000

Answer

196 How many Americans did the Census Board find lived in rural (ie non-urban) locations?

A. 246,440,000
B. 123,220,000
C. 58,560,000
D. 58,650,000

Answer

197 Is the projected area of growth between 2008 and 2050 in the US population?

    A. Less than the UN projected rate of increase in the world population 2008–
2050

    B. Greater than the UN projected rate of increase in the world population
2008–2050

    C. Neither less nor more than the UN projected rate of increase in the
world population 2008–2050 but the same rate – namely 37%

    D. Cannot tell

        Answer [   ]

198 How many residents are projected to be residents of either Texas or
California by 2050?

    A. 85,400,000
    B. 122,920,000
    C. 178,400,000
    D. Cannot tell

        Answer [   ]

199 If in 2050 people under 18 still make up a quarter of the population and
people 65 and over still represent 1/8 of the population, then how many
Americans will be aged between 18 and 64 years?

    A. 297,178,000
    B. 274,375,000
    C. 213,869,000
    D. 164,625,000

        Answer [   ]

200 If in 2008 the United Nations had estimated the world's population to be 7
billion how many people would they have expected to be alive in 2050?

    A. 8.75 billion
    B. 9.10 billion
    C. 9.30 billion
    D. 9.59 billion

        Answer [   ]

Spatial recognition and visual estimation

Below you will find practice for three types of spatial or visual estimation tests. In the first example your task is to identify the plan of a three-dimensional shape. A plan is the view of the shape, looking exactly down on it. In the second type you have to identify the shape that has been rotated but is otherwise identical to the question shape (all the others would have been rotated but changed in some way too).

In the last type of question you must identify the shape that could be contrasted if the two example shapes are combined. No other change should be made to the shapes other than combining them.

You will find hundreds more practice questions in *How to Pass Diagrammatic Reasoning Tests*, published by Kogan Page, from which these 15 examples have been taken.

Type 1

Identify the plan of the three-dimensional shape in the following five questions.

201

A

B

C

Answer

202

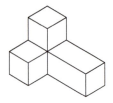

A

B

C

Answer

203

A

B

C

Answer

204

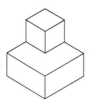

A

B

C

Answer

205

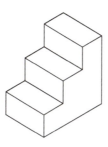

A

B

C

Answer

Type 2

Identify the shape that has been rotated but is otherwise identical to the question shape in the following five questions.

206

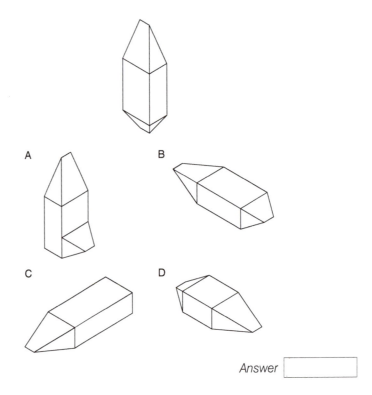

A   B

C   D

Answer

207

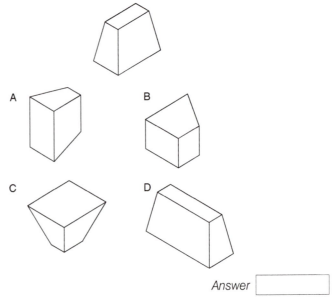

A   B

C   D

Answer

208

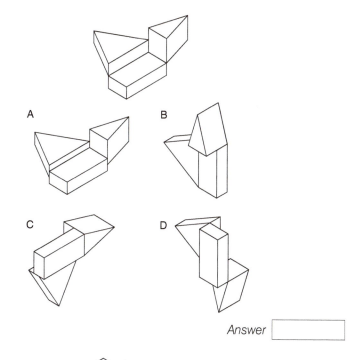

Answer

209

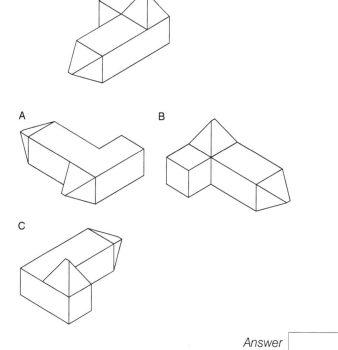

Answer

210

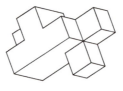

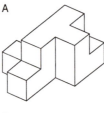

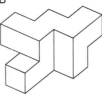

A   B

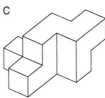

C

Answer [   ]

Type 3

Identify the new shape that could be constructed if the two example shapes were combined in the following five questions.

211

A   B

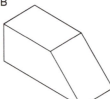

C   D

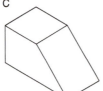

Answer [   ]

212

213

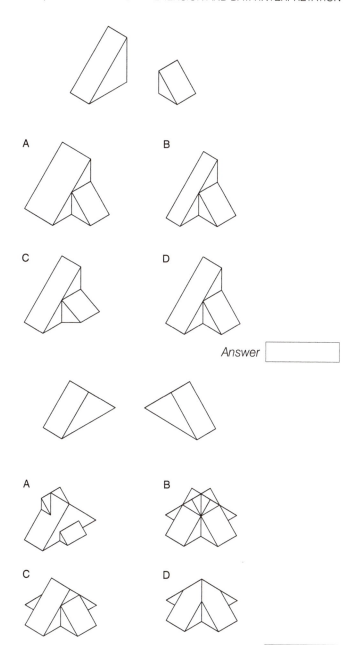

Answer

Answer

214

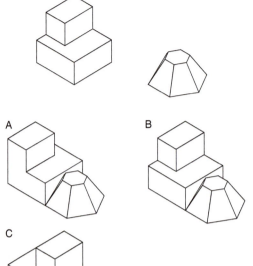

A

B

C

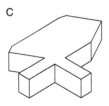

Answer

215

A

B

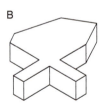

C

Answer

Input-type diagrammatic tests

These tests involve rules that must be applied to a sequence of shapes, numbers or letters. If you are applying for a technical job they will involve 'switches' that allow only certain changes to the sequence to occur. In the case of non-technical positions they are likely to involve symbols that change the figures, letters or objects that make up the sequence. For example, a symbol may signify that triangles must be replaced with squares. Alternatively, a code may reverse the letters, while another may signify that a letter must be dropped or added. All types require you to quickly visualize how the sequence will be transformed through a series of transformations and identify whether, and if so where, a fault in the application of the rules has occurred. Take the word 'quickly' seriously. Many candidates complain that there is insufficient time to attempt all the questions in this style of test. In many input-type diagrammatic reasoning tests the highest-scoring candidates are those who can maintain their accuracy while working quickly enough to attempt more questions than most other candidates. Whichever type you face, the practice below will help you prepare. The answer and explanation to the first question have been given. Remaining answers and explanations are provided in Chapter 7. You will find 100 more practice questions in *How to Pass Diagrammatic Reasoning Tests*, published by Kogan Page.

Rules Q1–5

AB	Delete the last character.
BC	Replace the third character with the next in the alphabet.
CD	Insert the letter P between the third and fourth characters.
DE	Exchange the first and last characters.
EF	Replace the second character with the previous letter in the alphabet.
FG	Replace the fifth character with the next in the alphabet.
GH	Reverse the whole sequence of letters.
HI	Delete the third character.

Q1   MOZLUCK → AB + FG + GH → (D)
             ↓   ↓   ↓
            (A)   (B)   (C)

(A) MOZLUC
(B) MOZLVC
(C) CVLZOM
(D) No fault

Answer [   ]

Q2   ULTIMATE → HI + EF + CD → (D)
                    ↓   ↓   ↓
                   (A)   (B)   (C)

(A) ULIMATE
(B) UKIMATE
(C) UKPIMATE
(D) No fault

Answer [   ]

Q3   ILLUSTRATE → DE + GH + DE → (D)
                       ↓   ↓   ↓
                      (A)   (B)   (C)

(A) ELLUSTRATI
(B) ETARTSULLI
(C) ITARTSULLE
(D) No fault

Answer [   ]

Q4   MEDITERRANEAN → AB + HI + EF → (D)
                          ↓   ↓   ↓
                         (A)   (B)   (C)

(A) MEDITERRANEA
(B) MEITERRANEA
(C) MDDITERRANEA
(D) No fault

Answer [   ]

Q5   DESTINATION → GH + CD + GH → (D)
                        ↓   ↓   ↓
                       (A)   (B)   (C)

(A) NOITANITSED
(B) NOIPTANITSED
(C) DESTINATPION
(D) No fault

Answer [   ]

Rules Q6–10

KL   Switch the second and fifth characters.

MN   Replace the last character with the letter X.

NO   Insert the letters SA between the six and seventh characters.

PQ   Exchange the middle and last characters.

RS   Switch the first and second characters.

TU   Replace the first letter with the letter B.

VW   Reverse the whole sequence of letters.

XY   Replace the middle character with the letter C.

Q6   UVEFGKLQ → TU + KL + MN → (D)

 ↓   ↓   ↓

 (A)   (B)   (C)

(A) BKEFGKLQ

(B) BGKEFKKLQ

(C) BGKEFKKLX

(D) No fault

Answer [ ]

Q7   XYTHMTCGG → PQ + XY + NO → (D)

 ↓   ↓   ↓

 (A)   (B)   (C)

(A) XYTHGTCGM

(B) XYTHCTCGM

(C) XYTHLTCSAGM

(D) No fault

Answer [ ]

Q8   NHTEEINPP → RS + VW + KL → (D)

 ↓   ↓   ↓

 (A)   (B)   (C)

(A) HNTEEINPP

(B) PPNIEETNH

(C) PINPEETNH

(D) No fault

Answer [ ]

Q9 TSTMTWNAS → PQ + KL + XY → (D)

$\qquad\quad$ ↓ $\quad$ ↓ $\quad$ ↓

$\qquad\quad$ (A) $\;$ (B) $\;$ (C)

(A) TSTMSWNAT
(B) TTTMSWNAT
(C) TTTMCWNAT
(D) No fault

Answer

Q10 MMDIAATIC → RS + MN + VW → (D)

$\qquad\qquad$ ↓ $\quad$ ↓ $\quad$ ↓

$\qquad\qquad$ (A) $\;$ (B) $\;$ (C)

(A) MMDIAATIC
(B) MMDIAATIX
(C) XITAAIDMM
(D) No fault

Answer

Rules Q11–15

AA Replace the third letter with the number 3.
CC Replace the last letter with the previous one in the alphabet.
GG Delete the third item in the sequence.
II Replace the fifth letter with the number 7.
KK Replace the first number with the letter Z.
MM Replace the first letter with the number 9.
OO Replace the fourth item with the letters WR.

Q11 BA2W3KEVQ → AA + KK + OO → (D)

$\qquad\qquad$ ↓ $\quad$ ↓ $\quad$ ↓

$\qquad\qquad$ (A) $\;$ (B) $\;$ (C)

(A) BA33KEVQ
(B) BA23KEVQ
(C) BA2WRKEVQ
(D) No fault

Answer

Q12 65LMMWE89 → CC + GG + MM → (D)

         ↓   ↓   ↓

       (A)   (B)   (C)

(A) 65LMMWD89

(B) 65MMWD89

(C) 65M9WD89

(D) No fault

Answer

Q13 BF442B7CR → II + AA + GG → (D)

         ↓   ↓   ↓

       (A)   (B)   (C)

(A) BF442B7C7

(B) BF44237CR

(C) BF4237CR

(D) No fault

Answer

Q14 BA97801SP → KK + OO + II → (D)

         ↓   ↓   ↓

       (A)   (B)   (C)

(A) BNZ27801SP

(B) BNZWR801SP

(C) BNZR801SP

(D) No fault

Answer

Q15 SU$KUK999 → AA + GG + MM → (D)

         ↓   ↓   ↓

       (A)   (B)   (C)

(A) SU$3UK999

(B) SU3UK999

(C) 9U3UK999

(D) No fault

Answer

Rules Q16–20

ZY Change the third letter to lower case.

XW Insert the letters Nr between the first and second items.

VU Exchange the second and sixth items in the sequence.

TS Change the first letter to lower case.

RQ Replace the second lower-case letter with the next in the alphabet.

PO Exchange the first and last items in the sequence.

NM Replace the second number with an upper-case P.

LK Replace the fourth lower-case letter with the next in the alphabet.

Q16 2007GMATgatQ → ZY + VU + LK → (D)

           ↓   ↓   ↓

         (A) (B) (C)

(A) 2P07GMATgatQ

(B) 2P07GMATgbtQ

(C) QP07GMATgat2

(D) No fault

Answer [   ]

Q17 N89jnwwwcom → ZY + VU + LK → (D)

           ↓   ↓   ↓

        (A) (B) (C)

(A) N89JNwwwcom

(B) Nw9jNwwcom

(C) Nw9jNwxcom

(D) No fault

Answer [   ]

Q18 DEC1341emb → NM + RQ + XW → (D)

          ↓   ↓   ↓

       (A) (B) (C)

(A) DEC1P41emb

(B) DEC1P41enb

(C) DNrEC1P41enb

(D) No fault

Answer [   ]

Q19 CKco7267td → NM + ZY + TS → (D)
　　　　　　　↓　　↓　　↓
　　　　　　　(A)　(B)　(C)

(A) CKco7P67td
(B) CKco7P67td
(C) CKco7P67cd
(D) No fault

Answer [   ]

Q20 784ursSPR → PO + ZY + TS → (D)
　　　　　　　↓　　↓　　↓
　　　　　　　(A)　(B)　(C)

(A) R784ursSPR
(B) R784uRsSP7
(C) r784uRsSP7
(D) No fault

Answer [   ]

ANSWERS AND EXPLANATIONS

Chapter 3 Situational judgement and personality questionnaires

Customer care

1. Answer

Most appropriate	B
Least appropriate	C

Explanation A store might have a policy on whether or not you should leave your work to help a customer but at the recruitment stage they are most likely looking for staff who shows a willingness to go that bit extra. For this reason, the most appropriate response would involve you walking the customer to where the milk is. Suggested answers C, D and E are all problematic. The least appropriate answer would involve directing them to customer services because they have asked where they can find milk not customer services!

2. Answer

Most appropriate	E
Least appropriate	A

Explanation

Retailers are in the business of selling things and a customer is more likely to buy when sales staff use positive language and clearly address the customers questions. Answer A starts positively but is the least appropriate because it doesn't tell the customer when they can buy the item. Answer E is the most appropriate because it answers the question positively and tells the customer when they can have the item.

3. Answer

Most appropriate	B
Least appropriate	A

Explanation

Retailers like their staff to take responsibility for errors irrespective of who makes them. For this reason, suggested answer B is the most appropriate because the worker takes responsibility and deals with the issue. Answer A is the least appropriate because customers first and foremost want a problem resolved and this response leaves the complaint unaddressed.

4. Answer

Most appropriate	D
Least appropriate	A

Explanation

When a client shares personal information you should show compassion and keep them at the centre of the conversation. This is why answer D is the most appropriate. To ensure that you are always customer focused you shouldn't move the conversation to talk about yourself or your situation. Avoid asking questions that risk the person disclosing more than they are comfortable with or are likely to take up more time than you may have.

5. Answer

Most appropriate	B
Least appropriate	D

Explanation Patients is an important quality in customer service and for this reason answer D is the most appropriate. Someone taking a call when you are serving them can be annoying but it might be really important or an emergency so the least appropriate response would be to interrupt them.

6. Answer

Most appropriate	C
Least appropriate	D

Explanation

Answer C is the most appropriate because you will be able to refer to some of the things they tell you when you explain which item will suit them best. Answer D is the least appropriate because they may interpret your eagerness as frustration.

7. Answer

Most appropriate	E
Least appropriate	C

Explanation

Many people suffer from anxiety especially if somewhere is crowded or noisy. The most appropriate way to support them is to ask if there is some way you can help. For example, they may want you to walk with them out of the store. The least helpful thing so the least appropriate would be to tell them to calm down.

8. Answer

Most appropriate	B
Least appropriate	C

Explanation

It is never ok for a customer to be rude or abusive but nor is it right to respond in kind. Answer A is incorrect because it is rude to hang up on someone and answer D is less than appropriate because you should always warn someone before you put them on hold. Yelling back is the least appropriate answer.

9. Answer

Most appropriate	A
Least appropriate	B

Explanation

Answer A is the most appropriate because it's always good to apologise when something has gone wrong even when it's the customer's mistake. Answer B is the least appropriate because it unnecessarily tells the customer they are mistaken and it may offend them.

10. Answer

Most appropriate	D
Least appropriate	E

Explanation

Employers want staff to be willing to learn and be open to training. The answer referring to a longer journey to collect your child is perfectly appropriate but it would be better if instead of say 'can't' attend because you have to be at the school it was said can I leave the course in time to get to my child's from school? For this reason answer D is the most appropriate.

11. Answer

Most appropriate	B
Least appropriate	C

Explanation

It's important to employers that you treat customers equally and let them know that they are valued. Situations such as the one in the question do arise and make it hard to uphold both these principles. The least appropriate answer is C because it risks making the regular customer feel like they've been told off. Neither answer A or D are ideal because they risk leaving either the new or regular customer feeling unappreciated. Answer B has the best chance of ensuring both customers feel acknowledged.

12. Answer

Most appropriate	E
Least appropriate	D

Explanation

Being able to recognize buying signals is a valuable skill in retail and this question reviewed several buying and not yet interested signs. The least appropriate answer to when you should approach a customer to try and make a sale was D because someone avoiding your eye contact is most likely not ready to buy. Answers A and C are clear buy signals, but Answer E is the most obvious sign.

Communicating with others

13 *Explanation:* Agreement suggests a candidate suitable for a customer-facing role and a sales-oriented, ambitious candidate; **14** *Explanation:* Agreement but not strong agreement would suggest a candidate able to show sensitivity to others; **15** *Explanation:* Agreement suggests someone uninterested in sales, and a strong preference in formulating strategy rather than its implementation; **16** *Explanation:* Agreement suggests suitability for many modern managerial positions. Disagreement would risk the suggestion that when under pressure the candidate was unable to maintain good relations with colleagues; **17** *Explanation:* Only agree strongly with this statement if the employer is seeking this quality, otherwise you risk giving the impression of a candidate who will be hard to manage and a potential liability when dealing with colleagues and customers; **18** *Explanation:* Agreement would suggest someone not suited to team working; **19** *Explanation:* Disagreement would be expected of an all-round candidate and anyone applying for a managerial role. Agreement would be acceptable for a candidate for a policy formation role; **20** *Explanation:* Disagreement with this statement would be expected; most employers would consider being opinionated at work as always a bad thing; **21** *Explanation:* Agreement would be expected for any role responsible for the communication of policy or the management of staff or change; **22** *Explanation:* Agreement might risk the impression of an employee who lacks commitment or who does not work fully towards the common aims of the organization. This is not an approach an employer would value in someone whom they have not yet employed; **23** *Explanation:* Agreement would support a candidate aware of the importance of relationships, personality and communication; **24** *Explanation:* Many employers are seeking staff who adopt this approach to team motivation and management. It would therefore be something with which to agree strongly if you are confident the organization values this approach; **25** *Explanation:* A bit of a trick question and, perhaps surprisingly, many questionnaires include such questions. To agree suggests a self-criticism but disagreement risks the impression that you do not recognize fully the value of lateral thinking and new ways of working. In some roles, such as strategy and senior management, agreement would be expected.

Your approach to decision making

26 *Explanation:* Disagreement might be appropriate if applying for a company that has a hierarchical style and for a non-managerial position. Strong disagreement would only be appropriate for candidates for executive positions; **27** *Explanation:* Employers would consider this an important question and they may not want to employ someone who disagreed as they may be unable to separate their personal views from those that represent the best interest of the organization; **28** *Explanation:* Agreement might be appropriate for applicants to professional roles or one where someone is expected to bring stature; **29** *Explanation:* Agreement might suit a position where you work unsupervised or a role where someone risk-averse is wanted; **30** *Explanation:* Agreement would be expected for a role where team working is essential and where policy formulation is a key activity. Consistent responses would be expected with questions 1 and 2; **31** *Explanation:* Agreement would suggest a numerate candidate for a position in a financial or analytical department. An all-round candidate might disagree; **32** *Explanation:* If applying for a policy or managerial role, then disagreement would be expected; **33** *Explanation:* Disagreement might suggest experience of the practical realities of business, strong agreement might suggest an over-cautious style; **34** *Explanation:* Agreement suggests a candidate happy to work in a hierarchical organization and if that is the type of organization to which you are applying, then it is the best response; **35** *Explanation:* Most employers would expect a candidate to disagree with this statement. A new employee with relevant experience or professional status would hold very valid views; **36** *Explanation:* Agreement risks the impression of a candidate unused to collective decisions and team working; **37** *Explanation:* Some employers would like a candidate who agreed, perhaps in a highly competitive field, but others might fear the person was too strong a personality and would fit badly in an existing team.

Your approach to planning

38 *Explanation:* Agreement suggests a strong proactive approach and an aversion to risk. These are qualities some employers value highly; **39** *Explanation:* Strong agreement would be expected of applicants for many managerial positions; it would of course have to be supported by experience detailed on your CV; **40** *Explanation:* Agreement might be taken to suggest financial acumen, strong agreement might be taken to suggest a risk-sensitive candidate, which may not be a bad thing, depending on the job; **41** *Explanation:* Agreement suggests a confident, reactive approach where greatest store is placed on hard work and experience rather than policy and planning; **42** *Explanation:* In some roles this may well be the case but many roles demand a compromise where maximum speed is realized with the minimum of errors; **43** *Explanation:* The statement describes the two most common approaches to work and management and your prospective employer will have decided which approach they prefer. So decide how you prefer to work and indicate that preference accordingly; **44** *Explanation:* An applicant for an all-round position would disagree but a specialist in sales or another customer-facing role who agreed might be exactly what an employer is looking for; **45** *Explanation:* Some industries have highly developed regulations and detailed procedures that staff are expected to follow. If you are applying for a position in such a company, then avoid any impression that you find those regulations inappropriate; **46** *Explanation:* Ambiguity is a fact of life in many roles. Yet people have to make good decisions despite that uncertainty. If the role to which you apply is one in which vagueness is a part of working life, then respond accordingly; **47** *Explanation:* Most employers would not like a candidate to indicate that they find an essential part of most roles demeaning; **48** *Explanation:* Agreement might be interpreted as suggesting a candidate who is inflexible and unwilling to work as part of a team with collective responsibility to get the job done; **49** *Explanation:* Delegation is a key skill expected in most demanding roles. Many employers might be concerned that an employee who does not delegate will not cope at very busy times.

Managing people and resources

50 *Explanation:* Agreement would suggest someone who is very sales-oriented but it would also risk the interpretation that they lack sufficient awareness of the need to maintain margins and cost controls; **51** *Explanation:* Every employer wants to know as soon as something goes seriously wrong, so most would expect prospective employees to agree with this statement; **52** *Explanation:* Strong agreement might be expected of someone in a financial or purchasing role or a managerial position. Agreement would perhaps be expected of all employees; **53** *Explanation:* Agreement would suggest someone able to deal sensitively with colleagues and clients and who will be a good team player; **54** *Explanation:* An employer seeking a hands-on manager will be looking for agreement with this statement but practitioners of other styles of management may disagree; **55** *Explanation:* Look for constancy of answer with the last question. It is possible to agree or disagree with both but they can be taken to represent aspects of different styles of management and in your responses you should try to give as clear an indication as possible of your preferred style; **56** *Explanation:* Agreement would suggest someone who is uncompromising in their commitment to a client-focused approach and this might well support an application for such a role but it would not be well received if management of people formed a significant part of the job; **57** *Explanation:* Another slightly tricky statement. Strong agreement might suggest a frustration with the widespread culture of targets and performance management and this could count against your application.

Motivating yourself

58 *Explanation:* This is a statement that most employers would want you to agree with. Do not worry about admitting to faults; after all, none of us is perfect; **59** *Explanation:* A self-confident applicant who recognizes the importance of continued personal development would agree with this statement. It would help create a winning impression with most employers; **60** *Explanation:* An independent-minded employee might agree but take care not to suggest that you might be difficult to manage or reluctant to accept the authority of others to set the criteria against which your performance might be judged; **61** *Explanation:* Agreement might suggest a candidate wanting a challenge and happy to work to achieve ambitious targets; **62** *Explanation:* Agreement suggests an empowering style of management and an acceptance of the value of performance management techniques; **63** *Explanation:* Be careful not to agree with too many statements that begin 'above all else' or 'I most want' as it implies it is a very significant issue for you and one the employer might or might not be looking for. Agreement would suggest a very ambitious candidate and that would please many employers but not all; **64** *Explanation:* A large salary, the latest mobile phone or computer do not motivate all employees. The mission of some organizations is social or altruistic and such employers may prefer to employ candidates who agree with this statement. But be careful not to agree too strongly because many roles, while contributing to a worthy objective, do not afford the post holder a clear perspective of what is being achieved and the employer may fear that the candidate has unrealistic expectations; **65** *Explanation:* This is exactly what some employers expect and like of a candidate. Others, however, might be frightened off by such up-front ambition; **66** *Explanation:* Agree with this only if the role to which you have applied offers it, but most do not and an employer might worry that they cannot meet the aspirations of the candidate; **67** *Explanation:* Meritocracy means a place of work where people are given responsibility or selected according to merit. Many organizations consider themselves meritocracies; **68** *Explanation:* Agreement suggests that you will bring a different perspective to a role, so you should only agree if this is the case and this is what the employer is looking for.

Features of your ideal role

69 *Explanation:* The question implies a high-pressure role and someone who can cope well in such an environment. So only agree if you want such a role and will thrive in it; **70** *Explanation:* Not all roles offer the opportunity to get stuck in and sort out a mess or see off a threat. Most employers are looking for someone to build on success or to continue the achievements of the past; **71** *Explanation:* Most employees would consider no distractions to be rather a luxury because in the real workplace distractions come thick and fast and still you have to get the job done. An employer might fear that they cannot guarantee a minimum of distractions and they might therefore reject a candidate who strongly agreed with this statement; **72** *Explanation:* Some employers want managers who are really hands on and some roles need this level of intervention, but not all, so be sure this sort of statement truly describes your preferred style of working and is what the role needs and what the employer is looking for; **73** *Explanation:* Unfortunately, this style of working does come with some territories and if you work in one of them, then you will agree with this statement; **74** *Explanation:* Many of us do, but it would perhaps be unwise to make such a negative point as it would do nothing to support your application; **75** *Explanation:* The first part of the statement is fine and something many employers value, but they cannot guarantee that things will always go to plan and so would be concerned if an applicant indicated that they tend to get stressed under such circumstances.

Your attitude towards risk

76 *Explanation:* Unfortunately, it is not always true that the higher the risk the higher the return, so it would be unwise to agree with this statement; **77** *Explanation:* Strong agreement might suggest someone who is risk sensitive, which may not be a bad thing; agreement may support the impression of financial acumen; **78** *Explanation:* It is a commonly held view but those working in even highly regulated industries still find room for creativity and an employer in one of these sectors might well be expecting a suitable candidate to disagree; **79** *Explanation:* In some industries success is dependent on taking chances or going further than the competition, in others it is not and such an approach would be unwelcome; **80** *Explanation:* A client-focused role or sales position would suit someone who agreed with this statement but it would be a less suitable response for an all-round position.

Appropriate responses in work

81 D or E, *Explanation:* An employer would want every customer, even the challenging ones, to receive the same high standard of service; **82** D or E, *Explanation:* To raise your voice when discussing something at work would be considered inappropriate behaviour by most employers; **83** D or E, *Explanation:* Lying is a form of dishonesty that most employers would not approve of. To describe it as a little lie does not change this fact; **84** A or B, *Explanation:* Employers want to be kept informed of any issues that affect performance. They can then take them into consideration when deciding what to do to address underperformance; **85** D or E, *Explanation:* To agree would suggest that you can prejudge people; this is to admit that you have prejudices against certain types of people which, if displayed in work, is inappropriate; **86** D or E, *Explanation:* At work we have to keep our employer, colleagues and customers informed whether the news is good or bad. If you are unsure whether or not you should tell someone something, ask your line manager for guidance; **87** D or E, *Explanation:* An employer wants to know as soon as something of significance goes wrong; you can always report at the same time what actions you propose to correct the situation; **88** D or E, *Explanation:* Everyone in work receives direction and an employer would want employees to be at ease both receiving and giving orders; **89** D or E, *Explanation:* Danger has no place at work. If you consider something dangerous, inform your line manager immediately and help find a way of completing the task that avoids unnecessary risk; **90** D or E,

Explanation: The correct action would be to inform the person upsetting you and, if this does not resolve the issue, your line manager. Otherwise implement the workplace grievance procedure which should be a part of your contract of employment; **91** A or B, *Explanation:* A serious issue such as bullying should be reported straight away so that it can be stopped; **92** D or E, *Explanation:* The passage implies that the joke is not appreciated by some colleagues and therefore it is inappropriate; **93** D or E, *Explanation:* Work should be organized so that both men and women can do every job equally well; **94** D or E, *Explanation:* Stealing is unacceptable no matter how little the value of the goods taken; **95** D or E, *Explanation:* If someone is not pulling their weight, then we need to find out if there is a reason that can be corrected; **96** A or B, *Explanation:* Such action is likely to appease the anger of the customer; **97** D or E, *Explanation:* Employers would want to be informed if you found your workload too great; **98** A or B, *Explanation:* This behaviour would be considered good team working; **99** D or E, *Explanation:* Employers want staff who are flexible in their working practice and will help address the unexpected. Anyway, most job descriptions include a last sentence that says the employee should be willing to undertake any other reasonable task; **100** D or E, *Explanation:* It may well be of concern to the employer if it affects your ability to undertake your work safely or if it adversely impinges on your performance; **101** A or B, *Explanation:* Most health and safety policies require this and they are likely to form a part of your contract of employment; **102** D or E, *Explanation:* Arguments at work are inappropriate and to argue until you are affected physically by the event would be unacceptable to employers.

Situational awareness

Situation 2 Answer

1	2	3	4
C	C	C	A

Explanation

Whatever the size of the business, your employer has a duty of care to look after your health, safety and welfare while you are at work. This duty of care includes making sure that ventilation, temperature, lighting, and toilet, washing and rest facilities all meet health, safety and welfare requirements. This includes providing somewhere for employees to get changed and to store their own clothes and an area set aside for rest breaks and to eat meals, including if necessary suitable facilities for pregnant women and nursing mothers. Response 1 is less than acceptable because you have tried to before and it has failed. Response 3 is less than acceptable because it is not the case that a small business does not have a duty of care for its employees. Suggested response 3 is also less than acceptable because a tribunal would expect you to have raised the matter formally with your employer. Response 4 is the most acceptable because you have tried to resolve the issue informally and failed and it is proper that you therefore raise the matter formally.

Situation 3 Answer

1	2	3	4
A	C	C	B

Explanation

You should first try to resolve disagreements with co-workers informally but if this fails and despite the passing of time the matter continues, then you should involve your supervisor or manager to see if they can resolve matters. If neither of these actions works and the issue continues to affect your work, then you should take the matter up formally. Do this using your employer's formal procedures for grievances. You should be able to find these in either your company's handbook or as an appendix to your contract of employment. Suggested response 1 is the most appropriate because it seeks to resolve the matter informally between the workers involved and then seeks to resolve it informally. Responses 2 and 3 do not follow the recommended procedure, so are less than acceptable. Suggested response 4 is acceptable but it is not the most appropriate because it does not first try to resolve things informally with your co-workers before involving management.

Situation 4 Answer

1	2	3	4
B	C	C	B

Explanation

Your employer should have systems and procedures in place to minimize the risk of pressures that create stress. When a member of staff falls ill due to stress at work, then the employer should review the person's role and look at ways to remove the causes of the stress and ill health. If you write to them informing them of a stress-related illness then they should respond by offering to meet with you and discuss ways to help you return to work and avoid the risk of the illness reoccurring. Responses 1 and 4 would allow the employer the opportunity to meet their responsibility to adjust your workload and provide a healthy place of work and so are both acceptable. Responses 2 and 3 are both less than acceptable. Response 2 is less than acceptable because the illness was due to the amount of work and not a lack of lunch breaks or extra hours worked. Response 3 is less than acceptable because it does not seek to address your workload, which is the cause of your ill health.

Situation 5 Answer

1	2	3	4
B	C	C	A

Explanation

You can expect your boss to be able to listen to someone distressed and be able to recognize signs of stress and have some understanding of possible ill-health outcomes. It is reasonable to expect your employer to have the systems and procedures in place to minimize the risk of pressures creating stress, and leading to ill health and to be able to accommodate events such as a bereavement by making adjustments to workloads. Suggested response 1 is acceptable but more is needed before it can be described as the most appropriate. Suggested responses 2 and 3 are less than acceptable because they do not secure the change necessary for you to cope with your return to work. Suggested response 4 is the most appropriate because it is likely to reduce the pressures on you.

Situation 6 Answer

1	2	3	4
B	C	A	C

Explanation

Your employer is probably trying to grapple with legal and business continuity issues. The work environment described in the situation sounds like a very difficult place and senior management would be trying to resolve it. It would not be right under the circumstance to discuss the matter directly with your manager but it is equally not appropriate that you put up with it because it is affecting your work and upsetting you. The most appropriate responses are 1 and 3 because they will ensure that management is informed of the additional problems and so can do something about them. Suggested response 3 is the most appropriate because of the professional and empathetic approach adopted.

Situation 7 Answer

1	2	3	4
B	C	B	B

Explanation

If there is bullying of any kind, or other behaviour which affects your health or ability to do your job, then a good employer will make changes to stop it. No employer should tolerate bullying of any kind and especially not of the sort described in this situation. If they cannot resolve it informally, then they should initiate disciplinary action against any harasser. If your employer does not take action against such an individual, you may be able to use the law to make your employer change their approach. Situations 1, 3 and 4 are acceptable responses because they support the individuals affected and should lead to a resolution. Situation 2 is less than acceptable because it is unlikely to result in a resolution.

Situation 8 Answer

1	2	3	4
C	B	C	C

Explanation

Response 1 is less than acceptable because while it is correct that the perpetrator should be challenged it would be wrong to call someone an idiot. Responses 3 and 4 are also less than acceptable because the fact that the event happened outside work does not mean that a code of conduct does not apply or that we have to accept inappropriate banter. Response 2 is appropriate in that it will result in supporting Jane; however, it is not the best possible response because it fails to challenge the behaviour of the perpetrator (which should be done in a non-confrontational way).

Situation 9 Answer

1	2	3	4
C	C	B	A

Explanation

Response 1 is less than acceptable because while you may feel that you have received enough instruction to operate the crusher it is the employer's responsibility to ensure that training and instruction are sufficient to ensure the safety of workers. Response 2 is also less than acceptable because an employer should not instruct you to operate equipment without proper instruction and or training – and this applies irrespective of the number of employees. Response 3 is acceptable but the best response is 4 because while you decline to operate the machinery you explain why and this gives the employer the opportunity to arrange the necessary instruction so that you can carry out your duties safely.

Situation 10 Answer

1	2	3	4
A	C	C	B

Explanation

Response 1 is the best approach given that you have tried and failed to resolve the matter informally and your manager is the most appropriate person to involve next. It may well be that your manager can stop all further discussion of the subject and advise Paul that he must stop. Response 2 is unlikely to succeed, so is less than acceptable because such an approach has already been tried and has failed. Response 3 is less than acceptable because it does not seek to resolve the problem. You might escape the problem but you will leave your colleagues to have to deal with it. Response 4 is acceptable in that it is reasonable that you approach a personnel officer; however, it would be better if you first took the issue to your immediate manager and then approached personnel only if he or she is unable to resolve the matter.

Situation 11 Answer

1	2	3	4
C	C	A	C

Explanation

Personal issues including family problems and emotional difficulties do sometimes impact on your work. Try as you might to keep your private life separate from your work life, inevitably when the personal issues are as great as those described in the passage, then one often runs into the other. In these circumstances you have no practical alternative but to inform your manager of the difficulties and request that they accommodate your situation wherever practical. Responses 1, 2 and 3 are all less than acceptable because they do not acknowledge the fact that your personal problems are impacting on your working life. Response 3 is the most appropriate because it acknowledges the impact of your personal problems on your work and seeks to deal with it.

Situation 12 Answer

1	2	3	4
C	B	B	C

Explanation

Response 1 is less than acceptable because it will leave the individual unaccompanied in the building. Responses 2 and 3 are acceptable (neither can be identified as the most appropriate response) as any potential breach in security will be avoided. Response 4 is less than acceptable because it will mean that a potential breach in security has been ignored.

Situation 13 answer

1	2	3	4
C	C	C	A

Explanation

Suggested response 1 is less than acceptable because it involves you disclosing personal details of your staff to a colleague. Response 2 is less than acceptable because a team meeting is not a suitable event in which to discuss with an individual an issue such body odour. Response 3 is less than acceptable because the fact that someone else has also noticed the odour means that you can no longer ignore the situation. Situation 4 is the best response because it will address the issue in a confidential and appropriate manner.

Situation 14 answer

1	2	3	4
C	A	B	C

Explanation
Response 1 is less than acceptable because a threat of violence is a serious matter and should not be ignored. Response 2 is the most appropriate because it will guarantee that the mater is dealt according to the correct procedure. Response 3 is an acceptable response because it will ensure that the matter is acted on. Response 4 is less than acceptable because it would be unreasonable to expect the person who was threatened to have to resolve the matter themself and without the support of management.

Situation 15 answer

1	2	3	4
B	C	C	A

Explanation
Response 1 is acceptable but may risk inflaming the situation so is therefore not necessarily the most appropriate response. Responses 2 and 3 are both less than acceptable because they do not prevent the person from using further bad language. Response 4 is the most appropriate because it will stop the inappropriate behaviour in the workplace.

Situation 16 answer

1	2	3	4
A	C	C	C

Explanation
Theft is a serious matter and response 1 is the most appropriate given that a theft has occurred. Responses 2 and 4 are less than acceptable because they do not attribute sufficient importance to the situation. Response 3 is less than acceptable because you may well not have the authority to search another

member of staff's personal belongings or property. It would be better to leave this to the police or in-house security.

Situation 17 Answer

1	2	3	4
B	C	A	C

Explanation

Response 1 is acceptable because it clarifies the team member's role and invites him to come and speak some more. Responses 2 and 4 are less than acceptable because they do not offer the support and help an employee can expect from a manager. Response 3 is the most appropriate because it invites his view on what might help and offers to organize things differently.

Situation 18 Answer

1	2	3	4
A	C	C	C

Explanation

Response 1 is the most appropriate because it offers to organize things in a way that accommodates the individual's differences, in this instance a disability. Response 2 is less than acceptable because equality of opportunity means that where practical we should make exceptions and arrange things so that differences can be accommodated. Responses 3 and 4 are less than acceptable because both present a disability as a problem and a matter of concern.

Situation 19 Answer

1	2	3	4
C	B	A	C

Explanation

Discrimination against an individual on the basis of gender is a matter that needs to be undertaken with a great deal of care to ensure it is fair (in the vast majority of cases it would not be). Responses 1 and 4 therefore are less than acceptable because they do not seek clarification or advice on such a serious matter. Response 3 is the most appropriate because it involves seeking the advice of a specialist. Response 2 is acceptable because it involves referring to the written document and procedures for guidance before making a decision.

Situation 20 answer

1	2	3	4
A	C	C	B

Explanation
Most organizations have clear written procedures for dealing with the press. Dealing with the journalist's request without referring to the organization's public relations procedure risks exceeding your authority, so responses 2 and 3 are less than acceptable. Response 1 is the best response because as well as finding out the correct procedure you obtain the telephone number of the journalist, which means their identify can be confirmed. Response 4 would be acceptable because it will result in the correct procedure being followed.

Situation 21 Answer

1	2	3	4
A	B	C	C

Explanation
Response 1 is the most appropriate because it prioritizes team building and so will ensure that the team and you will get to know each other. Response 2 is less acceptable because it places less emphasis on team building. Responses 3 and 4 are less than acceptable because they place no emphasis on the need to build the new team.

Situation 22 Answer

1	2	3	4
C	A	C	C

Explanation

If you are discontented in your role, then you should draw this to the attention of your line manager as soon as is practical so that they may have the opportunity to correct the situation. You should not wait until the annual review to do this or ignore your negative feelings toward the role.

Chapter 4 Verbal reasoning

Word link

1 B Purchase, E Acquisition; **2** A Recognition, D Acknowledgement; **3** B Liable, F Accountable; **4** C Flexible, D Variable; **5** C Supplement, D Attachment; **6** B Observe, E Respect; **7** C Adjoining, F Juxtaposed; **8** A Suspension, F Deferral; **9** C Arbitrate, D Negotiate; **10** A Fix, E Rectify; **11** B Counsel, D Advise; **12** C Outline, E Sketch; **13** B Beneficial, F Favourable; **14** C Oppressive, E Wretched; **15** C Preceding, D Prior.

Word link – synonyms

16 B aim; **17** C affiliate; **18** A every; **19** C ill-starred; **20** A platitudes; **21** C imprudent; **22** C incidental; **23** B outmoded; **24** A conclusion; **25** C proportion; **26** B portray; **27** B appraise; **28** A primary product, *Explanation:* A commodity is a raw material or product traded on specialist markets; **29** C competitor; **30** A agreement, *Explanation:* Both lease and agreement are types of contract; **31** B benefits; **32** A utilities; **33** C brusque; **34** B allocate.

Word link – opposites

35 C Descend; **36** A Jovial; **37** B Prohibit; **38** A Foolish; **39** B Rise; **40** C Direct; **41** C Pacify; **42** A Confirm; **43** B Despise; **44** B Progress; **45** D Accelerate; **46** B Irresolute; **47** C Exhaust; **48** C Question; **49** A Unprofitable; **50** B Lax; **51** A Confirm; **52** C Crude; **53** D Wrong; **54** B Work; **55** A Deter; **56** A agree; **57** B sophisticated; **58** C beneficial; **59** B dawdle; **60** A collect; **61** B poor; **62** C ignore; **63** A reality; **64** B pleasant; **65** A slack; **66** C direct; **67** B whole; **68** C imperceptible; **69** B junior; **70** C often; **71** C incapacitated; **72** A optimist; **73** B ancestor.

Find the new word(s)

74 tour; **75** idle; **76** teem; **77** only; **78** arid; **79** gene; **80** rely; **81** arch; **82** tilt (tormentil is a plant); **83** urge; **84** earl and hove; **85** onto; **86** rich and chum; **87** near; **88** dial; **89** duty; **90** sale; **91** seed; **92** term; **93** note; **94** calm; **95** chap;

96 real; **97** tale; **98** tear; **99** flag; **100** cult; **101** same; **102** meal; **103** push; **104** only; **105** hope; **106** bane; **107** last; **108** must; **109** zero; **110** race; **111** malt; **112** ally; **113** skin; **114** tone; **115** deaf; **116** palm and opal; **117** oust; **118** lame and nine; **119** etch; **120** gasp; **121** lush; **122** best; **123** that and hath; **124** sour.

Word swap

125 yourself and someone; **126** to and is; **127** money and squabbles; **128** American and generation; **129** result and work; **130** as and steady; **131** city and café; **132** a and each; **133** a and the; **134** from and on; **135** challenging and successful; **136** employees and leaders; **137** developed and diverse; **138** organization and organization's; **139** inflation and expansion; **140** supplied and powered; **141** human and unfashionable; **142** bar and suit; **143** bull and financial; **144** inflation and growth; **145** treaty and change; **146** 57,000 and 150,000; **147** route and signs; **148** and and out; **149** America and Mexico; **150** China and India; **151** Manufacturing and outsourcing.

Sentence sequencing

152 C, A, B; **153** B, A, C; **154** C, A, B; **155** C, D, B, A; **156** B, C, A, D; **157** D, B, A, C; **158** B, C, D, A; **159** A, C, D, B; **160** C, B, D, A; **161** C, A, B, D; **162** C, A, D, B; **163** B, F, D, A, E, C; **164** B, A, D, C; **165** C, A, B, D; **166** B, D, A, C; **167** D, C, B, A; **168** D, C, B, A; **169** D, B, A, C; **170** D, B, C, A; **171** C, B, A, D; **172** B, C, D, A; **173** A, C, B; **174** B, C, D, A; **175** C, A, D, B; **176** D, A, C, B.

Best word(s) to complete a sentence

177 compensation; **178** performing and level; **179** track and with; **180** failing and meeting; **181** the and promotional; **182** at and compromise; **183** renewed and in; **184** rallied and from; **185** in and slowing; **186** in and margins; **187** to and responding; **188** comparatively and if; **189** strategy, form and from; **190** growth spurt and convertible; **191** on, actuarial and insurance; **192** media, nor and commercial; **193** cautious, akin and positions; **194** unable, contraction and decline; **195** is, growth and rates; **196** measures, extremely and remaining.

English usage

197 A1 and B1, *Explanation:* Both bits of missing text are past tense, one continuous. Saw is past tense and sitting is a continuous action; **198** C in, *Explanation:* A preposition defines a relation. For example, in the sentence 'The girl is in the shop', 'in' is a preposition. In the sentence 'The book was written by her', 'by' is the preposition; **199** A2 and B1, *Explanation:* 'Had' identifies the sentence as in the past tense, so we use 'couldn't' and 'forgotten'. 'Can't' is the present tense; **200** C largest, *Explanation:* These are adjectives that describe the most or least in a group of similar things. My house is the smallest, your house is the largest; **201** A1, *Explanation:* A1 is correct because the speaker is concentrating at that time; **202** broken, *Explanation:* Past participles often end in -en or -ed; they are adjectives that serve as a verb in the sentence; **203** A1 and B2, *Explanation:* My brother and I went to a particular hospital, so 'the' is used to identify it. 'My mother is in hospital' does not need the term because in this case hospital is used in the general sense; **204** A2 and B2, *Explanation:* We are drawing comparisons and to do this with short words we add -er but for longer words we use 'more'; **205** A3 and B3, *Explanation:* 'Last night' requires the past tense of the verb and the action of Sam in the park requires the present participle; **206** ideas, *Explanation:* A noun serves to identify the thing, place, class or person; **207** B was, *Explanation:* A sum of money is singular, so we use 'was'; **208** B later, *Explanation:* Comparative adjectives allow us to draw comparisons between two similar items. 'Your train was later than mine.' 'I drove further than you.'; **209** A1 and B1, *Explanation:* Here 'so' is used for emphasis while 'as' is used to make a comparison; **210** A2 and B2, *Explanation:* 'In' is used for people and places. Superlatives usually take the form 'more' or -est, eg nicest, most beautiful, but 'far' is an exception as it becomes 'furthest'; **211** A4 and B1, *Explanation:* 'Must' is used to imply that something that follows is true; **212** cleaning, *Explanation:* A verb describes an action; **213** A2 and B1, *Explanation:* A verb such as 'like' is placed alongside the object, in this case animals. So it is wrong to say 'I like very much' as this separates the verb and its object; **214** A2 and B2, *Explanation:* When something changes we use the expression 'no longer' or 'any longer'. The rule is that we use 'no longer' in the middle of a sentence and 'any longer' at the end; **215** A1 and B3, *Explanation:* Both are the past tense. A2 is wrong because 'have watched' would be used to describe the present state. 'I have watched a lot of television.'; **216** A2 and B1, *Explanation:* We use 'in spite of' but not 'despite of', only 'despite'; **217** A1, *Explanation:* 'There' is used to refer to a location, 'their' when we are referring to people or their property. After 'while' when referring to the future we use the present tense, so not 'will'; **218** A3, B1 and C2, *Explanation:* The sentence states 'notes', so from the suggested answers it must be two notes; a ten pound note is a singular, so pound is correct and the number of hours worked is three, so we say hours' in the possessive plural form; **219** A1 and B1, *Explanation:* We use 'until' when an action continues but we use 'by' when something happens; **220** A1, B2 and C2, *Explanation:* We use 'at' for the time of day, 'on' for the day of the week and 'in' for the month of the year; **221** A3 and B2, *Explanation:* The apology is a completed action, so we use the past tense, but when describing an action that was continuing, we use a present participle (making); **222** A2 and B1, *Explanation:* When referring to people, an apostrophe s is used; for things the 'of the' structure is usually adopted; **223** A1, B2, C1 and D3, *Explanation:* We say 'on' a plane, 'on' a bicycle, 'in' a car and 'at' a party.

Identify the correct sentence or word(s)

224 B, *Explanation:* B is unclear as it is not stated whether he greeted one or two people as the two job titles could be held by one person; **225** A and B, *Explanation:* 'really carefully' is correct but it does not make sense to say that 'the police officer was both unimpressed'; **226** A3 and B1, *Explanation:* We say 'a friend of yours' or 'your friend and a friend of mine'; **227** A and B, *Explanation:* 'was' is used in the singular, 'were' for a plural subject. We share between two people and among more than two; **228** A2 and B1, *Explanation:* When describing an action in the past which was continuing, we use the present participle (going), but the act of smelling is completed, so we use the past tense; **229** A1 and B2, *Explanation:* It is said that we are in a country but on a beach; **230** slow, *Explanation:* An adjective adds detail to a noun; **231** A1, *Explanation:* 'them' serves to identify which persons are left-handed; it is used when referring to two or more people or things; **232** A3 and B3, *Explanation:* 'too' means higher than desired and 'enough' means as much as is necessary; **233** A3 and B2, *Explanation:* We sit 'on' the bus but we are 'at' the back of something; **234** 'I am doing', *Explanation:* This part of the sentence gives the time which is the present and it is continuous; **235** A3, B3 and C3, *Explanation:* We say get/arrived/travel etc to a place but we do not say 'to' home. For example 'go home', 'on the way home' etc; **236** A1, B1 and C2, *Explanation:* We say 'in my car' or 'by bus' and 'by car' and 'by cheque' but 'in cash'; **237** 4 – beautiful, young, blue, green, *Explanation:* Adjectives add detail, so beautiful and young add detail to what is known about the woman and blue and green add detail to what is known about the dress; **238** A and B, *Explanation:* Both sentences misuse the meaning of the word 'unique' which means one of a kind, unlike anything else; **239** A2 and B3, *Explanation:* 'so' and 'such' serve to add emphasis; 'so' is used with adjectives and 'such' with nouns; **240** A4, *Explanation:* Adjectives such as 'long' and 'red' are normally put in the order of size, then colour. We would only use 'and' if a list was formed, for example 'a long red and white coat'; **241** A1 and B3, *Explanation:* 'who' introduces the clause that provides the extra information about where Peter lives. 'Which' and 'what' refer to objects, 'who' and 'whom' to people. We use 'which' rather than 'what' because we are referring to something already mentioned; **242** F themselves, *Explanation:* 'my' and 'ours' are possessive pronouns. The rest are reflexive but only 'themselves' is plural; **243** A2, B2 and C1, *Explanation:* 'each' and 'every' are often interchangeable but in these instances we are referring to the teams in the particular games, not every rugby team. Also, when we describe how often something occurs we use 'every'; **244** A2 and B3, *Explanation:* 'much' and 'little' are used with unspecified quantities; 'much' is correct because the 'but' implies a tension with 'little'. 'Few' is used for plural subjects; **245** A2 and B2, *Explanation:* 'some' is used to make a positive point while 'any' is used in a negative situation; **246** A4 and B3, *Explanation:* When we introduce something for the first time we refer to it as 'there's'; for subsequent references 'it' is used. 'There's' is an abbreviation for 'there is'. 'Their' is used when the subject is a person, 'there' for a place.

Read a passage and evaluate a statement

Passage 1

247 C, *Explanation:* The passage makes no comment on how the world would be if there were no colours; **248** A, *Explanation:* 'Amalgamate' means mixture and the passage states that white light is a mix of all the wavelengths; **249** B, *Explanation:* The passage does not make this statement; **250** A, *Explanation:* The truth of this statement follows logically from the passage; **251** A, *Explanation:* The truth of this statement can be inferred from the passage.

Passage 2

252 A, *Explanation:* The period 1797 to 1815 totals 18 years; **253** A, *Explanation:* The passage states that Napoleon was the emperor of France, which conquered much of the continent of Europe; **254** C, *Explanation:* The passage states that the French army was the most powerful but you cannot safely infer that it was also the largest; **255** C, *Explanation:* The passage states that France was at war with these kingdoms but does not say whether France won battles against them all; **256** B, *Explanation:* No date for this battle is given in the passage.

Passage 3

257 B, *Explanation:* The passage states that this was true traditionally but that today medicine is also concerned with prevention; **258** B, *Explanation:* The passage describes the legacy of treatments and techniques pioneered centuries ago; **259** A, *Explanation:* This is stated in the passage; **260** C, *Explanation:* The views of the author are not disclosed; **261** A, *Explanation:* The passage states that doctors use treatments of many types and gives examples of both techniques (surgery) and technologies such as radiation and vaccines.

Passage 4

262 A, *Explanation:* The passage states that Asia was the birthplace of civilization; **263** C, *Explanation:* The passage does not provide any information on this point; **264** A, *Explanation:* The passage states that the people of Asia make up over two-thirds of the world's population; **265** C, *Explanation:* The passage states that the first economies to boom were Japan, Singapore, Taiwan and South Korea. It does not say in which of these it first occurred; **266** A, *Explanation:* The passage states that Asia is the world's largest continent, so the truth of this statement can be inferred.

Passage 5

267 B, *Explanation:* The passage states that the climate will be cooler, not the weather; **268** A, *Explanation:* The passage gives examples of causes and mechanisms of climate change; **269** A, *Explanation:* The passage states that in tropical rainforests the climate remains hot and damp all the year round; **270** C, *Explanation:* The passage does not provide information on this point and it cannot be safely inferred from the passage; **271** A, *Explanation:* The passage states that the Arctic is cold all year and that the polar zone is the only climate zone where it is always cold.

Passage 6

272 B, *Explanation:* The passage describes smaller particles; **273** B, *Explanation:* The passage describes matter as being either elements or compounds; **274** C, *Explanation:* A tricky one – the passage describes molecules as atoms bonded together but it states only that atoms are held together by bonds. The means by which molecules are bonded together is not stated; **275** A, *Explanation:* This is stated in the passage; **276** A, *Explanation:* The passage states that all matter is made up of atoms including molecules and that atoms are made from these smaller particles.

Passage 7

277 C, *Explanation:* The passage does not provide details of which type of fraud is the most common; **278** C, *Explanation:* No details of the new measures are given in the passage; **279** B, *Explanation:* The passage states that the new measures are not yet in place; **280** B, *Explanation:* Total card fraud has reached £500 million; most but not all of this fraud is committed as a result of intercepted cards; **281** A, *Explanation:* This is clear from a careful reading of the passage.

Passage 8

282 A, *Explanation:* This can be readily deduced from the passage; **283** A, *Explanation:* The passage provides details of the lives and injuries saved and details the cost in terms of the environment and delays to the ambulance service; **284** C, *Explanation:* The passage does not inform us of driver attitudes; **285** A, *Explanation:* The passage states that road humps disrupt the flow of traffic; **286** B. *Explanation:* The passage does not state that this is true, only that critics claim this to be the case.

Passage 9

287 B, *Explanation:* The 1,000 deaths result from hospital-acquired infections; **288** C, *Explanation:* The passage provides no information on how the antibiotic-resistant bacteria might have been countered in the 1950s; **289** B, *Explanation:* The passage states that the infection became established in hospitals and nursing homes since that time; **290** A, *Explanation:* The term is used to describe it in the passage; **291** C, *Explanation:* The passage does not provide information on the relative severity of these conditions.

Passage 10

292 C, *Explanation:* The passage does not say whether or not the administrators voiced their concerns to government; **293** A, *Explanation:* The passage states that widespread fraud would discredit the electoral process but that fraud is currently rare; **294** A, *Explanation:* The passage states that recent changes to the system have led to an increased fear of fraud. So the truth of this assertion can be inferred from the passage; **295** A, *Explanation:* The passage states that checks are made but the new system may not allow sufficient time to complete them; **296** B, *Explanation:* It is not clear as the views of the author are not given.

Passage 11

297 C, *Explanation:* The passage does not give details of the actual record price, only the range of prices and the current price; **298** B, *Explanation:* The most efficient fields currently extract oil at these prices; the new techniques will allow for more oil to be economically extracted but the price of extraction for these techniques is not given; **299** A, *Explanation:* While it is not explicitly stated in the passage it is a reasonable assumption from reading the passage; **300** B, *Explanation:* This is not explicitly stated in the passage; **301** A, *Explanation:* The results are described as unexpected and to have led to improved forecasts of both the amount of oil and the amount that can be economically extracted. It is fair therefore to conclude that analysts were impressed by the findings.

Passage 12

302 A, *Explanation:* It also mentions journalists but this does not affect the truth of the statement; **303** B, *Explanation:* The passage states that solicitors only have to report suspicions of money laundering; **304** A, *Explanation:* The passage describes exceptions for all the professions, including journalists, who might break their code under order of a court; **305** C, *Explanation:* Only four professions are covered in the passage, so we do not know if all professions have these codes; **306** B, *Explanation:* The passage states only that they must report such injuries, not that they can be prosecuted.

Passage 13

307 A, *Explanation:* 80,000 by benefit officers and 44,000 by local authorities; **308** B, *Explanation:* The passage states that the new lower total was the lowest for 10 years, so the level must have been lower 10 years ago; **309** B, *Explanation:* Housing benefit is also awarded to the low paid; **310** A, *Explanation:* In the passage the fall in false claims is described as spectacular; **311** A, *Explanation:* The passage states that the £½ billion drop is equivalent to 25%, so the level of fraud 12 months previously would have been £2 billion.

Passage 14

312 A, *Explanation:* Such growth does not occur in some parts of the developed world and the passage asks if it is realistic to assume that prices will always rise; **313** C, *Explanation:* Only the views of middle-class people in the United States, Spain, Ireland and the UK are detailed; we are not informed of the views of the middle classes from other countries and cannot infer this information; **314** B, *Explanation:* Home ownership would become less attractive, so we might expect more people to rent, not fewer; **315** B, *Explanation:* The passage states that prices have almost doubled; **316** A, *Explanation:* This is a fair summary of the passage.

Passage 15

317 B, *Explanation:* The process of depopulation is described as having reduced to a trickle, so it continues; **318** B, *Explanation:* Over half of the new jobs are public appointments; **319** C, *Explanation:* The city of Liverpool is described this way but no information is given or can be inferred as to the relative state of the region's economy; **320** A, *Explanation:* The subsidy is described as playing a significant part in attracting jobs and investment; **321** A, *Explanation:* Low living and housing costs have attracted jobs and as other cities have become expensive Liverpool has become more popular.

Chapter 5 Numerical reasoning

The key operations

Mental arithmetic

1 3; **2** 7; **3** 6; **4** 77; **5** 6; **6** 9; **7** 12; **8** 144; **9** 8; **10** 4; **11** 84; **12** 3; **13** 5; **14** 11; **15** 4; **16** 33; **17** 7; **18** 90; **19** 11; **20** 5; **21** 6; **22** 9; **23** 10; **24** 33; **25** 4; **26** 5; **27** 11; **28** 7; **29** 42; **30** 9; **31** 25; **32** 11; **33** 8; **34** 108; **35** 11; **36** 8; **37** 7; **38** 20; **39** 8; **40** 4; **41** 6; **42** 4; **43** 6; **44** 8; **45** 4; **46** 18; **47** 11; **48** 9; **49** 8; **50** 32; **51** 6; **52** 9; **53** 64; **54** 11; **55** 7; **56** 30; **57** 9; **58** 11; **59** 48; **60** 9; **61** 7; **62** 36; **63** 12; **64** 3; **65** 1, 2, 3, 6, 9, 18, *Explanation:* $1 \times 18 = 18$, $2 \times 9 = 18$, $3 \times 6 = 18$, $9 \times 2 = 18$, $18 \times 1 = 18$; **66** 1, 3, 9, 27, *Explanation:* 1×27, 3×9, 9×3, 27×1; **67** 1, 11, *Explanation:* 11 is a prime number, ie a number whose factors are only 1 and itself; **68** 1, 2, 11, 22, *Explanation:* 1×22, 2×11, 11×2, 22×1; **69** 1, 2, 3, 4,

6, 9, 12, 18, 36, *Explanation:* 1 × 36, 2 × 18, 3 × 12, 4 × 9, 6 × 6, 9 × 4, 12 × 3, 18 × 2, 36 × 1; **70** 6, *Explanation:* They are 1, 2, 4, 5, 10 and 20; **71** 8, *Explanation:* They are 1, 2, 4, 7, 8, 14, 28 and 56; **72** 2, *Explanation:* 19 is a prime number; **73** 1, 2, 3, 4, 5, 6 10, 12, 15, 20, 30, 60; **74** 4, *Explanation:* They are 1, 2, 7, 14; **75** 1, 2, 3, 6, 7, 14, 21, 42; **76** 2, *Explanation:* 37 is a prime number; **77** 1, 2, 4, 8, 16; **78** 10, *Explanation:* 1, 2, 3, 4, 6, 8, 12, 16, 24, 48; **79** 1, 2, 3, 4, 6, 8, 12, 24; **80** 6, *Explanation:* 1, 2, 4, 8, 16, 32; **81** 4, *Explanation:* 1, 2, 17, 34; **82** 4, *Explanation:* This is the whole number that divides exactly into both figures. 4 × 2 = 8 and 4 × 5 = 20; **83** 4, *Explanation:* The following whole numbers divide exactly into both these numbers: 1, 2, 3 and 6; **84** 7, *Explanation:* 7 × 3 = 21, 7 × 7 = 49; **85** 3, *Explanation:* They are 1, 2 and 4; **86** 1,270, *Explanation:* These are easy but be sure that you can do them by moving the decimal place to the right by the number of 0s for multiplication; **87** 163; **88** 3.76, *Explanation:* Move the decimal point by the number of 0s to the left; **89** 90,600; **90** 0.024; **91** 9.6; **92** 0.01502; **93** 3,002; **94** 0.007; **95** 3; **96** 18,400, *Explanation:* First multiply by the 2 and then move the decimal place. 920 × 2 = 1840 × 10 = 18,400; **97** 3, *Explanation:* First divide by 100 and then by 4, 12 ÷ 4 = 3; **98** 210,000, *Explanation:* 3 × 7 = 21, 1,000 × 10 = 10,000, 21 × 10,000 = 210,000; **99** 800, *Explanation:* 48 ÷ 6 = 8, 1,000 ÷ 10 = 100, 8 × 100 = 800; **100** 180,000, *Explanation:* 6 × 3 = 18, 100 × 100 = 10,000, 18 × 10,000 = 180,000

Percentages

Changing fractions to decimals

101 20%, *Explanation:* 100 ÷ 5 = 20 × 1 = 20; **102** 25%, *Explanation:* 100 ÷ 4 = 25 × 1 = 25; **103** 11.1%, *Explanation:* 100 ÷ 9 = 11.11 (recurring), so treat it as 11.1 × 1 = 11.1; **104** 8.3%, *Explanation:* 100 ÷ 12 = 8.333 = 8.3 × 1 = 8.3; **105** 12.5%, *Explanation:* 100 ÷ 8 = 12.5 × 1 = 12.5; **106** 6.25%, *Explanation:* 100 ÷ 16 = 6.25 × 1 = 6.25; **107** 66.6%, *Explanation:* 100 ÷3 = 33.3 × 2 = 66.6; **108** 60%, *Explanation:* 100 ÷ 5 = 20 × 3 = 60; **109** 37.5%, *Explanation:* 100 ÷ 16 = 6.25 × 6 = 37.5; **110** 62.5%, *Explanation:* 100 ÷ 8 = 12.5 × 5 = 62.5; **111** 66.6%, *Explanation:* First reduce the fraction to its lowest term. 4/6 = 2/3, 100 ÷ 3 = 33.3 × 2 = 66.6; **112** 75%, *Explanation:* 6/8 = 3/4, 100 ÷ 4 = 25 × 3 = 75; **113** 80%, *Explanation:* 12/15= 4/5, 100 ÷ 5 = 20 × 4 = 80; **114** 20%, *Explanation:* 4/20 = 1/5, 100 ÷ 5 = 20 × 1 = 20; **115** 37.5%, *Explanation:* 9/24 = 3/8, 100 ÷ 8 = 12.5 × 3 = 37.5; **116** 40%, *Explanation:* 8/20 = 2/5, 100 ÷ 5 = 20 × 2 = 40; **117** 18.75%, *Explanation:* 6/32 = 3/16, 100 ÷ 16 = 6.25 × 3 = 18.75; **118** 75%, *Explanation:* 1/28 = ¾, 100 ÷ 4 = 25 × 3 = 75; **119** 31.25%, *Explanation:* 25/80 = 5/16, 100 ÷ 16 = 6.25 × 5 = 31.25

Changing between decimals and percentages

120 50%, *Explanation:* 0.5 × 100 = 50; **121** 20%, *Explanation:* 0.2 × 100 = 20; **122** 60%, *Explanation:* 0.6 × 100 = 60; **123** 0.25, *Explanation:* 25 ÷ 100 = 0.25;

124 40%, *Explanation:* 0.4 × 100 = 40; **125** 0.9, *Explanation:* 90 ÷ 100 = 0.9; **126** 35%, *Explanation:* 0.35 × 100 = 35; **127** 0.05, *Explanation:* 0.5 ÷ 100 = 0.05; **128** 72%, *Explanation:* 0.72 × 100 = 72; **129** 0.024, *Explanation:* 2.4 ÷ 100 = 0.024; **130** 42.5%, *Explanation:* 0.425 × 100 = 42.5; **131** 160%, *Explanation:* 1.6 × 100 = 160; **132** 33.3%, *Explanation:* 0.333 × 100 = 33.3; **133** 1.2, *Explanation:* 120 ÷ 100 = 1.2; **134** 0.005, *Explanation:* 0.5 ÷100 = 0.005

Expressing values as percentage

135 60%, *Explanation:* 30/50 = 3/5, 100 ÷ 5 = 20 × 3 = 60; **136** 25%, *Explanation:* 10/40 = 1/4, 100 ÷ 4 = 25 × 1 =25; **137** 40%, *Explanation:* 100 ÷ 5 = 20 × 2 = 40; **138** 11.1%, *Explanation:* 3/27 = 1/9, 100 ÷ 9 = 11.1; **139** 15%, *Explanation:* 12/80 = 3/20, 100 ÷ 20 = 5 × 3 = 15%; **140** 25%, *Explanation:* 4/16 = 1/4 , 100 ÷ 4 = 25 × 1 = 25; **141** 30%, *Explanation:* 12/40 = 3/10, 100 ÷ 10 = 10 × 3 = 30; **142** 40%, *Explanation:* 14/35 = 2/5, 100 ÷ 5 = 20 × 2 = 40; **143** 83.5%, *Explanation:* 25/30 = 5/6, 100 ÷ 6 = (16.666 so treat as) 16.7 × 5 = 83.5; **144** 80%, *Explanation:* Get rid of the decimal 10/12.5 = 20/25 = 4/5, 100 ÷ 5 = 20 × 4 = 80; **145** 16.7%, *Explanation:* 0.5/3 = 1/6, 100 ÷ 6 = 16.7 × 1 = 16.7; **146** 33.3%, *Explanation:* 0.3/0.9 = 3/9 = 1/3, 100 ÷ 3 = 33.3 × 1 = 33.3; **147** 0.25%, *Explanation:* 0.2/80 (multiply top and bottom by 5) = 1/400, 100 ÷ 400 = 0.25 × 1 = 0.25; **148** 110%, *Explanation:* 3.3/3 = 33/30 = 11/10, 100 ÷ 10 = 10 × 11 = 110; **149** 18.75%, *Explanation:* 6/32 = 3/16, 100 ÷ 16 = 6.25 × 3 = 18.75

Percentages of quantities

150 £10, *Explanation:* 12.5 ÷ 100 = 0.125, 80 × 0.125 = 10; **151** 1 hour and 15 minutes, *Explanation:* 25 ÷ 100 = 0.25 × 300 minutes (5 hours × 60) = 75 minutes = 1 hour 15 minutes; **152** 4 m, *Explanation:* 25 ÷ 100 = 0.25 × 16 = 4; **153** 25 pence, *Explanation:* 5 ÷ 100 = 0.05 × 5 = 0.25; **154** 11 m, *Explanation:* 20 ÷ 100 = 0.2 × 55 = 11; **155** 12 minutes, *Explanation:* 1 hour 20 minutes = 80 minutes, 15 ÷ 100 = 0.15 × 80 = 12; **156** £43.20, *Explanation:* 12 ÷ 100 = 0.12 × 360 = £43.2 = £43.20; **157** 27 minutes and 30 seconds, *Explanation:* 3 hours 40 minutes = 220 minutes, 12.5 ÷ 100 = 0.125 × 220 = 27.5 = 27 minutes and 30 seconds; **158** 31.5 m, *Explanation:* 45 ÷ 100 = 0.45 × 70 = 31.5; **159** £9.18, *Explanation:* 45 ÷ 100 = 0.45 × 20.4 = 9.18; **160** 45 cm, *Explanation:* 15 ÷ 100 = 0.15 × 3 = 0.45 metres = 45 cm; **161** 7 hours and 12 minutes, *Explanation:* 24 hours = 1,440 minutes, 30 ÷ 100 = 0.3 × 1,440 = 432 minutes ÷ 60 = 7.2 hours = 7 hours and 12 minutes; **162** 30m, *Explanation:* 12 ÷ 100 = 0.12 × 250 = 30; **163** £271.25, *Explanation:* 17.5 ÷ 100 = 0.175 × 1,550 = 271.25; **164** 2 hours and 9 minutes and 36 seconds, *Explanation:* 72 × 60 = 4,320, 3 ÷ 100 = 0.03, 4,320 × 0.03 = 129.6, 129 ÷ 60 = 2 hours and 9 minutes, 0.6 of a minute = 0.6 × 60 = 36

Percentage increase

165 50%, *Explanation:* Increase = 10, 10 ÷ 20 = 0.5 × 100 = 50; **166** 20%, *Explanation:* 4 ÷ 20 = 0.2 × 100 = 20; **167** 40%, *Explanation:* 16 ÷ 40 = 0.4 × 100 = 40; **168** 12.5%, *Explanation:* 1 ÷ 8 = 0.125 × 100 = 12.5; **169** 60%, *Explanation:* 3 ÷ 5 = 0.6 × 100 = 60; **170** 25%, *Explanation:* 4 ÷ 16 = 0.25 × 100 = 25

Quantities and conversions

171 *Answer* 6.4 km, *Explanation:* 1.6 × 4 = 6.4; **172** *Answer* 8.75, *Explanation:* 5 × 1.75 = 8.75; **173** *Answer* $28AU, *Explanation:* 1US = 4AU, so 7US = 7 × 4 = 28; **174** *Answer* 105 oz, *Explanation:* 35 × 3 = 105; **175** *Answer* 175 fluid ounces, *Explanation:* 5 × 35 = 175; **176** *Answer* 25AU, *Explanation:* 1US = 2.5AU, so 10US = 10 × 2.5 = 25AU; **177** *Answer* 3,750 m, *Explanation:* 3.75 × 1,000 = 3,750; **178** *Answer* 6, *Explanation:* 6 drums if full would hold 6 × 120 = 720 litres, so you would need 6 to hold 700; **179** *Answer* 13 lengths, *Explanation:* 1/20 of a kilometre = 1,000m ÷ 20 = 50 metres and 50 ÷ 4 (the length of each timber) = 12.5 lengths. You would therefore need 13 lengths in total; **180** *Answer* 127, *Explanation:* 25.4 × 5 = 127; **181** *Answer* the 13th, *Explanation:* counting back from Saturday there are two days to Thursday and 15 minus 2 = the 13th; **182** *Answer* 17.6 pounds, *Explanation:* 8 × 2.2 = 17.6; **183** *Answer* $30AU, *Explanation:* 1US = 2AU, so 15US = 30AU; **184** *Answer* 1,202.3, *Explanation:* 1093 × 1.1 = 1093 + 109.3 = 1202.3; **185** *Answer* 7020 m, *Explanation:* 7.02 × 1,000 = 7020; **186** *Answer* 2.1 pints, *Explanation:* 1.75 × 1.2 = 2.1; **187** *Answer* 2,186 yards, *Explanation:* add 1093 to 1093 to arrive at 2,186; **188** *Answer* 20 km/minute, *Explanation:* 0.3km/s = 0.3 × 60 18 km/minute; **189** *Answer* 101.6, *Explanation:* 25.4 × 4 = 101.6; **190** *Answer* 15 km, *Explanation:* 180 ÷ 60 (the number of minutes in an hour) = 3km per minute × 5 = 15km in 3 minutes; **191** *Answer* $10.5AU, *Explanation:* 1.75 × 6 = 10.5; **192** *Answer* 11.2 km, *Explanation:* 1.6 × 7 = 11.2

Conversions

193 *Answer* $5EC, *Explanation:* 1EC = (16 ÷ 4) = 4T, so 20T = (20 ÷ 4) = 5EC; **194** *Answer* $4EC, *Explanation:* 1EC = (13.5 ÷ 6) = 2.25T, so 9T = (9 ÷ 2.25) 4T; **195** *Answer* $8HC, *Explanation:* 20 ÷ 2.5 = 8; **196** *Answer* $5HC, *Explanation:* 9 ÷ 1.8 = 5; **197** *Answer* $4HC, *Explanation:* 18 ÷ 4.5 = 4; **198** *Answer* $5HC, *Explanation:* 8 ÷ 1.6 = 5; **199** *Answer* $50HC, *Explanation:* 55 ÷ 1.1 = 50; **200** *Answer* $5EC, *Explanation:* 1EC = 2T, so 10T = (10 ÷ 2) = 5; **201** *Answer* $0.25EC, *Explanation:* 1.5 ÷ 6 = 0.25EC; **202** *Answer* $15EC, *Explanation:* 48 ÷ 3.2 = 15; **203** *Answer* $6.5EC, *Explanation:* 1EC = 4T, so 26T = (26 ÷ 4) = 6.5; **204** *Answer* $8EC, *Explanation:* 1 EC = 3T, so 24T = (24 ÷ 3) = 8; **205** *Answer* $5EC, *Explanation:* 3 ÷ 3.6 = 1.2 so 1EC = 1.2T and 6T = (6 ÷ 1.2) = 5EC; **206** *Answer* $6EC, *Explanation:* 1EC = 2.25T, so 15T = (15

÷ 2.5) = 6EC; **207** *Answer* $12EC, *Explanation:* 1T = 9.5EC, so 114T = (114 ÷ 9.5) = 12EC; **208** *Answer* $4EC, *Explanation:* notice that 7 is twice 3.5 so double 2EC to get the answer, otherwise 1EC = 1.75T, so 7T = (7 ÷ 1.75) = 4EC; **209** *Answer* $11EC, *Explanation:* 1EC = 2T, so 22T = (22 ÷ 2) = 11; **210** *Answer* $6EC, *Explanation:* 1EC = 3T, so 18T = (18 ÷ 3) = 6EC

Sequencing

211 12, *Explanation:* 5 is added each step in the sequence; **212** 34, *Explanation:* 8 is taken away each step in the sequence; **213** 1, *Explanation:* The previous sum is multiplied by 6 each step; **214** 35, *Explanation:* Add 5 each step; **215** 27, *Explanation:* Divide the previous sum by 3; **216** 37.5, *Explanation:* Multiply the previous sum by 2 each step; **217** 11, *Explanation:* The sequence decreases by 4 each step; **218** 27, *Explanation:* The previous sum is multiplied by 3 each step; **219** 522, *Explanation:* Add 87 each step; **220** 67.5, *Explanation:* Divide the previous sum by 3 each step; **221** 25, *Explanation:* Add the previous two values to find the next, ie 9 + 16 = 25; **222** 159, *Explanation:* Add 17 each step; **223** 251, *Explanation:* Minus 26 each step; **224** 100, *Explanation:* Divide the previous sum by 2.5 each step; **225** 70, *Explanation:* Add 14 each step; **226** 0.5, *Explanation:* The previous two values are added together each step, so to find the first value minus 2 from 2.5 = 0.5; **227** 1,504, *Explanation:* Add 101 each step; **228** 1, *Explanation:* Divide the previous sum by 10 each step; **229** −13, *Explanation:* Take away 71 each step; **230** 60, *Explanation:* Add together the previous two values, 21 + 39 = 60; **231** 4, *Explanation:* Multiply each sum by 0.4; **232** −56, *Explanation:* Minus 22 each step; **233** 12.5, *Explanation:* Multiply the previous sum by 5 each step; **234** 31, *Explanation:* Add the previous two values to find the next, 8 + 23 = 31; **235** 71, *Explanation:* It's a bit of a trick – 34 is added at each step from the starting number 107, but the sequence of numbers is then presented in a misleading way. It should look like 107, 141, 175, 209 but it has been presented as 10, 71, 41, 17, 52, 09; **236** 18, *Explanation:* Multiply the two previous values 3 × 6 = 18; **237** 60, *Explanation:* Each step the previous sum is multiplied by 1.5; **238** 999, *Explanation:* 333 is added each step in the series; **239** 173, *Explanation:* Add together the previous two values 81 + 92 = 173; **240** 62, *Explanation:* Minus 12 each step starting with 198, but the sequence has been presented as 19, 81, 86, 17, 41, 62 instead of 198, 186 etc; **241** 3, *Explanation:* Multiply the previous two values to get the next, 3 × 1 = 3; **242** 0.48, *Explanation:* Multiply by 0.2 each step; **243** 17, *Explanation:* Start with 91 and add 29 each step and misrepresent the series 91, 120, 149, 178, 207 as 91, 12, 01, 49, 17, 8,207; **244** 25, *Explanation:* The sequence is that of the first 6 whole square numbers (numbers multiplied by themselves), 5 × 5 = 25; **245** 13, *Explanation:* The sequence is the first 8 prime numbers (a number with only 1 and itself as factors); **246** 80, *Explanation:* Starting from 800 minus 20 each step and misrepresent the sequence 800, 780, 760, 740 as 80, 07, 80, 76, 07,

40; **247** 15:20, *Explanation:* The sequence comprises equivalent ratios starting with the lowest expression; **248** 4, *Explanation:* Multiply the two previous terms each step to get the second value, divide 8 by 2 = 4; **249** 108, *Explanation:* Multiply the previous sum by 6 each step, 6 × 18 = 108; **250** 53, *Explanation:* The sequence is the first six whole square numbers, 1, 4, 9, 16, 25, 36, presented in a misleading way; **251** 51, *Explanation:* Start with 155 and add 15 each step; the sequence is then presented in a misleading way; **252** 99, *Explanation:* Add the previous two sums, 41 + 58 = 99; **253** 192, *Explanation:* Multiply the two previous terms, 8 × 24 = 192; **254** 49, *Explanation:* Divide the previous sum by 7 each step; **255** 49, *Explanation:* The sequence is that of the square numbers starting with 6 × 6 = 36, 7 × 7 = 49; **256** 1, *Explanation:* The sequence is the whole number factors of 12; **257** 117, *Explanation:* 13 is added to the previous sum each step; **258** 3, *Explanation:* Each number is followed by its square root; **259** 32, *Explanation:* 2 is raised to the power of 22–27; missing is 2 to the power of 5 = 2×2×2×2×2 = 32; **260** 49, *Explanation:* Add the previous two values to get the next, 11 + 38 = 49; **261** 4:8, *Explanation:* The sequence starts with a ratio in its lowest form and is followed by the next equivalent; **262** 3, *Explanation:* The sequence is a list of the whole number factors of 15; missing is 3 × 5 = 15; **263** 1,000, *Explanation:* The sequence is that of the cubed numbers in the range 63–103; missing is 10×10×10 = 1,000; **264** 12, *Explanation:* Multiply the previous step by 4, 3 × 4 = 12; **265** 112, *Explanation:* Add 14 each step in the sequence; **266** 283, *Explanation:* Starting with 22, it is the sequence of even numbers presented in a misleading way; **267** 81, *Explanation:* The sequence is 3 raised to the powers 32–36; missing is 34 = 3×3×3×3 = 81; **268** 0.1, *Explanation:* The previous sum is multiplied by 0.2 each step; **269** 29, *Explanation:* Add the previous two values to find the next; **270** 100, *Explanation:* The sequence is the range of numbers 122–82; missing is 102 = 10×10 = 100; **271** 7, *Explanation:* This is the list of whole number factors of 14; missing is 7 × 2 = 14; **272** 256, *Explanation:* Multiply the previous two sums to get the next, 8 × 32 = 256; **273** 256, *Explanation:* The sequence is the value of 42–45; missing is 44 = 4×4×4×4 = 256; **274** 108, *Explanation:* Divide the previous sum by 3 each step; **275** 123, *Explanation:* Starting with 19, it is the sequence of odd numbers presented in a misleading way; **276** 0.25, *Explanation:* Multiply by 12 each step to find the first value; divide 3 by 12 = 0.25; **277** 025, *Explanation:* You should be able to recognize these by now; starting with 5 it is the sequence of multiples of 5 presented in a misleading way; **278** 4, *Explanation:* It is the sequence of whole number factors of 16; missing is 4×4 = 16; **279** 80, *Explanation:* The previous sum is divided by 4 each step; **280** 125, *Explanation:* The sequence is that of the values 52–55; missing is 53, 5×5×5 = 125; **281** 64, *Explanation:* 8 is added each step; **282** 0.2, *Explanation:* It is the sequence of first 5 whole number reciprocals of 1 (that do not produce a recurring number), ie 1 ÷ 2 = 0.5, 1 ÷ 4 = 0.25, 1 ÷ 5 = 0.2, 1 ÷ 8 = 0.125, 1 ÷ 10 = 0.1; **283** 3,

Explanation: It is a list of the whole number factors of 18; 3 is missing, 3 × 6 = 18; **284** 121, *Explanation:* This is a sequence of the multiples of 3 beginning with 3 and presented in a misleading way; **285** 11, *Explanation:* It is the sequence of prime numbers in descending order in the range 19–7

Number problems

286 D, *Explanation:* 55 × 5 = 275, 110 × 2 = 220, 275 + 220 = £4.95; **287** B, *Explanation:* 1.20 × 6 = 7.20; **288** C, *Explanation:* 30 × 60 = 1,800; **289** B, *Explanation:* 40 × 6 = 240, 240 × 12 = 2,880 (you might do this second sum like this: 24 × 12 = 2 (12 × 12) = 2 × 144 = 288 but then put the 0 back = 2,880); **290** A, *Explanation:* 12 × 18 = 216 (a quick way to calculate this is 10 × 18 = 180, 2 × 18 = 36, 180 + 36 = 216). 216 – 200 = 16; **291** C, *Explanation:* 200 × 15 = 3,000 (2 × 15 = 30, add the 00 = 3,000); **292** A, *Explanation:* 15 × 75 = 1,125 pence or 11.25 (a quick way to do this is to work out 10 × 75 = 750, 5 × 75 = 375, add then together = 1,125); **293** B, *Explanation:* 9 = 27 so each box weighs 300 gm (2,700 gm ÷ 9), 300 × 4 = 1,200 gm = 1.2 kg; **294** D, *Explanation:* Work out the rate for one minute, 2,000 divided by 8, and multiply by 9 = 2,250; **295** A, *Explanation:* Work out the cost per 100 gm, 750 ÷ 3 = 250 per 100 gm, 2,600 ÷ 10 = 260 per 100 gm; **296** C, *Explanation:* Remember to convert the shoes to pairs of shoes, 192 shoes = 96 pairs, 96 ÷ 8 = 12 (you should know that 12 × 8 = 96); **297** C, *Explanation:* 40 × 15 = 600 (4 × 15 = 60 then add the 0); **298** A, *Explanation:* Work out the cost of 5 pencils, 180 ÷ 10 = 18 for 5, 14 × 5 = 70 so 18 × 14 = cost of 70 pencils = 252; **299** D, *Explanation:* 132 ÷ 6 = 22 (work this out quickly by breaking the 132 down, ie 10 × 6 = 60, 20 × 6 = 120, add 12 = 132, so 22 × 6 = 132); 22 × 4 = 88; **300** C, *Explanation:* 6,000 ÷ 30 = 200 (6 ÷ 2 = 3, 1,000 ÷ 10 = 100), 200 × 5 = 1,000; **301** D, *Explanation:* Rental = £9 per quarter = £3 per month, so £11 is spent on calls (14 – 3) each month, 11 × 12 = 132; **302** B, *Explanation:* 0.70 × 250 = monthly cost of the cover = 175.00 × 12 to get the annual cost = £2,100; **303** D, *Explanation:* 5.20 × 35 = 182, 5.2 × 1.5 = 7.8 (hourly overtime rate), 7.8 × 5 = 39, 182 + 39 = 221; **304** A, *Explanation:* 18 × 16 = 288 + 29 = 317; **305** B, *Explanation:* 60 ÷ 5 = 12, 1.20 × 12 = 14.40 (cost of gas over 60-day period) + standing charge 0.9 × 60 = 5.40, 14.40 + 5.40 = 19.80; **306** B, *Explanation:* You need to express one number as a percentage of another, so treat the first number as a fraction of the second and multiply the result by 100. 30/500 = 3/50, 100 ÷ 50 = 2 × 3 = 6; **307** D, *Explanation:* 52/80 = 13/20, 100 ÷ 20 = 5 × 13 = 65; **308** C, *Explanation:* 18/60 = 3/10, 100 ÷ 10 = 10 × 3 = 30; **309** D, *Explanation:* 432/720 = 3/5, 100 ÷ 5 = 20, 20 × 3 = 60; **310** C, *Explanation:* 9.68/88 = 968/8800 = 11/100 (hcf 88), 100 ÷ 100 = 1 × 11 = 11; **311** D, *Explanation:* Don't be put off; if you are not allowed to use a calculator then the maths will be straightforward! 487.50/640 = 48,750/65,000 = 4,875/6,500 = ¾ (hcf 1,625), 100 ÷ 4 = 25 × 3 = 75; **312** A, *Explanation:* 120/4,000 = 12/400 = 3/100 (hcf 4) 3/100 = 3%; **313** C, *Explanation:* 63/420 = 3/20 (hcf 21), 100 ÷ 20 = 5 × 3 = 15; **314** D, *Explanation:* 126/6,300 = 2/100 (you should be able to see this straight away as 1% = 63 so 2% = 126), 2/100 =2%; **315** B, *Explanation:* 750 = 100, 1% = 750/100 = 7.5 × 4 = 30; **316** C, *Explanation:* 3 hours = 180 minutes, 100% = 180, 1% = 180/100 = 1.8, 1.8 × 15 = 27; **317** D, *Explanation:* You should be able to see this straight away, 600 = 100%, 1% = 600/100 = 6 × 12.5 = 75; **318** A, *Explanation:* Another easy one, 400 = 100%, 1% = 400/100 = 4, 4 × 9 = 36; **319** C, *Explanation:* 2,400 = 100% 1% = 2,400/100 = 24 × 2.5 = 60, 2,400 + 60 = 2,460; **320** B, *Explanation:* 14 = 100%, 1% = 14/100 = 0.14, 0.14 × 40 = 5.6, 14 + 5.6 = 19.6; **321** C, *Explanation:* 620 = 100%, 1% = 620/100 = 6.2 × 3 = 18.6; **322** C, *Explanation:* 3,550 = 100%, 1% = 3,550/100 = 35.5 × 20 = 710, 3,550 – 710 = 2,840; **323** A, *Explanation:* 4 hours 30 minutes = 270 minutes = 100%, 1% = 270/100 = 2.7, 2.7 × 5 = 13.5 minutes, 270 – 13 minutes 30 seconds = 4 hours 16 minutes and 30 seconds; **324** C, *Explanation:* 103% = 3,605, 1% = 3,605/103 = 35/1 × 100 = 3,500; **325** A, *Explanation:* 100% = 7,000, 1% = 7,000/100 = 70 × 8 = 560, 7,000 + 560 = 7,560; **326** B, *Explanation:* 4,300 =100%, 1% = 4,300/100 = 43 × 4 = 172, 4,300 – 172 = 4,128; **327** B, *Explanation:* Blue party obtained 30,000 + 8%, 1% = 30,000/100 = 300, 300 × 8 = 2,400, 30,000 + 2,400 = 32,400 votes; **328** D, *Explanation:* Red party received 22,000 – 18%, 100% = 22,000, 1% = 22,000/100 = 220, 220 × 18 = 3,960, 22,000 – 3960 = 18,040 votes; **329** B, *Explanation:* 92% = 552, 1% = 552/92 = 6, 8 × 6 = 48, 552 + 48 = 600; **330** A, *Explanation:* The length of metal was 2% longer before it was cooled. 2% of 1 m = 2 cm, so 2% of 3 m = 6 cm, so the original length was 306 cm; **331** A, *Explanation:* 300 m = 125%, 1% = 300/125 = 12/5 = 22/5 or 2.4, 2.4 × 100 = 240; **332** B, *Explanation:* 108% = 6.75, 1% = 675/10,800 = 1/16 (hcf 675) = 0.0625 × 100 = 6.25; **333** C, *Explanation:* yr 1 6,000 × 88/100 = 60 × 88 = 5,380, yr 2 5,280 × 88/100 = 52.8 × 88 = 4,646.40; **334** D, *Explanation:* yr 1 18,000 × 105% = 18,000 + 5 × 180 = 18,900, yr 2 18,900 × 105% = 18,900 + 5 × 189 = 19,845; **335** C, *Explanation:* It is an easy one so long as you sort out the task: 8 seconds as an improvement on the original time, original time = 8 + 12 = 20, so we must find 8 as a percentage of 20, 20 =100, 1 = 5%, 8 = 40%; **336** A, *Explanation:* 100% = 800 so we need to establish what 300 increase represents. 100 ÷ 800 = 0.125 × 300 = 37.5; **337** D, *Explanation:* It is an easy question and you will find some in real tests and not just at the start, so keep going if you hit a more difficult patch in a real test as they are often followed by easier questions. 2,000 loss / 8,000 × 100 = ¼ × 100 = 25; **338** C, *Explanation:* Profit = 8% of 25, 100% = 25, 1% = 25/100, 8% = 25/100 × 8 = ¼ × 8 = 2, selling price = 27; **339** B, *Explanation:* Loss = 4% of 120,000, 1% = 120,000/100 = 1,200, 4% = 1,200 × 4 = 4,800, purchase price = 120,000 +

4,800 = 124,800; **340** A, *Explanation:* Profit on 12 eggs = 15 × 12 – 150 = 30, % profit = 30/150 × 100 = 1/5 × 100 = 0.2 × 100 = 20; **341** C, *Explanation:* It's easy once you sort out your grams and kilos. 1 kg = 10 × 100 gm, profit = 60 × 10 – 300 = 300, % profit = 300/300 × 100 = 100; **342** D, *Explanation:* Purchase price = 20 × 2.5 = 50, so loss of 50 – 42 made, % loss = 8/50 × 100 = 0.16 × 100 = 16; **343** D, *Explanation:* Loss = 500,000 – 515,000 = 15,000, % loss = 15,000/500,000 × 100 = 15/500 × 100 = 1,500/500 = 3; **344** D, *Explanation:* Profit = 120 – 10 = 110, % profit = 110/10 × 100 = 11 × 100 = 1,100%, but this is a net profit and all the other costs of the establishment must also be recovered.

Chapter 6 Non-verbal reasoning, mechanical comprehension and data interpretation

Features in common

1 A, *Explanation:* The example shapes and A all contain one dot; **2** B, *Explanation:* All three examples are quadrilaterals (4-sided shapes) and B is a trapezium and also a quadrilateral; **3** A, *Explanation:* The question shapes all have an even number of faces (in the case of a three-dimensional shape a face is a flat surface), the cylinder has 2, the box 6, the pyramid 4; only A, the star, also has an even number (10); **4** C, *Explanation:* All the question shapes are constructed from equilateral triangles (triangles with 3 sides equal in length); only shape C shares this quality; **5** A, *Explanation:* These shapes are called nets and some, if folded, would form a solid object. All the question shapes, if cut out and folded, could form a cube; only suggested answer A would also do this; **6** C, *Explanation:* All the question shapes have dots which total a multiple of 3: 9, 3, 6. C has 12 dots and so is the only suggested answer that also has a total number that is a multiple of 3; **7** B, *Explanation:* All 3 question shapes have an odd total number of dots, 3, 5 and 5. Only B also has an odd number of dots, 3; **8** A, *Explanation:* The question shapes are all divided by a line from top left to right; only A shares this quality; **9** A, *Explanation:* Both question shapes contain 3 triangles; only A shares this quality; **10** C, *Explanation:* In the question shapes the outer arrows point in an anticlockwise direction while the inner arrows point clockwise. Only shape C shares this quality; **11** B, *Explanation:* Both question shapes have in common the fact that if you subtract the top number of dots from the bottom number the remainder is 3. Only shape B also has this quality; **12** C, *Explanation:* Both question shapes are divided into five triangles, as is shape C; **13** B, *Explanation:* The first question shape numbers 16 squares of which 4 (¼) are shaded and the second numbers 12 squares of which 3 are shaded and also ¼ are shaded. Suggested answer B also has ¼ of its squares shaded; **14** B, *Explanation:* The question shapes have only a single shaded circle in common and only shape B also contains one shaded circle; **15** C, *Explanation:* The question shapes are both made up of 11 shapes, as is suggested answer C; **16** B, *Explanation:* Both question shapes have shaded circles at the start and end of the line, as does suggested answer B; **17** B, *Explanation:* The two question shapes have two horizontal and three or more vertical surfaces. B is the only suggested answer that has more vertical than horizontal surfaces; **18** A, *Explanation:* The sum of the dots in each of the two question shapes is a prime number, as is 7, the number of dots on suggested answer A; **19** C, *Explanation:* Both question shapes have internal angles that add up to 180°; the two angles of C also add up to 180°; **20** B, *Explanation:* Both question shapes include two triangles, as does suggested answer B; **21** A, *Explanation:* The two question shapes both comprise 24 sides, as does the shapes making up suggested answer A; **22** A, *Explanation:* Both question shapes have rotational symmetry (they look the same when rotated); only A also has this quality; **23** B, *Explanation:* Both question shapes have a consistent cross-section (this is used to calculate their volumes); the cross-sections of A and C are not consistent but B's is; **24** A, *Explanation:* The number of dots in both question shapes total 6, as does suggested answer A; **25** C, *Explanation:* The question shapes are related in that the second is an enlargement of the first by the scale factor of 2. Suggested answer C is related to the question shapes because if enlarged by a scale factor of 2 it would be identical to the smaller of the question triangles; **26** A, *Explanation:* Both question shapes have one line of symmetry (where a line can be drawn through the shape and both sides are identical). A also shares this quality whereas N has no lines of symmetry and H has two; **27** C, *Explanation:* In both question shapes half the total shapes are shaded, as is the case in C; **28** A, *Explanation:* The values represented in the bar charts equal 16, as does the total described in pie chart A; **29** B, *Explanation:* Divide the top value of dots by the number below and we get 2 in both question shapes; this is also the case with shape B; **30** A, *Explanation:* Neither question shape has any lines of symmetry, nor does J. H has two and O an infinite number.

Find the shape that completes the series

31 A, *Explanation:* The bar across the circle is rotating in an anticlockwise direction; **32** C, *Explanation:* The smaller circle is sinking downwards while the line across the circle is rising; **33** A, *Explanation:* The direction of the arrow head is alternating; the number of dots is increasing by 2 each step; **34** A, *Explanation:* Each pattern comprises two right-angled triangles and three equilateral triangles forming a random pattern. In each case two of the triangles are shaded. The triangles that are shaded could be two right angled, two equilateral or one of each. In the question shapes we have two shaded equilateral triangles and one of each, so this leaves two shaded right-angled triangles as the next step in the series; **35** C, *Explanation:* The shaded segment is rotating anticlockwise around the circle, in turn covering up the shapes in the other segments; **36** A, *Explanation:* Both the shaded box and the two shapes are rotating around the shape in a clockwise direction; **37** B, *Explanation:* In the series the triangle becomes a square and then turns back to a triangle again; the arrow direction reverses each step; **38** A, *Explanation:* The number of triangles increases by 2 each step and the shading of the circles starts on the left and migrates across the shape, one circle each step in the series; **39** C, *Explanation:* The number of circles is increasing by one each step and half the total area of the circles is shaded; **40** A, *Explanation:* The shapes drop down the square each step, returning to the top of the square each fourth step. They also decrease by one each step, counting down 3, 2, 1, before becoming 3 again, the triangles are all shaded and the whole of the left-hand column is shaded alternative steps; **41** C, *Explanation:* The total number of sides of the shapes increases by 3 each step in the series, starting with 9 sides; **42** A, *Explanation:* At each step shapes transform; first squares become triangles then arrows become diamonds and finally circles become crosses; **43** C, *Explanation:* The number of circles is decreasing, 3, 2, 1 and back to 3 again, and they are moving down the square; the three wavy lines are moving up the square; **44** B, *Explanation:* The L shape rotates around the box in a clockwise direction; at each step a circle becomes a triangle and the shading alternates between the circles and triangles; **45** B, *Explanation:* The number of shaded squares increases by five each step, starting with five shaded squares; **46** C, *Explanation:* A new feature is added to the shape each step and the triangles become squares and then circles before becoming triangles once more; **47** C, *Explanation:* The number of shaded circles and crosses is decreasing by one each step while the direction of the line of circles and the position of the crosses are alternating; **48** B, *Explanation:* Shapes are transformed alternately from circles and squares into semicircles and triangles. The circles and squares are arranged to the left while the semicircles and triangles are arranged to the right; **49** B, *Explanation:* The number of triangles that form a random pattern alternate from 7, 14, 7, 14; **50** A, *Explanation:* The total number of sides of the shapes is increasing by 2 each step; the number of sides starts with 4; **51** C, *Explanation:* The number of arrows follows the sequence of square numbers, starting 4, 9, 16, 25 (2×2, 3×3, 4×4, 5×5); **52** A, *Explanation:* The squares decrease in number starting with 4 and alternate from the top to the bottom of the box; the circles increase from one each step and also alternate position; **53** B, *Explanation:* The sequence of segments in the circle follows the BOMAS rule, $6 \div 2 = 3 \times 2 = 6 + 2 = 8$. BOMAS is the order in which operations are undertaken: brackets, of division, multiplication, addition, subtraction; **54** A,

Explanation: The L shape rotates around the box in an anticlockwise direction; the shapes alternate between squares and triangles arranged left and then right; the wavy lines do not change; **55** B, *Explanation:* The second shape is the mirror image or reflection of the first, so the third image in the series must be the mirror image of the fourth which is B; **56** A, *Explanation:* The shading and unshading of the boxes is alternating and the number of shaded or unshaded boxes is increasing by 3 each step, starting with 9. So the series runs 9 shaded, 12 unshaded, 15 shaded, 18 unshaded; **57** C, *Explanation:* The number of sides of the shapes increases by one each step from 9, 10, 11, 12; **58** B, *Explanation:* The number of squares follows the sequence of prime numbers beginning 2, 3, 5, 7; **59** B, *Explanation:* At each step a square is transformed into two triangles and moves down the box; also, there is one less wavy line each step; **60** C, *Explanation:* The inner circle is rotating anticlockwise exposing two shapes each move, the outer circle is rotating clockwise; the shapes are following the sequence square, diamond, circle, triangle and back to square etc again; **61** B, *Explanation:* The numbers on the top line of the shapes count down from 6, 5, 4, 3, the numbers on the bottom of the shapes count from 0, 1, 2, 3; **62** B, *Explanation:* The hands of the clock are indicating the sequence 2, 3, 4, 6 (which are the factors of 12, excluding 1 and 12); **63** B, *Explanation:* At each step the figure is rotating and is the reflection of the previous figure; **64** A, *Explanation:* The number of squares is decreasing by one each step and rotating around the boxes in an anticlockwise direction; **65** B, *Explanation:* The shapes alternate between diamonds and squares and they are rotating clockwise; **66** C, *Explanation:* The shapes start in position C then make a 360° rotation then a 180° rotation then a 90° rotation; **67** B, *Explanation:* Each step in the series the shape is rotated a ¼ turn and then its reflection is represented; **68** A, *Explanation:* The sequence of shapes runs cross, triangle, circle and square and these shapes are uncovered as the semicircle rotates clockwise; **69** C, *Explanation:* The series of shaded squares are the sum of the multiples of 6, 5, 4, 3 up to 30, ie in the first step of the series the 6th, 12th, 18th and 24th squares are shaded, in the next step the 5th, 10th, 15th, 20th, 25th and 30th squares are shaded; **70** C, *Explanation:* The shape is rotated 90° each step and represented as the reflection of the previous figure; **71** B, *Explanation:* The shape is alternating between a hexagon and a square and the number of triangles represents the multiple of 7, 0, 7, 14, 21; **72** B, *Explanation:* The series runs along the top then the bottom of each shape and through the sequence 0–6 starting with 3, so the series runs 3, 4, 5 ,6, 0, 1, 2, 3; **73** A, *Explanation:* The two lines are progressing across the box from left to right; the smaller circle is descending while the line enclosed within the larger circle is ascending; **74** B, *Explanation:* The shaded squares represent the multiples of 7, 8, 9 and 10 up to 30. In suggested answer B the 7th, 14th, 21st and 28th boxes are shaded, the 8th, 16th and 24th in the second step in the sequence and the 9th, 18th and 27th in the next step; **75** A,

Explanation: In the series the circles have a value of +1, the diamonds –1 and the squares are the product of the sum at that point, so the series runs 4 –2 = 2 + 2 – 3 = 1 + 3 – 2 = the answer, 2 squares; **76** B, *Explanation:* The three shaded squares are moving in a clockwise direction around four adjacent squares; **77** C, *Explanation:* The number of lines and circles is represented; each is represented 1, 2 or 3 times, also either a square, diamond or triangle is represented; **78** B, *Explanation:* Triangles each have a value of +1, shaded squares = –1 and circles give the sum of the calculation at that point. So the series runs 4 – 2 = 2 + 3 – 1 = 4 + or – 0 – 2 gives the answer 2, or two circles; **79** B, *Explanation:* The shaded squares are moving up the grid diagonally from left to right; **80** C, *Explanation:* There are either one, two or three lines on the base of the figure and at the end of the 'arms' either a triangle, square or circle; the arms alternate in direction. The figure with three lines at its base and circles at the ends of the upward-facing arms correctly completes the series.

Completing the series in columns and rows

81 C, *Explanation:* Each row is made up of the three shapes; the square is missing in the third row; **82** B, *Explanation:* Each column and row comprises the three shapes (only the circles are shaded); **83** C, *Explanation:* Each column and row comprises the three shapes and alternate shapes are shaded; **84** A, *Explanation:* The first two shapes are combined to make the third in each column; **85** B, *Explanation:* A circle with no shading and two types of shading is represented in each row and column; **86** A, *Explanation:* The third shape in each column is the sum of the first shape minus the second. Column 1 has 4 squares – 1 square = 3 squares, column 3 has 1 square – 1 square = no squares; **87** C, *Explanation:* Each row comprises three identical shapes, one with a spot, one with a diagonal line; **88** C, *Explanation:* The middle number of lines in each column is divided by the first number of lines to give the third. So 111 ÷ 1 = 111 (3 ÷ 1 = 3), 6 ÷ 3 = 2; **89** C, *Explanation:* The lines attached to the first two shapes in each row are both present in the third shape; **90** A, *Explanation:* Each shape is represented in each column three ways: shaded, large and small; the line across the shapes does not change size; **91** C, *Explanation:* In each row the details within the first two shapes are combined to create the third shape; **92** B, *Explanation:* In each row the number of lines decreases by one; **93** B, *Explanation:* In the columns the shapes combine, except where the feature is repeated in which case it is deleted; **94** A, *Explanation:* The sequence relies on the following values across the rows, taking the first shape in the first column and the first shape in the second column, then the second shape in the first column and the second shape in the second column; a circle + a square = a square, a square + a circle = a square, a circle + a circle = a square, a square + a square = a circle. The answer obtained is square + circle = square, circle + circle =

square, giving answer A, square and square; **95** C, *Explanation:* Across the rows each shape rotates to have the other shapes connected to it. Starting on the left the shape at '9 o clock' has the other two shapes connected to it, it then appears at '12 o clock' and then at the '6 o clock' position; **96** B, *Explanation:* In the columns the shapes combine to form new shapes, except where features of the shapes are repeated in which case that feature is deleted; **97** C, *Explanation:* To work out the sequence you need to establish from the two complete rows that a triangle + a square = a triangle, a square + a triangle = a triangle, a square + a square = a square and a triangle + a triangle = a square; **98** A, *Explanation:* Going down each column the L shape is rotating in the first column anticlockwise, the second clockwise and the third clockwise; **99** A, *Explanation:* Going down the columns the shapes combine to form the third shape, except where the feature is repeated in which case it is deleted; **100** A, *Explanation:* Going across the rows, to answer the question you must establish from the two complete rows that $0 + x = x$, $x + 0 = x$, $x + x = 0$, $0 + 0 = 0$.

Mechanical comprehension

101 B, *Explanation:* The most accurate assessment is most likely to be obtained with the eye directly above both the scale of the measure and the mark on the item being measured; **102** A and B, *Explanation:* The radio produces heat (thermal energy), as a by-product, and sound waves (kinetic energy); it uses electrical energy but does not produce it; **103** B, C and D, *Explanation:* The chemicals in the firework will be transferred into heat, light and sound which are thermal, electromagnetic and kinetic energies; **104** Ice, *Explanation:* The stronger forces give the ice a definite shape; **105** A, *Explanation:* The attractive forces between the molecules forces a liquid into a spherical shape, which has the smallest area for a given volume; **106** B, *Explanation:* The adhesive force between the water and glass is greatest in the narrow tube and the water will rise highest; this is called capillary rise; **107 and 108** B and A, *Explanation:* The meniscus of mercury is convex while the meniscus of water curves downwards; **109** B, *Explanation:* The bar will expand as it is heated, so the pins will be pushed away from the blocks; **110** Winter, *Explanation:* In the summer the wires will expand and so slacken; if this was a summer scene, then, come the winter, the wires would break as they contracted with the cold; **111** A, *Explanation:* The thicker glass beaker is more likely to crack because the glass on the inside expands while the outside glass does not; **112** B, *Explanation:* When heated, brass expands more than iron, so the strip will bend with the brass on the outside as it will become longer than the iron; **113** A, *Explanation:* Water is unusual in that it is most dense at 4°C; most other liquids expand uniformly as they warm; **114** B, *Explanation:* Some water will rise up the tube as the air cools and contracts; this will cause the water level in the beaker to fall; **115 and 116** A and F,

Explanation: Once the switch is closed the circuit will be complete and the light will come on and the heating element will warm. As the bimetallic strip warms it will bend away from the contact point, breaking the circuit; **117** D, *Explanation:* The behaviour of a gas is described by Boyle's law which states that pressure × volume = constant figure; **118** The copper bar, *Explanation:* Glass is an insulator not a conductor of heat, metals are good conductors and copper is a better conductor than iron; **119** B, *Explanation:* Of the three liquids, mercury has the highest boiling point, alcohol the lowest; **120** B, *Explanation:* A flow of air would occur from the cool sea to the warm land, making the flag fly on the landside of the pole; **121** The shiny tin can, *Explanation:* The shiny can will reflect much of the radiated heat from the sun while the mat black one will absorb most of the heat; **122** B, *Explanation:* In the northern hemisphere the most effective direction for the solar panel would be south facing; **123** C, *Explanation:* The direction of North is given and from this you can work out the other directions; **124** C, *Explanation:* The latent heat of fusion of water is 340,000 joules per kilogram. This is the amount of heat needed to change 1 kg of ice into water without changing the temperature; **125** B, *Explanation:* Mineral salts lower the melting point of water, so the temperature of the salty water must be lower than 0°C; **126** C, *Explanation:* The pressure on the ice of the weighted thin wire will melt the ice immediately below the wire. The wire will move downwards but the water above the wire will refreeze. So the block will remain unchanged as the wire slowly passes through; **127** C and D, *Explanation:* Impurities such as salt will cause the boiling point of the water to rise, so the water will come off the boil, the temperature of the water will increase and it will come back to the boil; **128** B, *Explanation:* At sea level water boils at 100°C. When the pressure is lower, as it is at altitude, it will boil at a lower temperature; **129** B, *Explanation:* Weight is the force of gravity caused by the pull of the Earth. This effect is slightly greater at the poles, so the weight would be slightly heavier; **130** B, *Explanation:* The beams in both A and B can bend; however, in the triangle a bend in one of the lengths would cause tension or compression in another part of the same, making it much more ridged; **131** C the least, B the most, *Explanation:* Both ice and oil float on water, so they are less dense; **132** Bottom, *Explanation:* Pressure increases with depth; **133** C, *Explanation:* Pressure acts in all directions but the pressure at the bottom of an object is greater than at the top (this results in an upward force); **134** A petrol, B ice, *Explanation:* Ice is denser than petrol, so it will sink below the petrol; **135** A, 970 mbar, *Explanation:* The atmospheric pressure is usually lower when we experience a weather system that brings rain; **136** B, *Explanation:* Friction acts between two objects when they are in contact and resists movement; **137** D, *Explanation:* Friction can only act where contact exists; all the other forces listed can act at a distance; **138** Between 4 and 5, *Explanation:* The vehicle accelerates quickly between 1 and 2, more slowly between 2 and 3, slows dramatically between 3 and 4 and travels at a constant speed between 4 and 5; **139** All three, *Explanation:* All three are in equilibrium in that they are not moving; C is the least stable as it would take little to change its centre of gravity, A is in neutral equilibrium as its centre of gravity would not change if it was moved; **140** B, *Explanation:* The centre of gravity is the point at which a shape balances; it is the point where it seems as if the whole weight of the object acts; **141** C and F, *Explanation:* The potential chemical energy is transferred into kinetic energy (the moving bullet and sound), heat and light; **142** The force, *Explanation:* The large gear A makes one full turn, the smaller gears two full turns. It will therefore turn more slowly and with a greater force; **143** C, *Explanation:* C shows distance increasing against time, ie accelerating. B shows a constant speed and A is a stationary object; **144** Cannot tell, *Explanation:* Machine 2 brings greater mechanical advantage as the effort required to move a weight is around half that required by machine 1. However, we cannot know where the smaller effort is because we do not know the relative weights of the loads; **145** D, *Explanation:* The direction alternates between the cogs; the cog with 5 teeth is rotating at 60 revolutions per second, so the cog with 10 teeth is rotating at 30 revolutions a second; **146** C, *Explanation:* One side is concave, the other convex; **147** A and C, *Explanation:* Like poles repel, opposite poles attract; **148** 7, *Explanation:* They are red, orange, yellow, green, blue, indigo and violet; **149** A, *Explanation:* The incomplete diagram shows 4 A (amperes) going out, so 4 A must be supplied; **150** B, *Explanation:* The electrodes and current would cause electrolysis and break the water down to hydrogen and oxygen. The composition of water is H_2O, so for every oxygen molecule there are two hydrogen. There would be therefore twice as much hydrogen produced as oxygen. Experience shows that the hydrogen would be produced at the negative electrode (the cathode); **151** Circuit 1 and table 1, circuit 2 and table 2, *Explanation:* The light comes in circuit 1 only when A and B are both closed. In circuit 2 the light comes on when either switch A or B is closed; **152** At no point, *Explanation:* Gamma rays are highly energized and, while reduced by a thin sheet of lead, are not completely stopped; **153** B, *Explanation:* Betaparticles are fast-moving negative electrons that pass through cloth, paper etc but are stopped by dense substances such as aluminium; **154** A, *Explanation:* Alpha particles are positively charged and relatively large and slow. They are stopped by most materials, including paper; **155** C, *Explanation:* A hydroelectric energy source relies on water turning a turbine which is then converted into electric energy by a dynamo; **156** Both A and B, *Explanation:* The downward acceleration of the balls would be the same; the horizontal acceleration of ball B does not affect this, so they would hit the ground at the same moment; **157** Cannot tell, *Explanation:* If the tyres were inflated to the same pressure then you could tell that B carried the greatest load but without this information you cannot tell; **158** All equal, *Explanation:* The pressure is consistent throughout the fluid; **159** A, *Explanation:* The weight × distance in A is equal on both sides, all the others are unequal, so the seesaw would move.

Data interpretation

Data Set 1: The web-building company

160 B, *Explanation*: The graph provided data (revenue figures and forecasts) for 6 years: year 0 (actual) and years 1–5 (forecast); **161** C, *Explanation*: This figure can be read straight off the graph; **162** B, *Explanation*: To answer this question, 'picture' in your mind the figures as a curve and compare them to the 4 scenarios (otherwise calculate some of the revenues for particular years from the scenarios and see which best fit the figures). The figures are quite distinctive. The rate of increase noticeably slows and the largest increase is between Yr 1 and Yr 2 ($2.5m). These characteristics should lead you to select scenario B; **163** D, *Explanation*: The scenario with the least variation can be read from the graph. It is the curve that shows the least rise and fall, ranging from 105% in Yr 1 to 125% in Yr 5; **164** A, *Explanation*: Extend the line and estimate the point on it for Yr 6, otherwise calculate the increase between each year (it is consistently between 7 and 8%) and add this amount to the Yr 5 percentage; **165** D, *Explanation*: Calculate 140% of 26m = 26 × 1.4 = 36.4; **166** A, *Explanation*: Only suggested Answer A related directly to the scale of output. Lowering the unit price might result in greater sales but not greater output, extending the project range would in itself not result in greater production and better distribution may improve the efficiency of the organization but would not result in an increase in production;**167** C, *Explanation*: Find 105% of 26m and then find 110% of the new total. 26 × 1.05 = 27.3m × 110 = 30.03m rounded down to 30m; **168** B, *Explanation*: Scenario A will generate 26m x 140% in Yr 5 = 26 × 1.4 = 36.4m. The scenario with the next-highest forecast is B, which even if estimated generously amounts to 26m × 134% = 34.8m; **169** A, *Explanation*: The scenario that best fits the figures can be identified as the revenue for Yr 0 is provided. Find the answer by trial. Start for example by calculating the figures for Yr 5 and try the most convenient first. Scenario A = 26m × 140% = 36.4m so we can rule out scenario A. Scenario C = 26m × 130% = 33.8m. This should lead you to look further at C and the conclusion that Answer A best fits.

Data set 2: The mail order company

170 A, *Explanation*: Follow the flow diagram to the add $40 box; if you answered $65 then note that the question asks how much is added to the order, so the answer is $40 is added to the order value of $25 and not $65; **171** C, *Explanation*: $12 is added to an order valued over $75 with a US postal address that requires express delivery, $40 is added to an order with a value over $75 with a non-US postal address that does not require express delivery and the difference is $28; **172** D, *Explanation*: $80 is added to the non-US order, while the US order qualifies for free delivery, so no amount is added and the difference is $80 more; **173** B, C and D, *Explanation*: Follow the flow diagram along its various routes and you will see that an order under $75 for a US postal address without a promotional code is not given the option of express delivery; **174** C and D, *Explanation*: Free delivery is only an option for orders with a US postal address that do not require express delivery. Suggested Answers A and B are incorrect because orders under $75 with a promotional code may qualify and orders over $75 without a promotional code may also qualify.

Data set 3: Analysis of a population by economic activity and district

175 C, *Explanation*: You must find 30% of 17,500. Find this by multiplying 17,500 by 0.30 = 5250; **176** A, *Explanation*: You must find the sum of 58% of 17,500 and 39% of 10,000. 17,500 × 0.58 = 10,150, 10,000 × 0.39% = 3,900, 10,150 + 3,900 = 14,050; **177** B, *Explanation*: Find which is greater of 30% of 17,500 or 57% of 10,000. 17,500 × 0.30 = 5,250 and 10,000 × 0.57 = 5,700, so the unemployed population of district 2 is the greater; **178** D, *Explanation*: Find the sum of 12% of 17,500 and 4% of 10,000 = 2,100 + 400 = 2,500, add the total populations of both districts = 27,500, minus the combined number of economically inactive = 2,500 = 25,000. You must express the ratio 2,500:25,000 in its simplest form; do this by cancelling the zeros and dividing both sides by 25 = 1:10; **179** A, *Explanation*: It has already been calculated that 12% of 17,500 = 2,100 and 4% of 10,000 = 400. Now find 400 as a percentage of the total economically inactive populations of both districts, 2,500. Find this by dividing 100 by 2,500 = 0.04 and multiplying it by 400 = 16 or 16%.

Data set 4: What young people find most and least interesting

180 C, *Explanation*: Each young person responded to the four issues twice, once to indicate the issue that most interests them and again to indicate the issue that least interests them. Therefore the sum of responses presented in either graph identifies the number of respondents; **181** A, *Explanation*: Add the 41 responses to looking good to the 22 responses to what others think to get the sum, 63. Subtract from this the 30 who were most interested in doing well in school to get the answer 33; **182** B, *Explanation*: In question 1 it was established that 117 young people took part in the survey and 1/3 of this = 39, and the issue that received 39 responses was doing well in school (30 indicated it was the issue they were most interested in and 9 indicated it was the issue they were least interested in); **183** D, *Explanation*: 24 young people indicated that they were most interested in finding a job compared with 4 who were least interested. This gives a ratio of 24:4 which simplifies to 6:1 or 6 times as many; **184** B, *Explanation*: 63 young people indicated that they were most interested in looking good or what others thought of them and this compares to 54 who were most interested in doing well in school or finding a job. This gives the ratio of 63:54 which simplifies to 7:6 is you divide both sides by 9.

Data set 5: Global sales by world regions

185 A, *Explanation*: European sales are worth 20% of the global market, while the value of African sales is 5%, 20 / 5 = 4 so the European market is x 4 bigger; **186** C, *Explanation*: Find in its simplest form the ratio 56:7, divide both sides by 7 to get 8:1; **187** B, *Explanation*: The US share of the market is 56%; find the value of the whole market by dividing 224m by 56 = 1% of the global market = 4m and × 100 = 100% or $400m; **188** C, *Explanation*: In 2008 the global market was worth $260m and the value of the Argentinean share of the global market is 20% of 7%. First find the value of the 7% (the other share of the whole market), 260 × 7% = 18.2m × 20% (Argentina's share) = 3.64m; **189** D, *Explanation*: First find 20% of 260m (the value of the European market in 2008) = $52m, next find the value of the European market in 2009, $52m – $7m = $45m, now find 45m as a % of 500m (the forecast global value in 2009) 100% = 500, 1% = 5, 45 = 9%.

Data set 6: The recruitment agency

190 C, *Explanation*: Add 144 and 54 to get the combined total of sales and administrative applicants and find 50% of this total = 99; **191** A, *Explanation*: Express the ratio 36 : 54 in its simplest form by dividing both sides by 9 to identify the answer as 4:6; **192** B, *Explanation*: 36 professional applicants began the process of an online application and 27 (75% of 36) completed it, of these 33% passed and so 67% failed the interview, 67% of 27 = 18; **193** D, *Explanation*: 126 applicants began the online process and 63 (50% of 126) completed it, of these 44 (71.5% of 63) passed at the test centre and 27 (60% of 45) candidates passed the work sample stage; **194** C, *Explanation*: Find the total of all online applicants who started the application process = 360, divide 360 by 18 = 20 and divide this by half (see the first part of the question) = 10.

Data set 7: Population growth

195 A, *Explanation*: We are told that the board found 1/8 of the population of 305 million to be 65 or over. 305/8 = 38.125 or 38,125,000 people aged 65 or over; **196** C, *Explanation*: The board found that 80.8% of Americans lived in urban locations so 19.2% must live in non-urban (rural) locations. 305 million x 19.2% = 305 × 0.192 × 1 million = 58,560,000; **197** B, *Explanation*: The US population is projected to increase from 305 million to 439 million, an increase of 134 million. 305/100 = 3.05, 134/3.05 = 43.93, clearly more than the UN projected increase for the world's population of 37%; **198** D, *Explanation*: We are told that the trend of people moving to the most populous states will continue until a point is reached when 28% of the population are resident in those states but we are not told when this point will be reached so cannot calculate the number of Americans who will live in either Texas or California by 2050; **199** B, *Explanation*: The US population in 2050 = 439 million, ¼ will be under 18, 1/8 65 or over, so 5/8 of 439 million will be aged 18-64 years. 439/8 = 54.875 × 5 = 274.375 × 1 million = 274,375,000; **200** D, *Explanation*: We are told the United Nations expects the world's population to increase between 2008 and 2050 by 37%. 7 × 137% = 9.59. The answer can be estimated. For example a third of 7 = approx. 2.33 so 33% increase = close to 9.3 therefore the only suggested answer that can be correct is D.

Spatial recognition and visual estimation

201 *Answer:* C, *Explanation:* a) shows the right side b) shows the left side; **202** *Answer:* C, *Explanation:* a) shows the left side b) shows the right side; **203** *Answer:* A, *Explanation:* in b) the middle part is too long, and c) has too many edges (count them and compare with the original); **204** *Answer:* B, *Explanation:* a) shows the right side, and c) shows the left side; **205** *Answer:* A, *Explanation:* all you can see from above is the three steps; in b) this zigzag form is not part of the original, and c) shows the right side; **206** *Answer:* B, *Explanation:* in a) the small 'roof' shape has been moved, in c) the small 'roof' shape is missing, and in d) the central part of the shape is too small; **207** *Answer:* A, *Explanation:* b) is wrong because it represents an extruded irregular quadrangle, in c) the shape has been shortened, and in d) the shape has been lengthened; **208** *Answer:* D, *Explanation:* in a), b) and c) the rectangular shape has been moved; **209** *Answer:* B, *Explanation:* it is the only one with a 'roof' on the intersection of the 'L'-shape; **210** *Answer:* A, *Explanation:* b) has a 'W' shape instead of a 'T' shape, and c) has a 'Z' shape instead of a 'T' shape; **211** *Answer:* C, *Explanation:* in a) the tri-angular shape has been deformed, and in b) and d) the cube has been deformed; **212** *Answer:* D, *Explanation:* in a) the big triangular shape has been thickened, in b) the big triangular shape has been thinned, and in c) the small triangular shape has been deformed; **213** *Answer:* B, *Explanation:* in a) and c) the right triangular shape has been truncated; in d) both triangular shapes have had the edges cut off; **214** *Answer:* B, *Explanation:* in a) and c) the small cube has been moved; **215** *Answer:* A, *Explanation:* in b) and c) the hexagonal shape has been deformed.

Input-type diagrammatic tests

Q1 *Answer* D. No fault. *Explanation:* rule AB requires that the K the last character is deleted, rule FG sees the fifth character a U replaced with the next in the alphabet which is V, GH requires that the whole sequence is reversed. So the sequence has been correctly inputted and therefore there is no fault.

Q2 *Answer* C. *Explanation:* The first instruction (HI) requires the 'T' to be deleted, EF sees the L replaced with a K, finally CD should see a 'P' inserted between the 3rd and 4th character but it has been inserted between the 2nd and 3rd, so a fault occurred at C.

Q3 *Answer* B. *Explanation:* in step B all letters should have been reversed however the first and last letters have not been. So a fault occurred at B.

Q4 *Answer* C. *Explanation:* The letter D deleted at step B has returned.

Q5 *Answer* D. *Explanation:* the instructions have been correctly applied, so there is no fault.

Q6 *Answer* D. *Explanation:* the codes have been appled correctly, so there is no fault.

Q7 *Answer* C. *Explanation:* the SA at step C has been inserted between the 7th and 8th and not the 6th and 7th.

Q8 *Answer* C. *Explanation:* the 2nd and 4th not 2nd and 5th characters have been exchanged at C.

Q9 *Answer* B. *Explanation:* the second letter at step B should be a 'S' not a 'T'.

Q10 *Answer* D. *Explanation:* the codes have been correctly applied, so there is no fault.

Q11 *Answer* A. *Explanation:* the correct sequence should read BA233EVQ because the third letter is 'K'.

Q12 *Answer* C. *Explanation:* the forth not third letter has been replaced.

Q13 *Answer* B. *Explanation:* the firth letter has been reinstated after it was replaced at set A.

Q14 *Answer* D. *Explanation:* the codes have been implemented without fault.

Q15 *Answer* D. *Explanation:* the codes have been implemented without fault.

Q16 *Answer* C. *Explanation:* the first and last items have been exchanged but the changes at step B have been omitted.

Q17 *Answer* A. *Explanation:* the lower case 'n' should have remained lower case.

Q18 *Answer* D. *Explanation:* the codes have been applied correctly, so no fault.

Q19 *Answer* D. *Explanation:* the codes have been applied correctly, so no fault.

Q20 *Answer* A. *Explanation:* the first item has been duplicated rather than switched.

CPSIA information can be obtained
at www.ICGtesting.com
Printed in the USA
BVHW021155160919
558558BV00008B/33/P